Mark Watts is the son of Alan Watts. He is the founder and head of the Watts Foundation in America, an organization dedicated to furthering the teaching of Alan Watts.

John Snelling is a well-known writer and broadcaster specializing in Buddhism, and Asian history and travel. After travelling in the East in the early 1970s, he was General Secretary to the Buddhist Society from 1980 to 1984 and for eight years was Editor of *The Middle Way*, a journal which Alan Watts edited in the 1930s, when it was known as *Buddhism in England*. At present John Snelling lives and works at the Sharpham North Community in Devon.

Also by John Snelling

Buddhism in Russia
The Elements of Buddhism
Buddhism
The Buddhist Handbook
Memoirs of a Political Officer's Wife in Tibet,
Sikkim and Bhutan (with Margaret D Williamson)
The Sacred Mountain

(edited by John Snelling)

The Early Writings of Alan Watts
Buddhahood, P D Mehta
Holistic Consciousness, P D Mehta

SEEDS OF GENIUS:

The Early Writings of Alan Watts

Edited by Mark Watts

with John Snelling

ELEMENT
Shaftesbury, Dorset • Rockport, Massachusetts • Melbourne, Victoria

First published as *The Modern Mystic*
in the UK in 1990 by
Element Books Limited

This edition published in the UK in 1997
by Element Book Limited
Shaftesbury, Dorset SP7 8BP

Published in the USA in 1997 by
Element Books, Inc.
PO Box 830, Rockport, MA 01966

Published in Australia in 1997 by
Element Books and distributed
by Penguin Books Australia Limited
487 Maroondah Highway, Ringwood, Victoria 3134

Cover design by Mark Slader
Design by Jennie Liddles
Typeset by Footnote Graphics
Printed and bound in USA by Edwards Brothers, Inc.

British Library Cataloguing in Publication
data available

Library of Congress Cataloging in Publication
data
Watts, Alan, 1915–1973.
[Modern mystic]
Seeds of genius : the early writings of Alan Watts / edited by
Mark Watts with John Snelling.
p.   cm.
Originally published: The modern mystic. 1990.
Includes bibliographical references and index.
ISBN 1–86204–264–0 (pbk. : alk. paper)
1. Buddhism.   I. Watts, Mark.   II. Snelling, John, 1943–
III. Title.
BQ4055.W38   1997   9/-3//49
294.3—dc21   CIP

ISBN 1 86204 264 0

CONTENTS

•

CONTENTS

ACKNOWLEDGEMENTS

•

We should like to thank sincerely the staff of the libraries of the London branches of the Anthroposophical, Theosophical and Buddhist Societies for helping us obtain material for the present anthology; also for kindly providing information which was invaluable in composing the Introduction.
Particular thanks are due as well to Harry C. Rutherford of the New Atlantis Foundation for providing information about the activities of Dimitrije Mitrinović and his circle during the 1930s, when Alan Watts was an intimate member of that fraternity. Also for providing copies of material published in the journal *The Eleventh Hour* and unpublished material from the New Atlantis Foundation Archives, and for kindly giving us permission to republish it.
In the Introduction we have gone quite thoroughly into the life and work of Mitrinović and Alan Watts' brief association with both because these matters have been only scantily dealt with by Alan's biographers and commentators, who have mainly just paraphrased the material given by Alan himself in his memoirs – including some of the slight errors that crept into that account.
Thanks also to Alan Keightley for providing photocopies of elusive material; to Charles and Winifred Snelling for helping to research some of the notes relating to the 1930s; to Paul Stanjer, late of Watkins' famous London bookstore, who generously helped in many ways; and to Michael Mann of Element Books for his kind support of the project.

J.S. & M.W.

INTRODUCTION

———————————— • ————————————

Because of his fame as a star of the Californian counterculture, popular mythology would have us believe that Alan Watts descended fully formed to earth in San Francisco in the 1960s. Actually, in order to become a great writer and talker on Zen and Oriental religion, he had to serve a long and difficult apprenticeship, and he did so mainly in prosaic England, where he was born in the conventional way in 1915 and where he lived continuously until 1938.

A suburb south of London bearing the very English name of Chislehurst can claim the honour of being the birthplace of Alan Wilson Watts. From there, where the amorphous sprawl of the great metropolis begins to give way to the north Kentish downlands, office workers and allied types have for much of this century commuted daily to work in the bustling commercial heart of London, not so long ago the greatest city in the world. Alan's father, Laurence Watts (1880–1974), was just such a commuter, working variously as an employee of the Michelin Tyre Company and the Metropolitan Hospital Sunday Fund. His wife, Emily (*née* Buchan, 1876?–1961), on the other hand, was a somewhat strait-laced schoolmistress. They were a good, sound, lower middle-class couple, endowed with all the classic British virtues of thrift, respect for education and culture, responsibility and so forth, and they earnestly wished to do their best for Alan, their much-loved only son.

The Watts family lived together on remarkably good terms at the modest family home, 3 Holbrook Cottages (now Holbrook Lane), Chislehurst, a semi-detached cottage of brick and pebble-dash with a rowan tree in its pocket handkerchief front garden. Once, when hard times hit them, they did briefly move away to a house at Widmore Road in nearby

1

As a boy, Alan Watts wore spectacles, but later cured his eye trouble by doing special exercises.

The dapper young Alan Watts.

Number 3, Holbrook Lane, Chislehurst, (Alan Watts' childhood home, as it was in 1984.

Bromley, made available to them by Alan's uncle, Harry Buchan, father of his childhood playmate, Joy. During that brief gray interlude Emily Watts took in embroidery work (she had been trained at the Royal School of Needlework) to make ends meet.

After kindergarten, Alan received the benefits of a private education, firstly at St. Hugh's School in Bickley and then, in 1929, he won a scholarship place at King's School, Canterbury, one of the most prestigious and exclusive of the English public schools. King's is quartered in the hallowed Gothic precincts of Canterbury Cathedral, the very heart of the established religion in England. Its distinguished old boys include the novelist Somerset Maugham, author of *The Razor's Edge*, that classic study of a Westerner on a religious quest in the East. Both Maugham and Watts have disparaging things to say about King's – but this is par for the course. Writers and artists, looking back with hindsight, tend to dwell sourly upon the spartan régimes, sporting obsessions and homosexual undertones of their old schools. They often forget the immense advantages they also derived – sound classical education, the company of cultured people, and encouragement to develop leadership qualities and special talents. Eccentricities were even tolerated, for they were deemed to lend a touch of colour to an establishment character.

So no-one batted an eyelid at King's when in 1930, at the tender age of fifteen, Alan Watts declared himself publicly to be a Buddhist. He was even given encouragement in his strange religious inclinations in 1932 by being sent as an official school representative to a religious conference in Haywards Heath, Sussex, presided over by no less a Church dignitary than the Archbishop of York. He also gave papers at the Caterpillars Club and the Marlowe Society, two King's school societies; one was on 'The Romance of Japanese Culture', while in the other he compared the Japanese *haiku* poet Basho (author of the classic *Narrow Road to the Far North*) with Omar Khayyam of *Rubaiyat* fame. He also contributed a poem entitled 'Shambhala' to *The Cantuarian*, the school magazine, under the pseudonym 'Ronin'.

Alan's interest in Buddhism that blossomed at King's went back a long way. Only children have a tendency to be imaginative and drawn to the strange and exotic, so when the

Mysterious East first impinged upon Alan's consciousness it found fertile ground. The earliest impressions came by way of the orientalia brought into the family home by Emily Watts – presents given her by the grateful parents whose daughters she had instructed in physical education and home economics at a missionary school at Sevenoaks in the days before her marriage. Later came books: the Fu Manchu novels of Sax Rohmer and the writings of Lafcadio Hearn (1850–1904), an American journalist of Greek–Irish extraction who lived for many years in Japan and delighted in its folklore as well as its Buddhist and Shinto traditions. Hearn's books include *Kwaidan, Gleanings in the Buddha-fields* and *Glimpses of Unknown Japan*.

Alan moreover always had a penchant for friendship, particularly with colourful or unusual characters. Encouragement of his Oriental inclinations also came from a youthful friendship with a cosmopolitan character named Francis Croshaw, the father of a childhood chum, who had 'an enormous library, and, realizing my interest in the Orient in general and Buddhism in particular, began lending me books and engaging me in discussions which went on far into the night — mostly at his bungalow near Rye — drinking Moulin à Vent and smoking his dynamite stogies.' Croshaw was the first of a series of gurus who deeply influenced Alan during his formative years.

In one of the books lent to him by Croshaw, Alan discovered a publication put out by the Buddhist Lodge, a group founded in London in 1924 by a highly successful barrister named Christmas Humphreys (1901–83). Alan wrote to the Lodge and in 1931 contributed his first article to its journal, *Buddhism in England* (now *The Middle Way*). The high literary quality and depth of understanding displayed in these writings gave Toby Humphreys and his colleagues the impression that they were dealing with at least a senior master at King's. They were bowled over, therefore, when Alan at last turned up at the Lodge, a schoolboy of sixteen or seventeen in the company of his father. 'And he was talking Zen!', Humphreys used to declare with gusto in later years.

This image of a *wunderkind* stayed with Alan right up to the time he left England for the United States in 1938. During that period he produced an enormous number of articles for *Buddhism in England*, of which he was Editor between 1936 and 1938. We have already published most of these in our first collection, *The Early Writings of Alan Watts* (Berkeley, California and London, 1987), and a few more are collected in the last section of the present volume along with writings that he contributed to other periodicals and some previously unpublished items. This is a substantial body of work by any standard, but in addition he also produced a number of pamphlets and two books, *The Spirit of Zen* (London, 1936) and *The Legacy of Asia & Western Man* (London, 1937). He gave spirited lectures too, influenced in his platform style by Christmas Humphreys.

In all his early writings Alan displays quite prodigious talents. One cannot fairly call him an entirely original thinker, for he drew heavily on the ideas of others — D. T. Suzuki, for instance, Christmas Humphreys, Dimitrije Mitrinović, the psychologists C. G. Jung and Eric Graham Howe, J. Krishnamurti... His mentors were legion. But he always had, from a very early age, a special talent for getting at their nuggets of gold. His was the kind of mind that could cut straight through to the heart of any matter and extract the living essence, then re-express what he had discovered with a new clarity, lightness and humour. He could also quickly pick out cross-connections with other ideas, sometimes in different areas or disciplines, and so make fruitful syntheses. For instance, he was one of the first to publicly point out that useful links could be developed between Western psychology and Oriental religion.

Regarding the present collection of early writings, I can only repeat here, what I wrote in my Introduction to the earlier volume:

> ... it was in Britain that he was born, grew up and received his first formative influences. As this anthology clearly demonstrates, many of those influences were lasting ones, and many of the themes that emerged in these early writings were to recur throughout his life. In fact there is strong evidence here to support the view that most of Watts' major philosophical themes arose in those early years and that he later merely developed, refined and played variations on them.

What gives these early writings their unique fire is that, when he wrote them, Alan was certainly not idly toying with ideas for mere intellectual diversion. He was on an earnest religious quest of his own — hungrily searching for new directions, ways of taking his life into his own hands and shaping it into something better, more imaginative, more spiritually fulfilling than the English middle-class conventions of the day allowed. So he was living out — or trying to live out — the ideas he came across, and as a result there is all the earnestness, freshness and vitality of youth here ... and some of the callow brashness too, for Alan was always a bit of a show-off, at least after King's School had brought him out. He loved to take the stage and become the centre of attention — and to cut a stylish figure in public.

When he left King's in 1932, at the age of seventeen, Alan did not take the normal course and go on to Oxford or Cambridge. Straitened family circumstances prevented that, so instead he took a bread-and-butter job in London and in his spare time carved out a unique education for himself in the esoteric societies and salons of the great metropolis. His main base was at the Buddhist Lodge, where the august Founder-President, Christmas Humphreys ('Toby' to his friends), supplanting Francis Croshaw, became his principal guru. Humphreys was a large character by any token. A great prosecuting counsel — he led for the Crown in many famous and dramatic murder trials at London's Central Criminal Court, the Old Bailey — he had marvellous oratorical talents, and was something of an actor, too (his club was the Garrick). He also wrote a succession of pioneering and very readable books on Buddhism, and was a poet in the spirited pre-modernist style of Kipling and his ilk.

In the early 1930s the Buddhist Lodge held its meetings at Toby Humphreys' own premises in South Eaton Place, a marvellous Aladdin's Cave crammed with intriguing books, pictures, art objects and orientalia. There Humphreys lived with his wife Puck (*née* Aileen Faulkner), a slightly older and rather formidable lady. They had no children, so readily took the young Watts under their wing for, despite a tendency to be a little insensitive on occasion and steam-roller people around, Toby was at heart that *rara avis*, a truly magnanimous person who actually liked to see other people flower. His Buddhism was of a rather personal and eccentric sort, however, deeply permeated with (and hence slighly distorted by) the Theosophy to which he had originally been drawn whilst still a student at Cambridge. A deep veneration for H.P.B. (Madame Helena Petrova Blavatsky, 1831–91), author of esoteric classics like *Isis Unveiled* and *The Secret Doctrine* and a vital influence on the regeneration of Buddhism in Sri Lanka and its transmission to the West, held firm throughout Toby's life, even after he had encountered Dr D.T. Suzuki (1870–1966), legendarily the 'man who brought Zen to the West'. Being a large spirit, however, Toby was not confined by Buddhism and Theosophy only; his interests ranged widely among the arts, and even into bizarre marginal matters like the authorship of Shakespeare's works. (He favoured the idea that they were written, not by the 'man from Stratford', but by a cabal of cultured noblemen.) Toby shared various of these enthusiasms — which he always indulged with boyish relish — with his protégé, Alan Watts. Two great egotistical extraverts, they would strut off to the ballet together in opera capes, toting ivory-handled canes. Certainly, Christmas Humphreys was one to help a young man with potential realise himself!

But during the six years (1932–8) that he was a dapper young man about London town acquiring his unique freewheeling education, Alan Watts was not confined to Christmas Humphreys and the Buddhist Lodge alone either. He also frequented John M. Watkins' famous esoteric bookstore in Cecil Court (just off Charing Cross Road), where he came in contact with other ideas and influences. He crossed paths with the likes of the great modern Indian sage Jiddu Krishnamurti and the philosopher Frederic Spiegelberg (who later invited him to join his American Academy of Asian Studies in San Francisco). He got to know psychiatrists like Eric Graham Howe and Philip Metman; and — perhaps the least understood aspect of this formative phase — he was drawn into a libertarian political movement with a powerful spiritual–psychological dimension inspired by a mysterious Yugoslav savant named Dimitrije Mitrinović - of which more later.

1936 was the *annus mirabilis* for the young Alan Watts — in his own words 'that true year of grace in my life' — for he then took over the editorship of *Buddhism in England* from its founding editor, A. C. Marsh, and published his first full-length book. He also attended sessions of the World Congress of Faiths, held in London at the instigation of Sir Francis Younghusband, who in 1904 had led a British expeditionary force to the holy city of Lhasa, capital of Tibet – and, strangely, experienced a powerful mystical opening while in that great Buddhist country. At the Congress Alan met Dr D. T. Suzuki for the first time. Elsewhere he also met Krishnamurti and attended a great exhibition of Chinese art held at the Royal Academy – this last provided lasting inspiration. It was an exciting life for a young man of energy and enthusiasm, but at the end of every full day Alan had to scramble to get a late train back to Chislehurst, for he was too poor to afford a *pied à terre* in London and so was still living under his parents' roof. Yet there is no reason to believe that his parents disapproved of his slightly bohemian lifestyle; indeed, his sympathetic father shared many of his interests and even held office as Treasurer at the Buddhist Lodge for a while. A cultured and imaginative man himself, Laurence Watts seems to have liked the idea that his son was trying to make a different sort of life for himself and was proud of his precocious achievements. Emily Watts, on the other hand, did begin to have qualms about her son's activities the next year, for things began to keep him up in London at nights.

The cause of this occasional nocturnal absenteeism was the usual: sex – something for which Alan always showed great enthusiasm and which he was concerned to integrate fully in his life. The arid, puritanical repression of conventional religion was never for him! We are, of course, talking of a period long before the permissive society when sexual frustration was the norm for most young unmarried people. Alan had already had various flirtations but, beyond a little preliminary petting, no consummation. However, in 1937 an American lady named Ruth Fuller Everett came to London. She was a remarkable lady who aroused much interest at the Buddhist Lodge since she had sat at the feet of a *roshi* (lit, 'old master') in a Japanese Zen temple. But, more significantly from Alan's point of view, she had a nubile daughter in tow.

Eleanor Everett was almost all he could have wished for – young, passably pretty in a plumpish way, well-travelled, interested in Buddhism, sexually amenable, and connected with wealth. So Alan fell in love and was soon engaged to be married – whereupon his horizons began to expand

Christmas Humphreys.

D. T. Suzuki.

exponentially and the pace of his life to accelerate to almost breakneck speed. At the end of the year he was crossing the Atlantic and going by train across the United States to visit the Everett family home in Chicago; then back to England again on the same ship, the *Bremen*, waltzing crazily on a heaving dance floor in rough seas, playing drunken chess with a dypsomaniac German professor and indulging in the delights of the table. However, the date of the projected marriage had to be brought forward on his return home. Eleanor was going to have a baby.

After their wedding, Eleanor and Alan moved into 'an almost palatial duplex' at Courtfield Gardens in fashionable Kensington. Alan went on with his spiritual questing and writing, but already the storm clouds of the impending World War 2 had begun to gather. He had long since decided that there was nothing intrinsically heroic about war; in fact, it was nothing short of collective criminal madness to which the only sane response was to opt out. In 1938 he adumbrated his latest thinking on the subject in an article he published in *Buddhism in England* entitled 'The Unimportance of War'. There he argued that the wise would do well to spirit themselves out of the cockpit of any conflict to safe retreats; they might be called cowards and escapists, but in the long run they would be doing society a favour, for they would be the ones who would help rebuild a new and hopefully better world out of the debris of the old. Clearly, in this article Alan was rehearsing his own rationalizations for what he himself would do in the event of the war that by 1938 was inevitable. As he admits in his memoirs, he was by then married to an American citizen and so had the necessary 'wings' to fly to the relative safety of the USA if danger threatened.

This is, in fact, what he did do. He and Eleanor left for New York late in 1938 and it was there that their first child, Joan, was born in November. Alan does not seem to have been entirely clear about his future when he sailed from British shores, for he did not at once relinquish his editorship of *Buddhism in England* and the people back at the Buddhist Lodge were half expecting him to return. Perhaps he would have returned if the political climate had relaxed. Instead events took their fateful course and by September 1939 a state of war existed between Britain and Germany.

Subsequently Alan never returned to live in his native land again, although he always valued his Englishness. Some back home saw his defection as cowardice, but in fact it was quite consistent with his declared convictions. He had, after all, first argued the case for conscientious objection at a debate at King's School years before, and he had never publicly deviated from that position. This, in its way, is therefore further proof that Alan Watts was no dilettante but fully prepared to live out the ideas that he took on board.

———————————— • ————————————

In the first part of this collection we have anthologised the articles that Alan Watts contributed to *The Modern Mystic (and Monthly Science Review)*, a lavish esoteric journal that ran for three years between January 1937 and January 1940. It formally proclaimed itself as 'A Monthly Journal Devoted to the Study of Mysticism and the Occult Sciences' and its publishers were quoted as King, Littlewood and King Limited of 35 Great James Street, Bedford Row, London WC1, later of 6 Bear Street, Leicester Square, WC2.

According to our information, *The Modern Mystic* was edited by a gentleman named Dagg, who at one time owned a bookshop in York. He was interested in all the contemporary occult movements but was not absolutely clear about all of them, though he favoured Anthroposophy and attended the Anthroposophical summer schools held in Britain, some of which were also attended by Rudolf Steiner[1] himself, the famous founder of the movement. Dagg never formally became an Anthroposophist, however, but he certainly used leading Anthroposophical writers like Eleanor C. Merry[2] in the columns of *The Modern Mystic*. Over the years other writers included Bernard Bromage, W. Johannes Stein, William le Quex, Eugene Kolisco, Rom Landau, Henry Miller, Clare Cameron (who succeeded Alan Watts as Editor of *Buddhism in England*), Alan Watts himself – and others with enigmatic soubriquets like Thales 11, Justicia and John W. Seeker. Besides Anthroposophy, subjects touched on included Rosicrucianism, Theosophy, Buddhism, Alchemy and Astrology.

That *The Modern Mystic* was intended to be a thoroughly serious journal, not pandering in any way to the grosser superstitions (among which it included Spiritualism and anything requiring the services of mediums), was made abundantly clear in the forthright Editorial of its very first number. There it boldly proclaimed itself 'the herald of the New Age', though at the same time denying that there was such a thing as a 'new age' at all, merely 'the periodicity of cycles'. A telling sign that cyclic change was afoot was the 'passing of Victorian materialism'. Nothing would appear in its columns that would 'offend the susceptibilities of the most ardent religionist', however. Nor did it despise science, for objective scientific investigation was the only sound approach to the study of mysticism. But it would not bow down to science as the ultimate arbiter; and while it thoroughly appreciated the powers of the intellect, it was not blind to the limitations of that faculty either.

The Modern Mystic would in fact open itself to the objective exploration of 'the many hundred ways which the Buddha said "lead to the One" '.

> We are in need of information as to the actual nature or underlying purpose of the ancient rites of initiation, the initiation not only of Egyptians, Chinese, Indians, but of those Mystics nearer home – the Druids. We need some idea of the real meaning of the Arthurian and other legends, and some deeper understanding of Merlin and of the nature of the Holy Grail.

It would also give attention to all kinds of paranormal phenomena: 'levitation, telepathy, healing, psychometry and the occult sciences of astrology and numerology, etc... [also] the possibilities of the one-time existence of such forgotten lands as Atlantis and Lemuria...' The arts, especially music, would not be debarred either. But while it repudiated allegiance 'to any sect, society, "ism" or "osophy" of any kind', its thinking seems to have been basically rooted in the classic Theosophical notion that all genuine manifestations of religion were 'offshoots of a single stem of Wisdom whose origin extends long into "pre-historic" times' and that 'in the course of time the original teachings were perverted, or possibly never divulged to the multitude' (i.e. kept esoteric).

Alan Watts' contributions to *The Modern Mystic* are of special interest in that they touch largely on his extra-Buddhist interests during the period. The English writers G.K. Chesterton and L. Cranmer-Byng[3] receive enthusiastic attention, as do C.G. Jung and J. Krishnamurti. There are a few sideswipes at some of the less appealing religious manifestations of the day, notably Frank Buchman's Oxford Groups, which later developed into the Moral Rearmament movement[4]. And there is also a quite charming and unique piece, 'The Old Man on the Downs', which vividly describes a chance meeting with an unsung and unselfconscious mystic — Buddhists might perhaps describe him as a *pratyeka buddha*, a reclusive buddha who does not proclaim himself or teach — during a ramble in the open hill country to the west of London.

Finally, there is an interesting note in the February 1938 issue of *The Modern Mystic* to the effect that Alan Watts would be resuming his articles on his return from America next month. Also, a notice to the effect that he would be lecturing at the Belfry, a 'centre of a new kind' opening in January 1938 in West Halkin Street, London SW1. 'The complete independence for which this journal stands,' the notice declared, 'is an attitude which the new centre will consider its basis...'

———————————— • ————————————

Generally Alan Watts tended to portray himself as apolitical — or at least not political in the conventional sense — and certainly no ideologue, whether of right or left. There is hardly anything surprising about this. Politics, with its strong collective slant, tends on the whole to be inimical to individual fulfilment, which was what Alan was primarily interested in. Yet between 1934 and 1935 he did for a time deviate from his usual course a little and produce a small body of writings with socio-political content, and these we have collected for the first time here in Part Two. They were written for *The Eleventh Hour*, a 'less ambitious weekly' produced under the inspiration of Dimitrije Mitrinović after the demise of the more substantial *New Britain* in August 1934. As the name suggests, the whole tenor of the magazine was urgent. Hitler and the evil of fascism were rising fast; war was inevitable; Europe, and indeed the world, were on the brink of disaster and must be awakened to their true spiritual and historical destiny before it was too late.

Dimitrije Mitrinović (1887–1953) was another of Alan Watts' mentors during this vital formative period in London. He was born in Herzegovina, now part of Yugoslavia, and as a young man became prominent in the Young Bosnian movement, which opposed the Austro-Hungarian takeover of Bosnia-Herzegovina. Later he studied in Munich, where he came in contact with Wassily Kandinsky and the *Blaue Reiter* school of artists. He also met philosophers like Erich Gutkind and Frederik van Eeden, with whom he joined in the Blutbund (lit. 'Blood Brotherhood'), an association of cultural luminaries dedicated to the initiation of a utopian future of peace and harmony. Finally, World War 1 forced him into exile in London, where he lived and worked until his death.

Starting with local, nationalistic concerns, Mitrinović's consciousness gradually widened to panoramic proportions. Early on he had awakened to the insight that liberation for Bosnia-Herzegovina had to be more than a no-holds-barred struggle for independence; a spiritual, cultural and moral regeneration was demanded too. Eventually he came to see that such a regeneration was necessary on the global scale if the world was to escape the nemesis towards which, in the 1930s, it was charging like a blind man on a sightless horse. To the chagrin of some of his old comrades, who inevitably viewed his position as a kind of defection, he proclaimed that the time of reductionistic tribal and nationalistic thinking was past and that the human race now had to think and act as one species inhabiting a single, organically interconnected world. The latter part of his life was accordingly dedicated to various attempts to initiate some sort of new millenarian regeneration that would lift the world out of its state of abject crisis. This was not so much about forming political parties or inaugurating movements — though indeed a movement, the New Britain Movement, did emerge under his inspiration and momentarily gathered a fair degree of momentum in the mid-30s — as about what he called 'initiatives'. These were forms of catalytic activity conducted through a series of magazines, public talks and group work, all aimed at galvanising the generality into new consciousness and action.

In his book, *The Yogi and the Commissar* (London, 1945), Arthur Koestler introduced that antagonistic duality: the yogi, concerned with inaugurating change from within, and the commissar, concerned with inaugurating change from without by a transformation of social institutions. Mitrinović,

*Dimitrije
Mitrinović.*

*Caricature of Dimitrije
Mitrinović by Alan Watts.*

15

however — and this was one thing that must have attracted the young Alan Watts — differed from the other ideologues of the day in that he was of the view that the demands of the individual to complete fulfilment on all levels (including the spiritual) and the demands of the collective did not have to be at odds but could be fully reconciled in a higher organic harmony. It was not a matter of yogi or commissar but of yogi and commissar. So his acolytes were involved both with inner psychological and spiritual work on themselves and with external concerns of a social and political nature.

Some of the personal work included what today we would describe as psychotherapy. Mitrinović was influenced by the ideas of Alfred Adler (1870–1937), the founder of Individual Psychology, along with Freud (of whose Viennese circle he was at one time a member) and Jung, one of the pioneers of modern psychology. Adler placed rather less emphasis than his currently more famous colleagues on depth analysis and rather more on reorientating an individual's lifestyle and attitude to life. Andrew Rigby in his study of Mitrinović (see Bibliography) has suggested that Adler's was essentially a holistic approach and that Mitrinović may have been drawn to it precisely for that reason; also because its stress on individual freedom and responsibility resonated with his own view that people should be encouraged to forge a brave new world on their own initiative. Mitrinović himself wrote that he shared Adler's concern for weaning people from neurotic addiction to power — achievement, not personal power, was in his view the true goal of human striving — and the consequent need to become some kind of special person at the expense of others.

In 1927 Mitrinović established an Adler Society in the lower storeys of a house at 55 Gower Street in the Bloomsbury district of north London, not far from his own dwelling at 38 Bloomsbury Street. Here, rooms were allocated for public functions like lectures and open meetings, and others for private study. The society survived until about 1933, when Adler himself dissociated himself from it because of a drift away from psychology towards social and political concerns and activities.

Mitrinović was also influenced by the American Trigant Burrow, author of *The Social Basis of Consciousness* (1927) and

Phyloanalysis (1933), where, according to Alan Watts, 'he contended that the ego personality was a socially implanted fiction and not a psychophysical entity'. Group sessions inspired by Burrow's ideas were held at Gower Street during which what Alan describes as 'a no-holds-barred mutual psychoanalysis' took place when 'for some months, we resolutely destroyed and rebuilt each other's personalities.' Alan adds, a little ruefully perhaps, that 'these meetings were not then, as sometimes now, held by both sexes in the nude'. On the socio-political front, Mitrinović's concerns ranged widely and radically. What he envisaged was a kind of specialized socialist millennium, an 'organic', non-authoritarian ordering of things that would incorporate devolution — that is, the investment of control of various activities and functions in small, local, self-governing groups — and also federalism on various levels – the national, the continental (he was an early advocate of a European federation), and ultimately the global. Social life he meanwhile saw as being subject to a tripartite division into the economic, cultural and political spheres. The so-called 'Social State' or 'Threefold State' based on such an ordering would have a three-tiered parliament comprising an Economic Chamber, a Cultural Chamber and a Political Chamber. These would be filled with representatives from the local levels. The balance would be maintained by Senate, 'a group of persons representing every function in the community, who would be respected for their understanding of and genuine concern for the interests of the whole, and their ability to act as a catalytic function without invoking any superrogatory power' (Harry Rutherford).

Mitrinović's ideas on industrial and economic matters were derived from his association with the distinguished journal *The New Age*, to which incidentally he contributed his famous 'World Affairs' series under the pen-name M. M. Cosmoi when A. R. Orage (later a prominent disciple and supporter of Gurdjieff) was Editor. For industry, he advocated a system of Workers' Control that owed much to Guild Socialism as propounded by such thinkers as S. G. Hobson and G. Stirling Taylor. He also advocated monetary reform, inspired initially by the ideas of Major C. H. Douglas on Social Credit and later by the more concise approach of Professor Frederick Soddy.

Mitrinović saw money as possessing a function analagous to that of blood in the human organism, helping to distribute vital energies to where they were needed. Harry Rutherford, one of Mitrinović's close colleagues, writes:

> He saw that with modern technology the problem of producing all the wealth which humanity needs is in principle soluble, but one of the main hindrances to achieving this is the way in which money is issued by banks as interest-bearing debt. When the debt is repaid the money is destroyed, unless it is re-lent to someone else. It is as if blood was only lent to the rest of the body on payment of interest and destroyed every time it was re-circulated. Ideally money should not be paid either as interest or wages, but as a social income to everyone.[5]

Or in Mitrinović's own more colourful words:

> *Release the credit of the community!* Let the social blood of the community flow more freely through the body of the New Community! Conceive the New Seed, the new historic will, and rejuvenate the blood of the Community! Decide to release the wealth of human inheritance, the riches of society, riches rotting and wasted![6]

Words that would surely make any committed Monetarist of the 1980s or '90s turn apoplectic and begin foaming at mouth!

All these fine ideals and practical proposals were subsumed under the vast umbrella of Mitrinović's all-encompassing spiritual system, which incorporated its own cosmology. This was founded on the centrality of Christianity, but Christianity of a rather unusual sort that contains distinct echoes of Vedanta as well as of the ideas of writers like Vladimir Solovyov, Rudolf Steiner and H. P. Blavatsky. The Divine, which is spiritual and immaterial, does not exist in some rarefied 'elsewhere' apart from man, but in man's own 'inwardness' – that is, in his consciousness or awareness. Man, both individually and collectively, is therefore a divine being and there is no divinity apart from man.

The significance of this can best be understood in relation to Mitrinović's own interpretation of the Athanasian Creed's doctrine of the Trinity, where God the Father represents the unconscious, and God the Son represents consciousness, reason, the Logos. This Eternal Son he identifies with humanity, whose attainment of self-consciousness he calls the 'Sin Primordial and Eternal which is the Fall of Man'. In Jesus

Christ, by virtue of his becoming conscious of his divine nature, the Eternal Logos was incarnated (the Word was made flesh) in individuated form – 'The Universe has become single'. Thus the divine centre of man is at once individual and universal.

As a religion, Christianity is 'the principle, and oracle of ripeness and coming of age of the human race', for it challenges each person to follow Christ's example and realise that he is himself the Second Person of the Trinity. As Mitrinović put it in characteristically apocalyptic style:

> Of the holy three-foldness of God, every man, through Universal Humanity, is the Second Person – every man, not by his organism but by the very fact of his being self-conscious; for the message of the Christian Dispensation to Earth is Personality, Filioque. Every man is a Son and is himself Universal Man and the Universal Humanity *sub specie aeternitatis*. Every son of man is truly and entirely Anthropos himself...[7]

When this is realised on a general scale, humanity will slough off the coils of blind unconscious evolution and graduate to true history, where it will responsibly and consciously participate in its own development 'in obedience to Providence and heroism against Destiny'. It will indeed usher into incarnation on earth the Third Person of Mitrinović's Triune God: Sophia or the Holy Spirit, 'proceeding equally from the Unconscious Power and from Divine Reason' (Harry Rutherford). And so a new millenium, a higher creation, will be inaugurated – the Kingdom of Heaven on earth, no less:

> Our generation is that one of the human generations whose destiny is to become collectively and generally conscious. Our age is the entrance of the Universal Socialism of Humanity into both the history of mankind and its evolution. Nothing less, not anything less. But by Socialism we do not mean any particular system of organisation, dictatorial or anarchist, but a self-ordering of man based on the nature of the individual and collective soul of mankind. Far from being a life plebeian or vulgar, Socialism is the dispensation of a life elevated, life seraphic and resurrected.
>
> The incarnation of Universal Humanity on earth is a mystery equal in abysmal greatness to the appearance of the Logoic incarnation [i.e. Christ] in the world. Humanity as a kingdom feels the need of supra-humanness. For Universal Humanity is the goal of mankind. The world is in need of its own organic

functioning, of its own organism. And in the problem of the organic wholeness of the world all the problems of classes, races, sexes, even of individuals are included.[8]

And if all this magnificence was to be realised and impending nemesis averted, it should be noted, there was no point in waiting for a new messiah. To wait for leaders is to evade responsibilities,' Mitrinović declared unequivocally. The time for 'great men' was anyway past. Now people themselves had to take responsibility for bringing the new theophany to pass.

–––––––––– • ––––––––––

How did Alan Watts become involved with these rather (for him at any rate) unusual bedfellows?

The initial connection was made around 1934 through another Alan Watts, to whom he was introduced by Nigel Watkins, son of the founder of the famous occult and religious bookstore in Cecil Court. This namesake, 'a bright-eyed, light-hearted, breezy man', was about 12 years older than Alan and, with his 'exquisite paramour' June, very much a man of the world. He instructed Alan in all those things about sex he had never been taught at home or at school. He also introduced him to the psychoanalytic ideas of Freud and Adler – and to Mitrinović.

It is clear from the way Alan writes about him in his memoirs that the Yugoslav savant impressed him mightily. Like his other mentor, Christmas Humphreys, here was a larger-than-life character with a touch of the bohemian about him. He was a cultured man too, who frequented museums, bookshops and art galleries but, unlike Humphreys, he was cosmopolitan, and much more widely and deeply versed in world religion and philosophy. Probably most of all, however, Alan was struck by Mitrinović's style, for he dwells with almost sensuous delight on the details of his appearance, habits and tastes: his stout Slavonic figure, the shaven head, the 'black winglike eyebrows', the 'power of his voice and eyes', his humour and 'oracular way of writing'. In the street he wore extremely formal clothes – a cutaway morning coat, striped trousers and high bowler hat; and he carried an amber-handled walking stick. In his 'sanctum sanctorum' in Bloomsbury Street, on the other hand, he would sit on the bed clad in loose robes and discourse at length — perhaps all night — to his acolytes, who felt immensely privileged to be allowed to be present. He smoked 'very fat Virginia cigarettes' and drank 'formidable amounts of whiskey [sic]'. His bills meanwhile were settled with crisp new £5 banknotes, 'which in those days looked like legal documents'; and he liked to entertain his friends to dinner in the Hungarian, Greek and Russian restaurants of Soho, where he would order half a dozen different dishes and then mix them all up together. Always he was surrounded by 'devoted disciples' — a misnomer, for Mitrinović did not want his colleagues to be slavish followers — many of them 'adoring women', Alan notes with admiration. Believing him to be 'probably a high initiate into the mysteries of the universe', Alan loved him... and feared him at the same time, for Mitrinović was thought by some in Buddhist and Theosophical circles to be a black magician, no doubt of the sinister Aleister Crowley type.

Alan compares Mitrinović most closely, however, with G. I. Gurdjieff. Both were, he says, 'rascal gurus'. It is hard to know precisely what he means by this. Perhaps he felt both had a salting of Jung's trickster archetype in their characters – that they manipulated and played games with their devotees, and/or retained venal character traits not exactly consistent with the popular view of what is appropriate in religious teachers. This is perhaps not quite fair in Mitrinović's case, and one could take Alan to task for the playful, even frivolous way in which he deals with the man in his memoirs. Certainly people I have spoken to, whose judgement I respect, speak highly of Mitrinović. He was definitely no charlatan but a man of very deep wisdom and high vision. Alan's account moreover contains various small inaccuracies. It was not true, for instance, that he 'invariably began his activities late at night, and would arrive among his disciples about 11 p.m.'.

According to his own account, Alan's work with Mitrinović 'involved meetings, bull sessions, public lectures and even selling our magazines on Piccadilly Circus'. He also worked at book reviewing, proof-reading, typography and lay-out on *The Eleventh Hour*. And though he does not mention it himself, he also formed a Bromley Group of the New Britain movement. On 27th June 1934, a notice of the group's regular meetings appeared in *New Britain*, in which Alan is described as the S.E. London Area Secretary. Such notices continued until the paper stopped publication on 8th August 1934. *The Eleventh Hour*, which took over from *New Britain* and for which Alan wrote and worked, did not publish news of New Britain groups; it appeared until 17th July 1935.

Alan also attended the second New Britain Conference that took place in August 1934 at Glastonbury, a magical place with strong Arthurian resonances in the west of England. He in fact reported on his group's activities to the nearly 200 people present. Then, in September 1934, the first and only issue of a duplicated broadsheet called *ALLIANCE for New Britain – Journal of the London Groups* appeared, containing notices of Bromley Group meetings on 5th, 13th and 19th September; also of a 'members only' meeting on 21st September when 'immediate action' was discussed. Alan is finally mentioned in connection with a series of meetings that took place under the aegis of The New Order between September and December 1935. He spoke on December 3rd on 'The New Spirit and the New World'.

In Part Two we have collected all Alan's writings for *The Eleventh Hour*, which include two articles and some fourteen book reviews. With the kind help and permission of Harry Rutherford and the New Atlantis Foundation, which currently continues the work that Mitrinović started, we have in addition been able to reproduce two letters that Alan wrote, one in his capacity as Secretary of the Bromley Group and one 'for and on behalf of the S.E. London Area Council'. But perhaps most interesting is a statement by Alan entitled 'The New Order', which was written in response to a questionnaire circulated to New Britain members.

These writings, particularly the last, show clearly the extent to which Alan was influenced by Mitrinović and how actively he was collaborating in the Yugoslav's work – until the end of 1935, when he began to drift away. He gives as reasons for this that he was still very much involved with the Buddhist Lodge, Christmas Humphreys was still his principal guru and moreover events in Europe, like the German reoccupation of the Rhineland, had made him disillusioned with the effectiveness of the political side of the work. Harry Rutherford believes that in any case the political and economic aspects of New Britain interested Alan far less than 'the spiritual idea of a national renaissance which it put forward'. It must also be added that the New Britain Movement was at this point winding down, for Mitrinović had withdrawn his energy from it in order to concentrate on working with small groups, which could only be done on the personal level. *The Eleventh Hour* also ceased publication. Almost simultaneously, things were picking up for Alan on the Buddhist front. In the next year, 1936, he published his first book, assumed the editorship of *Buddhism in England* and attended the sessions of the World Congress of Faiths.

Yet, before he finally drifted away, a highly exotic event took place. As Alan recounts in his autobiography, one day two of Mitrinović's colleagues, Harry Rutherford and John Harker (the nephew of Gordon Harker, the actor), rushed over to his office in the city and announced that it was absolutely necessary that he drop all plans for that evening and meet them in a pub on the corner of Tottenham Court Road and New Oxford Street. There, having gulped down beers, they took a taxi to the sanctum in Bloomsbury Street where a berobed Mitrinović was waiting for them, a glass of straight whisky in one hand and a fat Churchman's No. 1 cigarette in the other.

'Alan Watts, I love you but I do not like you,' the Yugoslav, who admitted to being 'a bit whiskey', declared. 'Nevertheless, I am going to invite you to join an eternal and secret fellowship which will watch you, guard you and keep track of you wherever you may go in the world. We call it the Wild Woodbines, named after the cheapest cigarette in England. Every member is to carry a package, and the sign of recognition is to produce your package and say, ''Have one of mine''. Now if you are inclined to enter into this masonry you must confer with the Jehovah which is in your heart of hearts, and answer me yes or no.'

Alan paused for a moment. Realizing how much he admired Mitrinović and how many close friendships he had made in his circle, he could make only one answer – 'Yes I will'. He was then initiated into the mysteries of a mandala, a key to many ancient symbologies, which more than thirty five years later he refused to divulge because of a grave oath of secrecy that he had taken. That accomplished, Mitrinović took out a packet of Woodbines. 'Have one of mine!' As Alan took a cigarette, all the people in the room rushed up and embraced him.

In fact the real name of this 'eternal and secret fellowship' was 'Woodbine', not 'the Wild Woodbines', the humble brand name of W. D. & H. O. Wills' famous working class cigarette 'standing for Universal Humanity or Human Household incarnated, as it were, in a group of persons who were only united by their humanity – but, as Mitrinović said, he couldn't call it Universal Humanity because it would have sounded too pompous!' (Harry Rutherford). Furthermore, the mandala incident was not an inherent part of the ritual but peculiar to Alan's initiation; and, though he seems to have overlooked the fact, he also took an equally grave oath not to mention openly the word 'Woodbine', though the point of secrecy was not in any way macabre but essentially to underscore the personal nature of initiation.

This dramatic initiation in 1936 was a final flourish to Alan's connection with Mitrinović's circle. Or almost. In 1973 he was again in touch with Harry Rutherford, who had written to him querying a point in his autobiography. They spent a very pleasant afternoon drinking warm vodka in the Charing Cross Hotel. After this meeting, Alan republished under the imprint of his Society for Comparative Philosophy a New Atlantis Foundation lecture by Rutherford on Mitrinović's writings on Christianity. In the Foreword Alan declared:

> In publishing this lecture, I am not implying that I agree with it in every detail. *De minimis non curat lex*. The point is that this man's work was seminal and should be brought into the light of day and carefully considered, especially by those involved in the wobbling Christian tradition. My own style and approach is very different from his, but not contrary... I am not quite so enthusiastic about the centrality of Christianity, even though this word may mean something very different from what has been taught in church, and I do feel that Asian points of view have altogether underestimated the value of the individual.[9]

Although he tends not to be quoted in Alan's later writings, there is no doubt that Mitrinović was a powerful influence at this formative stage and that much of his teaching went into that great melting pot from which Alan later drew the inspiration for his own books and lectures. Take one concrete example. This firstly from Alan Watts:

The individual is an aperture through which the whole energy of the universe is aware of itself, a vortex of vibrations in which it realizes itself... – not alone, but as central to all that surrounds it.[10]

Well, if one looks into Mitrinović's writings one finds the following:

We are individuations of reality and its centres. The centre of all centres is within each of us humans. Existence itself is aware of itself in us humans. Our own reason and awareness is the awareness of Existence itself about itself...[11]

———————————— • ————————————

We begin Part Three, a miscellaneous section, with 'The Whole and its Parts' (subtitled 'New Tendencies in Modern Psychology'), an article that Alan published in the *Occult Review* in 1937. This forward-looking piece anticipates ideas that have only recently gained wider acceptance. Alan in fact argues for holistic thinking and against the reductionism (he calls it the 'disintegration') which in medicine and psychology means that parts are treated rather than the whole. Such notions certainly indicate the influence of Mitrinović's concept of 'organism', which the Yugoslav savant applied quite generally, but Alan only refers specifically to the writings of Dr. Eric Graham Howe[12], the Harley Street psychiatrist whom he met in 1936 and who was for a time another formative influence. It is interesting that Alan concludes the piece with a quote from Howe's book *I and Me* extolling the virtues of a playful approach to life.

By the time that the next two articles anthologised here appeared in 1939, a major watershed had been passed. Late the previous year, with war clouds gathering ominously over Europe, Alan had departed for the United States with his young wife Eleanor, and had been established in style by his affluent mother-in-law, Ruth Fuller Everett, in a suite adjacent to her own in the Park Crescent Hotel at 87th Street and Riverside Drive, 'overlooking the Hudson, and in the heart of Jewry'.

Alan's ever-susceptible senses were ecstatic at the plethora of marvellous stimuli that assaulted them in the bustling labyrinths of towering Manhattan. Yet, though he does not make much of it in his memoirs, it is clear that things were beginning to close in on him. While in London it had been perfectly all right for an unattached young man, with all the outward trappings of gentility, to adopt the lifestyle of an amateur, dabbling in esoteric matters and generally living as the spirit moved him, this was not so acceptable in more hard-headed, commercially conscious New York – and especially not for a married man with a baby on the way. Living off the Everett family money was all right for the time being, but it was clearly expected that he should sooner rather than later put himself on his own feet and 'be a man'.

One thing that Alan tried early on was to deepen his understanding of Zen. Fortuitously, his mother-in-law was also supporting a Japanese Zen priest, Sokei-an Sasaki[13], who had trained under Suzuki's old master, Soyen Shaku, at Engaku-ji in Kamakura. To all intents and purposes this was a golden opportunity, but Alan's native inability to take the second place and bow before a master quickly asserted itself, and soon he was taking an independent line. He then set up as a teacher of sorts himself, lecturing at the (Jungian) Analytical Psychology Club of New York and holding freelance seminars in Oriental philosophy at the new apartments on West 77th Street ('a furnished apartment, Bauhaus style') and then at 435 East 57th Street, to which he and Eleanor moved with their new baby, Joan. The Analytical Psychology Club lecture was published as a pamphlet under the title 'The Psychology of Acceptance', and later expanded into a full-length book, Alan's third, *The Meaning of Happiness*. Even so, the more conventional and censorious of the Everett family were not impressed.

'Pheel*os*ophy!' one elderly matron trumpeted, waving a metaphorical lorgnette in the air *à la* Lady Bracknell. 'Why, you can't make a living out of pheel*os*ophy!'

'...But *then* I nearly believed her!' Alan comments – ruefully.

Following the publication of *The Meaning of Happiness*, Alan records that '*Asia* magazine bought two articles from me'. We have anthologised them here: 'The Rusty Swords of Japan' and 'How Buddhism Came to Life' (subtitled 'A Study in the Death of a Philosophy' and 'The Wide Differences in the Practice of an Ancient Indian Philosophy in China and Japan', respectively). Both deal with Zen. In the latter Alan specifically celebrates his love of the classic Chinese Zen

(Ch'an) of the T'ang dynasty masters. Here, he feels, through the fruitful interaction of the Chinese genius with the teachings that had been transported all the way from India, Buddhism was transformed and fully vitalized. He has a point! 'Rusty Swords', on the other hand, is given a contemporary relevance. Alan contrasts the brutal militarism of the Japanese invasion of China with the noble spirit of the samurai of the Kamakura period, who were deeply influenced by Zen. One feels that here, however, he was probably being a little starry-eyed!

The problem of a career loomed large, however. Ruth Everett, who was probably growing a little tired of funding her freewheeling son-in-law, suggested that Alan should qualify himself for a teaching career by getting a Ph. D. Back in Britain long before, he had decided against seeking entrance to Oxford or Cambridge; now he stalled again – and in this he was supported by Marguerite Block, then Editor of the *Review of Religion*, which was published under the auspices of Columbia University. She was a 'cheerful white-haired, beady-eyed woman [who] was a member of the Analytical Psychology Club and an authority on Swedenborg'.

'No, it isn't worth it,' Ms Block declared, her hyperbolic words no doubt falling on very receptive ears. 'I simply wouldn't waste your time with all that picayune [insignificant – as a 5 cent piece – Ed.], myopic-minded, long-drawn-out, mole-eyed academic ritual. Just write a long and learned article on some new wrinkle in comparative religion and we'll publish it in the *Review*. That should do instead.'

We have included this 'long and learned' article here: 'The Problem of Faith and Works in Buddhism' (1941). It certainly has all the obligatory academic embellishments, including copious footnotes and, for the Oriental terms, the correct accents and diacriticals. But it is also undoubtedly a highly significant article, even a crucial one, pointing directly forward to the next decisive step in Alan's always original life. He says as much in his memoirs: for him 'the work had momentous consequences'.

What he explored in this article was the possibility of finding common ground between Buddhism and Christianity. No small undertaking, to be sure! According to his own account, he saw that in both these great world religions there was a fundamental dichotomy between those who argued that salvation was a matter of individual will and effort, and those who argued that it was all a matter of grace. In Christianity there were the Pelagians 'who held salvation to be the result of good works', and the Augustinians (including Luther) 'who held that it came solely by faith'. In Mahayana Buddhism likewise, there were those who believed that Enlightenment was only possible through 'self power' (*jiriki*) and those who believed that it could only come through 'other power' (*tariki*). The latter were the followers of the devotional Pure Land sects, which originated in India but really reached full development in China before being transmitted on to Japan. Central to them is the cult of Amitabha (Japanese, Amida), the Buddha of Infinite Light, who resides in the 'Pure Land' of Sukhavati, a celestial realm which devotees hope to reach after death solely through faith in Amitabha's divine compassion. In the Elysian circumstances prevailing in Sukhavati, full Enlightenment is easily achieved.[14]

Alan wrote:

> ... I saw that if you substituted 'Christ' for 'Amitabha', Zen, Jodo Shin-shu [one of the principal Japanese Pure Land sects], and Christianity were all approaching the same point by different routes. It thus might be possible to develop a deeper and more intelligible form of Christianity which would, however, have to bypass that religion's imperialistic claims to be the one true and perfect salvation. At the same time, Christianity would be strengthened in being seen as a form of the common religious experience of mankind. It would have more validity by being less of an oddity.[15]

He also managed to work in cross-connections with a thesis he had propounded in his 'Psychology of Acceptance' pamphlet and the subsequent book. Belief in 'other power' means that we must have faith that we are acceptable for Enlightenment *as we are*, warts and all. We do not have to do anything to reform ourselves to be saved, for we are already saved, already Enlightened – only, until our eyes are opened, we do not know it. Of course such notions, themselves not unknown in Christian theology, raise ethical questions. If we are saved all along, why do anything at all – why even restrain oneself from living an antinomian life? As always, for Alan himself these ecumenical ruminations did not bear solely upon his spiritual life. They had ramifications in the personal sphere too, for they pointed towards a solution to the crisis that had for some time been gathering. He need no longer be a cranky outsider; he could resolve the difficulties he had with Christianity and Western culture generally; he could at last *fit in* and have a credited social role, a career and a regular income...

He could, in short, become a Christian priest – not of just any Christian sect, to be sure. It had to be the most liberal on offer. And that turned out after some investigation to be the Episcopalian Church ('the awkward denominational label for the American branch of the Anglican Communion'), within whose 'charitable embrace... you can be a Roccoco Catholic, a stately High Churchman, a virtual Presbyterian, a Marxist, and even a Theosophist – just as long as you keep loosely to the Book of Common Prayer, and take care not to play around openly with any of the ladies on the altar guild'.

It is hard to know just when this new trend towards Christianity really began in earnest for Alan. Certainly Mitrinović, while being prepared to take cognisance of all the great religions, had always thought Christianity central. C. J. Jung too, who Alan quoted extensively in *The Meaning of Happiness*, was always of the opinion that a person should stick with his own native traditions. Indeed, in the book Alan had himself declared that 'Christianity is our traditional faith; it is in our blood and bones'. Ultimately, of course, the Christian connection was something that ran right through his life, back to his King's School days and his parental home in Chislehurst.

Another personal factor reinforced the new direction. Eleanor, Alan's wife had become deeply depressed since returning to the United States. Part of this, Alan admits, might have been the result of living with an off-beat individual like himself, who could neither get himself a regular job nor settle down to a regular lifestyle. She also worried about money a great deal, ate too much and became overweight. In her unhappy condition, she suddenly found herself drawn to St Patrick's Cathedral while shopping in Manhattan one day, and there she was graced with a 'vivid vision of Christ'. Afterwards, she and Alan began exploring the Episcopalian churches of the locality together – they were still very close at the time. Alan predictably found his senses delighted with the ritual and the music that they encountered in one particular church, St Mary the Virgin, on West 46th Street. Going there was a spiritual homecoming.

Though some of Alan's friends were not so sure about the wisdom of his entering the priesthood, he himself became set on taking 'the STEP'. The major hurdle, the lack of a degree, was overcome when, by force of the impressive reading list that he drew up, he was accepted as a Special Student at Seabury-Western Theological Seminary at Evanston, Illinois, by the Dean, Bishop McElwain. So he and his family moved to the mid-West and a new suburban, middle-class life. Two years later, on the Feast of the Ascension, May 18th 1944, the Reverend Alan Wilson Watts was ordained to the Sacred Priesthood at the Church of the Atonement, Chicago, by no less a figure than the Right Reverend Wallace Edmonds Conkling, Bishop of Chicago.

●

We should very much like to have republished in Part Three two articles that Alan is reputed to have contributed to a presumably long-defunct British journal called *The Sufi* in 1936: 'What is Zen?' and 'The Birth of a Divine Son'. However, neither the British Library nor the libraries of the Anthroposophical and Theosophical Societies in London have any copies or records of this journal. If any reader of this book has information about either the journal or the articles, we should be very pleased to hear about it and can be contacted via our publishers.

●

Finally, Part Four anthologises the articles Alan contributed to *Buddhism in England*, later *The Middle Way*, the journal of the Buddhist Lodge, later the Buddhist Society, after he ceased to be Editor and had settled in the United States. That he maintained a connection with the journal — which did not pay its contributors — for so many years indicates the

The Right Reverend Wallace Edmonds Conkling,
Bishop of Chicago, will ordain
The Reverend Alan Wilson Watts
to the Sacred Priesthood
at the Church of the Atonement, Chicago,
on the Feast of the Ascension,
May 18th, 1944, at 10 a. m.

✝

First Mass at the Church of the Atonement,
Saturday, May 20th at 10 a. m.

Alan Watt's Ordination card.

Rev Alan Watts at Canterbury House, Evanstow, with his wife Eleanor, daughters Joan and Ann, and parents Laurence and Emily Watts.

affection that he had for both it and its illustrious founder, Christmas Humphreys, with whom he kept in contact right up to his last European lecture tour just before his death in 1973. But then Humphreys and the journal had set him up as a figure of note in the spiritual/esoteric subcultures, as well as providing him with generous opportunities for developing his literary and lecturing skills – and much else besides.

These articles reflect some of the changes that Alan went through during their seventeen-year span. Most were published in the period 1939–41, and two of those, 'The Buddhist Way of Life' and 'Tomorrow Never Comes', give little tell-tale hints of Alan's impending U-turn into the Christian priesthood. He talks in one place, for instance, about Christianity being Western man's 'own religion', and elsewhere refers quite freely to God — who was and still is not always *persona grata* in Buddhist circles — though it is clear that this is a God with a Buddhist/Vedantist/Taoist as much as a Christian complexion. 'The Mystery of Shin' meanwhile reiterates many of the arguments to be found in 'The Problem of Faith and Works'. There is also the fable, 'The Second Immortal', a whimsical piece of *Chinoiserie* that, for this reader at any rate, suggests affinities with lines from the 'What the Thunder Said' section of T. S. Eliot's *Waste Land*: 'Who is the third that walks always beside you?/ When I count, there are only you and I together/But when I look ahead up the white road/There is always another one...'[16]

There is then a hiatus of nearly ten years between 1941 and 1950/1, during the latter part of which period Alan was a 'paradox priest', ministering in his own original and flamboyant way to the faithful on the Evanston campus of Northwestern University. But of course the church could not contain Alan's anarchic energies for long, and in 1950 he quit holy orders under something of a cloud. His first marriage came to an end at about the same time. Then, after a brief introspective interlude at Thornecrest Farmhouse, Millbrook, New York, during which he wrote *The Wisdom of Insecurity*, he lit out for the golden vistas and opportunities of California, where he no longer had to negotiate with compromises but could return to Buddhism and the other Eastern religions. Our last two items, from 1951 and 1956, therefore show him back on home ground once again, doing what he did best –

but with perhaps a new maturity. For, despite all their freshness and vitality, Alan's early articles up to 1941 always have a dash of callowness about them. He sounds for all the world like some brash sixth-former at a public lecture, contriving with every trick of gesture and rhetoric to make his words sound substantial and grown-up – yet never quite succeeding. During the decade of the 1940s, however, he encountered for the first time the harsh face of life; he suffered a great deal – and our final pieces attest to that. The *wunderkind* had at last come of age.

We take our leave of Alan Watts just as he stands on the brink of fame and discovery after following his off-beat vocation for more than twenty bumpy years on two continents. Soon he will be immortalised by Kerouac as Arthur Whane in *The Dharma Bums* and, as a luminary of the Californian counterculture, be adjudged a star 'as big as Lennon'. As Alan himself told Theodore Roszak, it was as though he 'had pressed the electric light switch... and the whole roof had fallen in'.

But all that is another story...

——————— • ———————

One cannot help feeling, when one reads the writings from the 1930s collected here, how lucky the young Alan Watts was to come into contact at an impressionable age with such a range and calibre of influences. Also that the inter-war period in London was a particularly richly endowed milieu for a young man of his tastes and inclinations.

True, the world was struggling with dark forces. World War 1 had left its traumatic aftermath, there had been the Wall Street Crash and then the Depression, fascism was on the rise in Germany, Italy, Spain and Japan, Stalin was ravaging Russia... All the demonic forces that would eventually precipitate World War 2 were inexorably constellating themselves. And yet it was a time too of intellectual ferment, when 'solutions' were actively sought to global, national and individual problems. People were enquiring, studying, debating, discussing – and prepared to put their theories and programmes into practice. Nor were the options on the table few and simplistic – a dull flip-of-the-coin choice between dogmatic ideologies like capitalism, fascism, communism...

Many saw that a political regeneration was impossible without individual regeneration – and that the spiritual dimension could not be left out either. Elemental to the best hearts and minds of the day too was the crystal spirit of freedom – a refusal to be intimidated but rather to take one's stand firmly in one's own centre. It was a time, in short, when people could still hope, believe, project and work for a better world.

How strongly this contrasts with the climate of the techno-consumer society of the 1980s and early '90s. In our contemporary Ship of Fools we have an unprecedented degree of affluence and material comfort; we can indulge ourselves in sensual pleasure and electronic entertainment to surfeit. Yet underlying the glitzy surface there is a yawning abyss of emptiness – a kind of Doomsday mentality. We no longer believe in the future, or that the awesome ecological, environmental and political problems that threaten global nemesis can be solved. For the most part, the educated young, who once would have been the most vociferous critics of the prevailing political, moral and spiritual bankruptcy, have been bought off with prodigal quantities of cash. They dance while the *Titanic* sinks. And all the time essential freedoms and idealistic social institutions are being eroded or destroyed with a frightening degree of acquiescent passivity on the part of the general population. Western governments right now seem able to snatch away enlightened social advances which in the past men struggled hard and even died to gain.

Yet even today, when one meets the occasional visitor from an Eastern bloc country like Russia, where for years people have lived materially hard lives under the cloud of savage repression, it is amazing and chastening to see how they still have the old kind of optimism in the possibilities of a better future. Despite all they have suffered, perhaps even *because* of all they have suffered, they have not lost faith – or humanity... At the time of writing, the only figure of discernible stature in the field of world politics is Mikhail Gorbachev. Set beside him, the Western 'leaders' are a sorry bunch whose vision seems to extend no further than trying to tease out material affluence, for the increasingly few, for as long as possible, while the planet withers; and for whom the

Alan in his post-priest phase discussing Zen with D. T. Suzuki at the Rembrandt Hotel, London, in 1958.

Alan with his daughter Ann and father Laurence in the garden at Rowan Tree Cottage, Chislehurst during the 1950's.

apogee of human potential is not the adventurer, artist, scientist or sage, but the businessman, whom public relations has spuriously ennobled as a 'generator of wealth'. The only possible conclusion is that material affluence is at least an insidious soporific, more probably as virulent a toxin as any of the chemicals with which it pollutes our planet's land, sea and air.

In this anthology, however, we can find something of that old spirit of vision, faith and freedom. It is not simplistic or naive or dogmatic either, but comes from a deep place of inspiration, beyond mere reason. If this book can begin to revive the seeds of those inspiring qualities in our own decadent and cynical hearts, then Alan Watts will have left us a golden legacy indeed.

Sharpham, Devon
May–October 1989

Notes

1 Rudolf Steiner (1861–1925); originator of the panoramic Christian-based esoteric teaching called Anthroposophy, who was born in the old Austro-Hungarian Empire and lived latterly at Dornach in Switzerland. Conscious of anti-life forces at work in the modern world, Steiner sought to infiltrate regenerative spiritual insights and energies into a wide range of human activities, but in a manner appropriate to the times and consonant with the findings of science. Thus emerged new approaches in farming (e.g. the so-called Biodynamic methods), education (the Waldorf schools), architecture and the arts (Steiner developed the system of movement known as Eurythmy as well as a theory of colour), medicine, the social sphere (he propounded the notion of the four-fold state and the necessity of reconciling community and individuality, both of which Dimitrije Mitrinović later developed), the community care of the disabled, etc. etc. He also lectured and wrote extensively on religious matters; his esoteric Christianity, however, was liberal enough to accommodate Eastern notions like karma and reincarnation. Books include *The Philosophy of Freedom* (1916), *The Philosophy of Spiritual Activity* (1922), *Occult Science – An Outline* (1909).

2 Eleanor C. Merry: see note 31 of Notes on the Text.

3 G. K. Chesterton and L. Cranmer-Byng: see notes 24 and 26 of Notes on the Text.

4 Frank Buchman and the Oxford Groups: see note 21 of Notes on the Text.

5 *Certainly Future, Selected Writings of Dimitrije Mitrinović,* edited by Harry C. Rutherford, Boulder, 1987; p433.

6 ibid., p366.

7 Quoted in *The Religion of Logos & Sophia from the Writings of Dimitrije Mitrinović,* by Harry C. Rutherford, Sausalito, 1973; p13.

8 ibid., p19

9 ibid., Foreword, page unnumbered.

10 *Cloud Hidden, Whereabouts Unknown,* by Alan Watts, London, 1974; p167.

11 *Certainly Future, Selected Writings of Dimitrije Mitrinović,* as above; p284.

12 See also note 55 of Notes on the Text.

13 See also note 97 of Notes on the Text.

14 See also note 80 of Notes on the Text.

15 *In My Own Way,* by Alan Watts, Vintage paperback edition, New York, 1973; p177.

16 *Selected Poems,* by T. S. Eliot, Faber paperback edition, London, 1973; p 65.

NOTE

•

In the following collection of writings, author's notes appear as footnotes against appropriate marks (*, †, ‡) in the text. Editor's notes, however, are numbered in the text and glossed in the Notes on the Text at the end of the volume.

In the case of specialist Oriental terms, accents and diacriticals have in the main been left out of the Introduction and Notes on the Text in the interests of simplicity and accessibility. This follows Alan Watts' usual practice. However, in the case of 'The Problem of Faith and Works in Buddhism', where he expressly set out to be academically punctilious, we have left the technical embellishments in place.

PART ONE:

Writings for

The Modern Mystic

.

THE SPIRIT OF ASIA AND MODERN MAN (1937) (*Series*)

—————————— • ——————————

1   A TREE WITHOUT SOIL

World movements do not begin abruptly, and it is mainly for the sake of convenience that we say that the history of modern man begins with the Renaissance. Thus essentially modern characteristics may be found in the thought both of the Middle Ages and of Ancient Greece. It is not surprising, therefore, that the Renaissance arose out of the Middle Ages and turned to Ancient Greece for much of its inspiration. But if there is anything which differentiates modern man from his mediæval ancestors, it is, generally speaking, this: the faith of modern man in his own reason, as distinct from mediæval man's faith in God. Hence it is significant that the greatest philosopher of the Middle Ages, St Thomas Aquinas, should have founded his philosophy on faith, and used reason simply to prove it, whereas the first of the modern rationalist philosophers, Réné Descartes, should have gone a step further and begun just with the fact of his own existence. Aquinas began with God and His Revelation in Christ, and Descartes with the proposition *Cogito, ergo sum* – 'I think, hence I am.' This change is reflected nowhere better than in the difference between pre- and post-Renaissance drama. The Mystery Plays of the Middle Ages were concerned with the story of Divine Revelation, with Adam, Moses and Christ, whereas the plays of Shakespeare are concerned with the doings of man. This preoccupation with man and his reason is known as humanism, and its attitude may be summed up in that passage from *Hamlet*:

> What a peece of worke is man, how noble in reason, how infinit in faculties, in form and moving, how expresse and admirable in action, how like an Angell in apprehension, how like a God!

In other words, 'The proper study of mankind is man'; to which should be added 'conscious, rational man,' for humanism is at heart the faith that man can ultimately solve all problems by his own unaided reason. Thus in modern times almost every great philosopher, Kant, Hegel, Berkeley, Hume, Leibniz, has sought to understand the mysteries of the universe by reason alone. In the same way we find in science the attempt to solve all physical problems by the same rational technique, and in the dreams of H. G. Wells we find this faith in science carried to its wildest extreme – the complete mastery of nature both in and around us by the sole power of reason.

But this faith is almost at an end. It reached its climax at the close of the nineteenth century, to which period H. G. Wells really belongs, when the ideal of Progress nearly became a substitute of religion. It was believed that, through science, civilisation would go forward to greater heights of mastery, until through human reason the Kingdom of Heaven was established on earth. And then came a shock. The Western world suddenly went mad. It was as if the forces of unreason suddenly burst the dam which man had been building against them for so many centuries, for faith in human wisdom was suddenly hurled aside by a revelation of human devilry. World War 1 proved once again what the Church had always taught – the doctrine of original sin, of man's inability to achieve salvation by his own conscious efforts. At the same time, faith in pure reason began to reach its logical conclusion – the subjection of man to machinery. Man worshipped reason and ended by being ruled by it. For he forgot that reason is not his God but his instrument, that essentially it is no more than a machine – certainly a useful machine, but a machine with definite limitations. This subjection of man by the machine may be seen in the ideal of the totalitarian state, in Marxism and Fascism, and especially in the present tendency to centralise, organise and regulate all communal life, all business, in bureaucracy, and all attempts to ensure efficiency by perfect organisation. But systems are all very well so long as they can be changed. They are man-made and should remain man's servants; the danger is that man should become system-made, and that is the avowed aim of much modern thought.

There are, however, certain highly important things which systems, intellect, reason and logic cannot do. If you rely on them alone you reduce life to a purely mechanical process which runs eternally on its logical course like a Metropolitan train going round the Inner Circle[1]. It becomes no better than a Metropolitan train; it is as steely and as woodenly dead. You explain life, you unveil all its mysteries, you subject it to logical order until it is as dead and dull as any piece of clockwork. In fact, by explaining it in terms of reason you explain it away. It ceases to be life and becomes dead, even damned. For the logical faculty, reason, is made to order life, not to understand it. If you ask an adding machine whether there is a God, it will give you an answer in pounds, shillings and pence, and if you believe it you will become a successful financier. You may spell out as many questions as you like on the dial of your automatic telephone, and you will probably get, not information about God, but a great deal of advice about Hell. For these instruments are made for a specific purpose and can only answer questions in their own terms. Therefore, if you rely exclusively on intellect, you will see all life in terms of intellect, which is to say in terms of machinery.

This will have one of two results, the second of which will probably follow in time from the first. Either you will become so unbendingly rational, so strictly moral, so aggressively well-regulated and so much like a machine that your friends will be able to calculate what you will think on any subject or do in any circumstances. Or else you will go mad. It is a characteristic of many lunatics that they have a reason for their least actions. We say that lunatics are those who have lost their reason; it would be much more true to say that they have *become* their reason, for the easiest way to go mad is to imagine that you are a machine. You must get up every morning in exactly the same way, touch exactly the same trees on your way to work, eat exactly the same lunch, and so on – this is a common enough form of lunacy. But instead of trying to get rid of this, we encourage it by making everyone's life as monotonous as possible by systemisation. And perfection, as understood by the reason, is the most monotonous thing in the world; it means perfect order in all things, which is to say the same order. In the ancient myth, Ixion was punished by being bound to a wheel which was to revolve for ever;

nowadays we consider what is only an extension of this not a punishment but something to be desired. The only difference is that our monotony is more complicated, that we have machines more intricate than the wheel. But they are all based on going round and round, and if going round and round is our ideal, the thing we worship, then we might as well be dogs and spend our days chasing our tails. This may be rational, but it is just intolerable.

In fact, it has led us to a state of spiritual bankruptcy. For to live on one's own reason is like living on one's own body, like consumption. It ends by killing itself. It has killed Christianity and the ancient dogmas of the Church; it has explained them away, and now it is explaining itself away. Man exchanged God for reason, and the result was that he was no longer made in the image of God but in the image of reason; he made himself like one of his own rational creations. If he believed in God at all he thought, as it were, 'God made me; I make machines, therefore I am like a machine. If I, who make machines, am a machine, therefore God, who makes me, is also a machine. Q.E.D.'

But now the reaction has set in; reason is either carried to its wildest extreme or utterly cast aside, and modern man is left rootless and bewildered. For his old traditions have been exhausted; the life which we drew from Greece, Rome and Israel through the medium of the Church means little to us now, and humanism has ended in its own contradiction. Yet, like a tree, civilisation must draw nourishment from the remains of older trees; it must not feed upon itself. If we have absorbed the legacy of classical antiquity, there is still left a vast and almost untouched soil for our roots – a soil which has only in recent years been made known to us. It is the legacy of ancient India and China. Its philosophies, unlike traditional Christianity, do not ask for belief in things which reason may deny; for rather than creeds they are psychologies, requiring not belief but experiment. But what is most important is that they open up a way to the understanding of life which surpasses reason without requiring unquestioning faith in a revelation. They do not deny reason but relegate it to its proper place; they do not deny revelation, but insist that you cannot understand it until you have experienced it for yourself.

Therefore the purpose of this series of articles is to show what the spiritual legacy of Asia can mean to us at this present stage in our evolution; how it can point out a middle way between reason and unreason, between unbelief and superstition, between the living death of pure logic and the unrestrained chaos of pure nonsense. In short, we have to learn over again what is meant by man being made in the image of God, but in a way which the Church never taught.

————————— • —————————

2 THE NEW HUMANISM

It has been said that to unite one must first separate, and whatever the faults of humanism as an ideal, it has this virtue as a means: that as a separation of man from nature it must necessarily precede his return to nature. It must not be imagined, however, that this has anything to do with what is usually understood as the 'back-to-nature' movement[2]. It is no more a matter of returning to the condition from which we started than the Prodigal Son returned to his former relationship with his Father. On the contrary, he returned to a very much more intimate and conscious relationship, so much so that it was for him, and not for the son who had always stayed at home, that the fatted calf was killed. Thus man as the primitive, as the savage, is like the son who has never left his home; he is so closely in touch with nature that the distinction between natural and artificial does not arise for him, and yet, if we may alter the words of Kipling, we must say of him, 'He does not know nature who only nature knows.' Indeed, so close is his union with nature in and around himself that he attributes personality to wind, rocks and trees and is almost unable to distinguish between dreams and waking life. In his own moods and impulses he sees the 'outward and visible signs' of gods and demons, and the whole animate and inanimate universe is one with him in the kinship of personality. But he has not the civilised man's sense of personal identity; he has not one soul but many. He has not the same sense of personal responsibility, for to him all his emotions, feelings and obsessions are distinct beings dwelling in his own body.

But with the development of consciousness and the sense of

identity, man becomes estranged from nature; he becomes self-conscious and uses the word 'I' instead of referring to himself in the third person. For just as the child says, 'Peter wants it,' the savage says, ''Mbongo faithful servant,' because neither can distinguish clearly between subject and object, between themselves and the external world. But when he becomes self-conscious, man rejects the idea that his moods and impulses are distinct beings of unpredictable behaviour, and accepts some responsibility for them. He finds that through reason they can, to some extent, be controlled, and that the natural forces of the external world can also be made to submit in some measure to his conscious will. Hence there follows the struggle for mastery between man and nature, and as man feels himself more and more a distinct and isolated being, so the struggle increases. In this way the philosophy of humanism is evolved, for man places his trust in the growing power of his own reason as against the irrational forces of nature. He glorifies himself by the measure of his separateness from and his rulership over the non-human world. To persist in this attitude, however, involves, as we have seen, a number of unfortunate consequences. For carried to its extreme, isolation is the equivalent of lunacy, and every mental specialist knows that the lunatic is the most isolated person on earth. The part only has meaning in some constructive and harmonious relationship with the whole, and no-one would think much of the steering-wheel of a car if it suddenly decided to step outside and inspect the front tyres. Nor would it be considered especially useful if it was so far unable to preserve its identity as to become involved with the gear-box, for in all things there is a Middle Way, which means simply a sense of proportion and relationship.

Hence, the separation of man from nature called humanism is in fact a preparation for a more intimate and fruitful union, a matter of *reculer pour mieux sauter*, a standing-away from the trees in order to obtain a view of the wood. In childhood there is no fruitful distinction between male and female; therefore children do not produce children. Thus before man can bear fruit he must become fully aware of the division between the two sexes. In adolescence this division is the cause of estrangement; the boy is somewhat contemptuous of the girl; he no longer plays with her as in childhood, but seeks companions of his own sex. Yet later on this estrangement gives way to the new union of marriage, and a child is born. There is this difference, however, between the union of marriage and the union of childhood: that in the latter the distinction between male and female has no meaning and is therefore not recognised, whereas in the former the distinction is not only recognised but also has meaning. And the meaning is the child, for the child is the *raison d'être* of the otherwise absurd division. Thus there are three stages: the first where there is no distinction, the second where there is distinction but conflict, and the third where there is distinction and harmony, and, as a result of harmony, meaning.

What is true of man's sexual life applies also to his spiritual life. This is not to say that religion is an expression of sex, but that both conform to certain laws or principles which operate alike on every plane of activity. At the present time Western civilisation is just coming out of the adolescent period; masculine reason is beginning to realise its inadequacy without feminine nature. In terms of individual life, our task is now to resolve the conflict between ourselves and the outside world (and for that matter the inside world of our innumerable emotions, impulses and desires). Socially, the task is to replace the conflict between man and nature by fruitful union, which must involve the end of that mere exploitation which degrades the exploiter to no more than a wealth-making machine. Thus we must try to succeed where the short-lived cultures of Greece and Rome failed. There were some few Greeks and Romans who overcame slavery to the intellectual and military machines (hence the Sacred Mysteries) but their influence was too slight to save their peoples from degeneration and conquest by barbarian masses. In humanism Greece and Rome were splendidly successful, and it was only right and natural that modern humanism should have derived its inspiration from them. But if we are to preserve ourselves from their fate we must look to those ancient cultures which lived beyond adolescence to maturity and old age – to India, China and Egypt. Of Egypt much is already being said in these pages, and therefore we shall confine ourselves to India and China.

Although generalisations are dangerous we have to use

them in any brief discussion of world movements. Thus when we make any general distinction between East and West, we do not deny exceptions, but in the main it will be agreed that whereas the West has glorified man by separating him from the universe, the East has done so by bringing the two into unity. In this union we have the basis of a new humanism. For the Buddha, the Avatar[3] and the Man of Tao are not supermen, not splendidly isolated beings ruling the world like gods, but great simply because they embody the principles on which the universe depends, because they express its meaning, because they are what in Christian terms we should call the Incarnate Word. This union is quite distinct from the union of primitive man, for before India and China reached spiritual maturity they had passed through the stage of reason, through the period of ordering and subjecting nature. For, nearly 2000 years before Christ, India had evolved the highly reasonably Laws of Manu[4], and it would seem that somewhere in the same period China produced the cultivated personal and social principles of her ancient classics.

Thus it is the greatest mistake to imagine that the important mystical philosophies of Asia – Vedanta, Buddhism and Taoism – advocate simply the absorption of man into the universe; that is chaos, mere formless vacuity, not cosmos. They do not wish us to return to the primitive condition of being unable to distinguish between ourselves and nature, to our 'first birth' when there is no division between man and woman. They seek instead the 'Second Birth' wherein man and woman unite while remaining different and produce a child, wherein man and the universe unite while remaining different to bear a Holy Child, to realise a Tao, a Dharma, a Meaning between opposites which were formerly in conflict. For just as the child gives meaning to man and woman and is the cause of love between the two, so also there is a Child which gives meaning to oneself and the world, which also calls forth love between the two. Eastern philosophy is the art and science of bringing that Child to birth, and although the whole secret is already contained in Christianity, it is only in symbol form. The wisdom of Asia will help us to pass from the form to the substance, to understand the story of Christ, the Holy Child, less as a historical event than as a personal experience. For what is important is not so much that Christ was born in Bethlehem some 2000 years ago, but that he should be born in us now so that we may say with St Paul, 'I live; yet no longer I, but Christ liveth in me.'

———————————— • ————————————

3 KRISHNA THE AVATAR

In our two previous articles we have discussed the wisdom of Asia in a general way, relating it to the present condition of life and thought in the West. But now we must turn to particulars, and this and the following two articles will be devoted to the three most important mystical teachers of the East – Krishna, the Buddha and Lao-tzu. Each of their systems will be considered by itself, but in the last article of the series we shall try to relate them to one another and express their common and basic theme in a way suited to the modern mind. In case anyone should be alarmed, we do not use the word 'modern' in the same sense as used by those people who like to describe themselves as 'modern.' For by modern people we mean people who are living today, not people who think they are especially clever *because* they are living today.

*   *   *

In one sense, however, it is always today, and though the capacity of man's intellect may develop with time, we have evidence that the quality of his soul has changed little in 3000 years. Some people may say that it has changed slightly for the worse, but we will not enter the misty realms of comparative morality. But sometime about 1500 years before Christ the inhabitants of northern India had evolved a social code which a few of the leading thinkers of the present day are beginning to recognise as the product of a supreme understanding of the social organism. And not long afterwards those same people began to chant verses which embrace almost every important problem known to philosophy. Upon the ancient foundation of the Code of Manu[4] and the Upanishads rests the great and rich tradition of Indian thought, which, in the form of Buddhism, has spread to nearly every part of Asia.

So far as we know the authors of the Upanishads were, economically speaking, mere peasants who could not even write[5]. These verses were committed to memory and passed down from generation to generation; yet in almost every line of even those acknowledged as the earliest there is a depth of wisdom equal to anything written in later times in any part of the world. It is not just ethical wisdom; it is philosophy and mysticism of the highest order.

The Upanishads, together with Shankara's[6] enormous commentaries thereon, may at first be too formidable a matter for the ordinary reader. Therefore as a beginning it may be more profitable to consider what is in some ways an epitome of the Upanishads – the *Bhagavad-Gita*. This is a later work, part of that great epic, the *Mahabharata*, which is supposed to be the discourse given to the warrior Arjuna on the field of battle by Krishna the Avatar, or incarnation of Vishnu. *Bhagavad-Gita* means 'The Song of the Lord,' for the *Gita* is less a discourse than a poem. The term 'discourse' may suggest the dry-as-dust philosopher who makes an 'analytical study'; but Krishna *sings*:

> I am the sapidity in waters, O son of Kunti,
> I the radiance in moon and sun; the Word of
> Power in all the Vedas, sound in ether, and
> virility in men:
>
> The pure fragrance of earths and the brilliance
> in fire am I; the life in all beings am I,
> and the austerity in ascetics. . .
>
> I am the gambling of the cheat, and the
> splendour of splendid things I; I am victory,
> I am determination, and the truth of the truthful I.
>
> Of rulers I am the sceptre; of those that seek
> victory I am statesmanship; and of secrets I
> am also silence; the knowledge of knowers am I.*

What is this 'I' which Krishna makes himself? It is the same thing which the Upanishads call the Self, the Brahman, the Atman[8], the central principle of almost every Indian philosophy. For India has always sought the answer to that greatest problem: 'What is That in me which is more than my emotions, my thoughts and my deeds? What is That which is

---

* The translation quoted throughout is Annie Besant's.

aware of my feeling, thinking and acting? What is That which brings all these operations into being and yet is not affected thereby?' They perceived, as it were, two selves in man, one which is composed of all those qualities, attributes and sensations which make up the personality, and another which is just the spectator of these things. Without the spectator we could have no knowledge of life, and to that extent it would no longer exist. Yet the more we think of it, the more our essential Self seems to be detached from all that we know objectively. Everything which we ordinarily call ourselves, everything which distinguishes us from other people and things, we can know as objects. But behind these there is always the Subject which knows, and this does not appear to have any distinct form or attributes. But in our ordinary way of living we identify this Self with the various parts of the personality; we think, 'I am angry,' not, 'I am aware of anger,' and in this manner the Self becomes virtually involved in the changing world of forms. When change comes upon us, when we are about to die and when we suffer, we fear, because we do not see that it is only the personality which changes, dies and suffers. In fact, the Self remains in all these things the untouched witness.

In the *Gita* Arjuna shows fear of the slaughter of battle, and this is an allegory of the world. But Krishna says:

> As a man, casting off worn-out garments,
> taketh new ones, so the dweller in the body,
> casting off worn-out bodies, entereth into
> others that are new.
>
> Weapons cleave him not, nor fire burneth him,
> nor waters wet him, nor wind drieth him away.
>
> Unmanifest, unthinkable, immutable, he is
> called; therefore knowing him as such thou
> should'st not grieve.

Krishna then goes on to describe the discipline of yoga, the means whereby man can discriminate between the two selves. He must learn to recognise that in action he does not act, but that the senses move about among the objects of sense. He must think not, 'I do this' but, 'The body, the senses, the mind, do this' and in this way he becomes detached from both action and its results. That is not to say that he ceases to act, but rather that he acts and renounces the fruit of action. He causes the lower aspect of himself to move only in accordance with Dharma[7] or duty; he acts in such and such a way because it is Dharma, and not because it will bring any reward. For the Self is beyond both reward and punishment; the one is adding and the other is taking away, and this can only concern that which has form, which is made of component parts. Thus the more man realises his identity with the Self, the more he becomes superior to change and circumstance.

This withdrawal into the Self may seem something like a tortoise pulling its limbs inside its shell – a manœuvre which to most of us seems the essence of cowardice. But it would be the greatest mistake to imagine that the *Gita* is the gospel of escapism. For it should be obvious that if we try to become detached from life through fear, the one thing from which we are *not* detached is fear itself. The fear may subside into latency, but its seed remains, and there is no true union with the Self until it is what is called 'union without seed' (*asamprajnata*). Thus the yoga which results from fear of life is perhaps the worst form of self-deception; the only right motive for seeking the Self is because it is in accordance with Dharma, with each man's duty to the universe. Needless to say, such purity of motive is hard to attain; indeed, it can only be attained when we have reconciled ourselves to the world of life which we fear by the complete acceptance of all experience. Ultimately, therefore, the one true motive for yoga, for union with the Self, is love for the world.

And yet it must seem strange that love for the world is the motive for withdrawal and detachment from it. But here we have to understand further what is meant by the Self. For the central principle of Vedanta, the philosophy of the Upanishads, is that the Self of man is the same being as the Self of the universe – Atman *is* Brahman, not a part of Brahman, but Brahman in its entirety. Therefore this withdrawal into the Self is the preparation for a great expansion; it is the inbreathing which precedes the outbreathing, for this breath rhythm runs through all our life. Indeed, Brahman means the One who breathes. In the womb our breath is, as it were, drawn in; we are born, we identify ourselves with experience, and our breath is thrown out; we seek the Self and it is drawn in again; we understand that the Self is Brahman, and this time our breath expands throughout the whole universe, so that we may say with Krishna:

> And whatsoever is the seed of all beings,
> that am I, O Arjuna; nor is there aught,
> moving or unmoving, that may exist bereft
> of Me.

But there is danger in this doctrine, as in all profound truth. For it has such a subtle temptation for our desire for personal power, for the egoism and spiritual pride in us which would claim lordship over the universe. Rightly interpreted the *Gita* is the road to supreme wisdom, but just such a slight perversion makes it an entry to madness. For in all spiritual adventure the penalties are as great as the rewards, and the rewards are only ours when we do not claim them – when we do not even desire to claim. Therefore, at the bginning, it is well to consider long and deeply the words of the Upanishads:

> Whatever lives is full of the Lord (Brahman).
> Claim nothing; enjoy, do not covet his property.

And again:

> The man who claims that he knows, knows nothing;
> but he who claims nothing, knows.

———————————— • ————————————

4 GAUTAMA THE BUDDHA

The story of the Buddha's Enlightenment would make an interesting subject for a symphony. It is divided into four distinct movements: the quest for happiness in the delights of sense, the awareness of suffering inherent in all pleasure, the quest for wisdom through asceticism, and finally the three previous themes are cast aside, for the tense striving of the ascetic yields. Even the longing for wisdom for oneself is seen as one of the desires that blind, and with this realisation there comes upon the Buddha that vast insight which was the reason of his title – Buddha, the Enlightened One.

Some time in the fifth century before Christ he was born as the son of a king in northern India, and the legend tells that he grew up and was married in circumstances as good as any man could desire. But a number of small incidents showed him that in wealth and pleasure there was no lasting happiness, for pleasure is a coin whose other face is pain. Whereat he stole away by night from his home and became a wandering ascetic, seeking in the pains of fasting and mortification the happiness which no luxury could give. But even here he found no consolation, for he had simply turned his life upside-down to find that pain is a coin whose other face is pleasure. There is no wisdom in cleaving to one extreme and rejecting the other, for the two can no more exist without each other than there can be front without back or flower without root. Therefore he stilled in himself the common desire of man for one side of life without the other, and with this letting go discovered the great principle of the Middle Way. But the Middle Way is not compromise; it is no mere principle of moderation, of being not very good and not very evil, of having no great pleasures in order that there may be no great pains. It has been rightly said that the Golden Mean is more mean than golden, but the Middle Way is less the Golden Mean than the Golden Meaning.

That is to say, just as the child is the meaning, the *raison d'être*, of man and woman, so the Middle Way is the meaning of life expressed as a changing rhythm of opposites. Music is a meaning whose father is sound and whose mother is silence; there is no meaning in sound alone or in silence alone, but when the two are wedded in a rhythmic sounding and silencing of notes there emerges a melody. Thus we may see that the Buddha's Enlightenment is the full understanding of the meaning of life. Unenlightened people do not perceive this meaning, for they are always seeking life as apart from death, and pleasure apart from pain; it is as if they desired a tune which was just one long uninterrupted noise, or a world in which there were no women. (Some of them actually do desire this latter monstrosity.) Therefore the Buddha's Middle Way is no more a compromise than a child is a hermaphrodite. It is neither a static condition of balance between the opposites nor a merging of the two into one. On the contrary, it is relating them to one another in such a way as to give them meaning. The marriage ceremony is not held to celebrate the mutual identification of bride and

54

bridegroom, although in England we have a legal fiction that the two are one person. Its whole point is that it is a union of wholly different beings, and if they ceased thereby to be different the affair would be without interest

Many of the Buddha's followers have tried to maintain that his teaching involved the rejection of both opposites; that if he rejected the pleasure of his father's palace he rejected also the pain of the ascetic. They would hold that as you cannot have pleasure without pain, pleasure is not worth having, which is rather like the old story of the sour grapes. It requires no Enlightenment to adopt this attitude to life; it means simply that you would have pleasure if you could have it without pain, and the fact that you renounce it does not change your inward desire. Such a philosophy, however, would have gained little respect in a land which reverenced the teaching of the Upanishads, and it is significant that as this negative interpretation of Buddhism developed it rapidly lost influence in India. It went southwards to Ceylon where its negativeness increased, and northwards to China where a highly practical and cultured people swiftly perceived its true meaning. They saw that, so far from being a denial of life and death, it was in fact a tremendous affirmation, and from this understanding grew the way of life which is today known as Zen.

If we examine the teachings of the Chinese Zen masters, we find that their Buddhism was by no means an escape from pain. Thus a disciple came to his master and asked, 'It is terribly hot, and how shall we escape the heat?' And at once the answer came, 'Let us go down to the bottom of the furnace.' So the perplexed disciple asked again, 'But in the furnace how shall we escape the scorching fire?' To which he received the surprising reply, 'No further pains will harass you.' This seems to be another way of saying that evil is overcome by acceptance as distinct from denial. Thus, if you try to avoid death you enter a living death, for life only lives, only moves, because it is at every moment dying. The more you run away from your shadow, the faster it follows, and it does not cease to exist because you turn round and look the other way.

Buddhism is therefore the art of understanding the shadow, of coming gladly to terms with the night as well as the day. For it is only when the day looks at the night and loves it for being different that a meaning is born between them, and only when we say YES to all experience that we find any meaning in life. We cannot have the flower's beauty without the root's ugliness, the light and colour above without the dirt and darkness below, and Enlightenment is the understanding that both are supremely right in their own places. Ignorance is trying to have one without the other, and sin is to put the flower in the dirt and the roots in the air. But the flower is not any less in beauty because the root feeds on mud, and it is well to remember that if the delights of the table did not undergo a relatively unpleasant transformation in the stomach, we should suffer from dire indigestion.

Thus Enlightenment is no matter of mere knowledge. You may study the internal workings of the body until you can take an honours degree in physiology, but that does not necessarily imply that you are not wholly repelled by your inside. Nor is it something to do with one's method or technique of living, for the greatest master of technique may be a poor artist if his technique expresses no meaning. Hence the method of living is simply the vehicle for expressing the meaning of life, and unless this is first understood no amount of occult study, yoga practice, asceticism, ritual, learning or mental gymnastics will bring you one whit nearer to Enlightenment. In Christian terminology, no amount of 'good works' avail without the Grace of God. The same must therefore be said of morality, for it is so often thought that morality is the way to religious understanding. The truth is that morality is a pure sham unless it expresses a previously felt religious experience. For this reason a great Chinese Buddhist once made the following alarming statement: 'Nirvana and Enlightenment are dead stumps to tie your donkey to. The twelve divisions of the scriptures are only lists of ghosts and sheets of paper fit to wipe the dirt from your skin. And all your four merits and ten stages are mere ghosts lingering in their decaying graves. Can these have anything to do with your salvation?' In other words, all the knowledge in the world and the most scrupulous attention to rules and regulations will not be of the least benefit without some measure of the wisdom which no words can describe. Mere ideas about Enlightenment are just stumbling blocks without the thing itself, and if we must put the matter into a slogan we might say, 'Means are dead without Meaning.' Certainly the artist's technique is a means to his full artistic triumph, and in the same way morality and religious observances are a means to the supreme Enlightenment. But of themselves they do not create the meaning to be expressed; they enable it to shine out in all its glory, but if it is not felt as existing within us in latency no technique can produce it.

Now Buddhism teaches that the Buddha-nature, the germ of Enlightenment, exists in every single thing in the universe. In other words, the deepest meaning is present in each one of us, and the first step is to realise its presence. Then, and then only, can technique be used with effect. But how do we realise (i.e. make real) its presence? The answer is that it will come of itself if we let it – and the stress is on the word 'let.' Just as the Grace of God is given to all who open themselves to receive it, the Buddha-nature can be realised by all who relax the fierce grip on life which is called 'I.' For when we cease the struggle to hold one extreme and push the other away, to keep life and reject death, to save ourselves from change and loss; when this frantic effort to stop up the conduit pipe of our being is made to cease; when we allow the stream of life to flow on without trying to hold it with a dam, then only can the Buddha-nature come through, for it is the very movement of the water. Hence the moment we relax to experience we realise the presence of a meaning in death as well as life, in pain as well as pleasure. And the paradox is that we do it by not doing but by letting go and renouncing the self-assertive effort to grasp and keep what can only live if it moves and passes away.

It is just this particular grasping desire which is expressed in that keyword of Buddhism — *trishna* — for the essence of the Buddha's teaching was that salvation comes through absence of desire. Herein is a matter of supreme importance for all seekers after truth: Enlightenment is not for those who desire it, for Enlightenment is the absence of desire. But be careful what is meant by 'desire,' for it is also said that when desirelessness has been achieved through desire the secret is understood.

———————————— • ————————————

5 LAO-TZU, THE MAN OF TAO

It is seldom that the founder of a great religion ever commits his own teaching to writing[70]; in almost every instance his words are memorised and recorded by his disciples. This is perhaps one of the reasons why our most venerated spiritual teachers always seem to us rather serious people. For their disciples regarded them as gods, and so intense and almost fanatical was their devotion that only rarely does anything human, not to say humorous, creep through those barriers of solemn words. There are perhaps one or two instances in the Gospels where Jesus might just be suspected of having made a joke, though none of the great Christian artists has ever painted a laughing Christ. So far as we can remember there are two distinct jokes in the Buddhist scriptures, but the images of the Buddha seldom do anything more than smile. But it is quite another matter when we come to the sages of that ancient religion of China known as Taoism. Curiously enough both Lao-tzu and his great exponent, Chuang-tzu[62], are supposed to have written down their teachings themselves, and throughout their writings is a refreshing and subtle humour. In Lao-tzu it is slightly veiled, but in Chuang-tzu there can be no mistaking it, while in Chinese art a solemn picture of either is the exception rather than the rule.

There is a legend that the Buddha, Confucius and Lao-tzu were once assembled round a barrel of vinegar. Each dipped in his finger and licked it, and while the Buddha pronounced it bitter and Confucius sour, Lao-tzu chuckled and declared it sweet. Although this is not quite a fair comment on either the Buddhist or Confucian attitudes to life, it does stress the important point that Taoism is anything but a world-denying and solemn philosophy. For the Chinese are, as a whole, a humorous and practical people, and had they not seen the real point of the Buddha's teaching and wedded it to Taoism in that astonishing cult known as Zen, Buddhism would probably have remained the most dismal religion on earth. A Chinese Buddhist sage was once asked: 'When the body crumbles all to pieces and returns to the dust, there eternally abides one thing. Of this I have been told, but where does this one thing abide?' Now an Indian teacher would probably have replied with a ponderous discourse of several thousand words, but the Chinese sage just remarked quite casually, 'It is windy again this morning.' It seems such a pity to have to try to explain this remark, because as a rule when we try to explain the great mysteries of life we only explain them away. But perhaps we shall understand just a little of the mind of that Chinese sage by learning something of Taoist principles, for nothing else can give so clear a revelation of the Chinese mentality.

The fundamental concept of Lao-tzu's philosophy is that almost untranslatable word 'Tao.' Originally it meant 'speech,' and therefore the first words of Lao-tzu's book, the *Tao Tê Ching*, contain the pun: 'The Tao that can be *tao*-ed is not the real Tao.[9] This is usually rendered, 'The Tao that can be put into words (or 'described') is not the real Tao.' (This, incidentally, should carefully be held in mind when reading what follows.) There have been many attempts to translate this word, some of our efforts being 'The Way,' 'God,' 'Reason,' 'Law,' 'the Logos,' 'the Spirit' and 'Meaning.' The last, which is Richard Wilhelm's translation, is in many ways the best because the Tao is really the essential meaning of life, or, to use the French expression, its *raison d'être*. That is not to say, however, that the Tao is the Principle of Reason, for reason (the characteristic of intellect) must always fail to grasp it. For Tao is the living meaning of life and death. Life cannot exist without death, for things move and change only because they are at every moment dying. Life and death are therefore like man and woman; without each other they are meaningless, but that which gives meaning to the two sexes is the child. In this sense the child is both the cause and the result of man and woman ('The child is father to the man'), and in the same way the Tao is the cause and result of life and death, and, furthermore, *is* life and death.

The important thing, however, is that the Tao is something living; it is the movement of living and dying, and the moment we try to catch hold of it, either in actuality or in thought, it is no longer there. If life were to stand still and not move towards death so that we could enjoy it for ever, it would at once cease to live. If the wind could be captured and shut in a room, it would cease to be wind; and if you try to clutch water in your hands, it will just slip through your fingers. In the same way you can never catch hold of the present moment. Before you can wink an eyelid it has vanished into the past, and the more you think about it, the more you try to analyse it and say just when and where it is, the more elusive it becomes. It is like a dog running round after its own tail: the faster it runs, the faster the tail escapes, and if it tries to run away from the tail, the tail follows as fast as it runs. The Tao seems to behave in just the same way. It is present in everything; it *is* everything; yet when we look for it it seems to run away, for we ourselves are Tao and to look for it is like turning round to see our own eyes. And yet Lao-tzu says that we must realise the Tao. This realisation he calls *Tê* or 'virtue,' although it is not what moralists understand as virtue, for Lao-tzu says:

> The superior virtue is not conscious of itself as virtue;
> Therefore it has virtue.
> The inferior virtue never lets off virtue;
> Therefore it has no virtue.
>
> (Trans: *Chu'u Ta-kao*)

That is to say, if you try aggressively to be virtuous you are just like the dog running after its tail. In the same way, if you try self-assertively to concentrate on what you are reading here, you will find that you are only concentrating on yourself trying to read. And if you think about that for too long, you will be concentrating on yourself concentrating on yourself trying to read, and so on in an infinite regress. But you will not read anything.

How then are we to realise the Tao? Another Chinese sage was asked, 'What is the Tao?' He replied, 'Usual life is the very Tao.'

And again he was asked, 'How, then, do we bring ourselves into accord with it?' 'If you *try* to accord with it,' he answered, 'you will get away from it.'

'But,' his questioner went on, 'with no trying, how can we know that it is Tao?'

'Tao,' said the sage, ''belongs neither to knowing nor not knowing. Knowing is but a dream; not knowing but an absence of memory. When we really attain to the doubtless Tao it will be as clear as the vastness of the sky. What is the necessity of calling it in question then?'

In other words, you cannot find the Tao in mere knowledge

about it such as you might gain from this article. Nor are you any better off if you have never heard about it at all. Therefore Lao-tzu taught a way of life known in Chinese as *wu-wei*, which literally means 'non-assertion' and is sometimes erroneously translated as doing nothing. It has two aspects, negative and positive. Negatively, it might be called non-possessiveness, letting go, or giving up one's own particular purpose.

'When purposelessness has been achieved through purpose,' says a Taoist book, 'the thing has been grasped.'

That is to say, we must give up chasing the Tao, and we must also give up running away from it. We must no longer try to possess and keep for ourselves either life or anything that lives in this present moment. In the same way, we must no longer try to run away from death; the seeds of death are in ourselves, and no amount of running can put them any further away. Tao is ourselves and our every thought and deed, and sin only enters our lives because we do not understand this, because we chase the Tao or flee from it in one or other of its countless forms. Indeed, the Tao lives in us in spite of ourselves; we cannot, whatever our efforts, make it come to us or go away from us. And if perchance we suddenly realise the Tao, that is no cause for pride; rather we should laugh at ourselves for not having seen that it has actually been realised all the time.

Therefore, positively, *wu-wei* means what is sometimes called 'going straight ahead.' To the question, 'What is the Tao?' a sage replied simply, '*Walk on!*'[63] For Tao is right before us at every moment; if we stop to catch it, it eludes us. Time moves on and never waits, and while we think about it and try to grasp it it leaves us behind. Therefore Chuang-tzu said, 'The perfect man employs his mind as a mirror. It grasps nothing; it refuses nothing. It receives, but does not keep.' In fact it reflects the Tao as it moves instantly and immediately, but does not cling to it. To change the simile, the man of Tao neither pursues himself nor flees from himself; if his shadow falls behind he does not hasten forward; if it falls in front he does not turn away. He just walks straight on. It is as if the dog had stopped worrying about its tail, having discovered that it was his *own* tail, and had simply gone right ahead instead of running in circles. There is no need now to worry about whether you have or have not found the Tao; if you walk on it goes with you, and try as you like you cannot get away from it.

Here, surely, is the cause of Taoist laughter. You know how often you must have laughed at yourself for looking all over the place for something you were carrying round with you. The Chinese sometimes speak of it as the story of the lunatic who went all over the world in search of his head, which he had never lost. Before and after his realisation his head is there just the same. Nothing has changed, and yet somehow everything has changed.

It is rather like Chuang-tzu's famous story of *Three in the Morning*.

Tzu-chi said, 'Not recognising the fact that all things are One – this is called *Three in the Morning*.'

And what,' asked Tzu-yu, 'is *Three in the Morning*?'

'A keeper of monkeys,' replied Tzu-chi, 'said with regard to their rations of chestnuts, that each monkey was to have three in the morning and four at night. But at this the monkeys were very angry, so the keeper said they might have four in the morning and three at night, with which arrangement they were all well pleased. The actual number of the chestnuts remained the same, but there was an adaptation to the likes and dislikes of those concerned.'

•

6 IN PERSPECTIVE

Our treatment of the wisdom of Asia has of necessity been brief. Indeed, we have done little more than to indicate the essential principles of her three greatest teachers — Krishna, the Buddha and Lao-tzu — and we have seen that when their teachings are reduced to their elements they are remarkably similar. All three embrace a fundamental principle which may be called the principle of 'surrender.' For Krishna, it is detachment from one's own personality as distinct from the Higher Self which uses that personality as an instrument. For the Buddha, it is the giving up of *trishna*, the desire to cling to things, to keep them from changing, to hold to life and reject death, to seek pleasure and shun pain. For Lao-tzu, it is *wu-wei* or 'non-assertion,' which is to cease to seek for the Tao through the knowledge that one has always had it. Furthermore, Lao-tzu's 'non-assertion' may be described in exactly the same terms as the Buddha's giving up of the desire to possess. These are three negative precepts, but we have seen that in each instance they have an essentially positive result. For in truth it is their opposites which are really negative, for the paradox is that to cling violently to the forms of life is to deny and to kill them, just as a living, running stream is no longer a stream if we try to shut it up in a reservoir. Therefore if we imagine that the Eastern religions would have us deny life just because they ask us to give up life, we miss the point entirely. On the contrary, it is only when life is given up that it can live. There is a saying, 'Live and let live'; we should do well to ponder the word *let* and consider that we can never give ourselves a chance unless we can first let our selves go.

This, then, is the fundamental principle of the Eastern wisdom, and for that matter of Christianity also. In applying it to our lives there are two things to be remembered: the first that it can be applied in a great multitude of ways corresponding to the vast diversity of human types, and the second that it can be applied on every plane of spiritual development. With regard to the first, we have said little as yet about the astonishing variety of Eastern religions, or even of the still more astonishing fact that so many different forms of religion can exist together with so little conflict. To understand this we must go to the foundations of the religious life of India – a land which has been in so many ways the spiritual fountain of Asia. For the ancient Indian Code of Manu is based on the fact that the universe, the life of society and the life of man are unities in diversity. Unless all the divers elements are cared for the whole will not be complete, and, conversely, no one element is of any account apart from the whole.

If we begin from the physical body, we shall see that man had three main organs – stomach, heart and head. These correspond approximately to man's three relationships to the world – to substance (economics), to other people (politics) and to ideas (culture)[39b]. The Code of Manu therefore divided society into three castes or functions corresponding to each of these three relationships. The Vaishya or merchant caste cared for substantial needs; the Kshattriya caste of warriors and rulers was responsible for political order; and the Brahmana caste of priests cared for the needs of the spirit. These three divisions corresponded in turn to the three essential qualities (*gunas*) of life – Tamas, the earthy and inert; Rajas, the fiery and active; and Sattva, the watery, the level and balanced. In the same way the Code of Manu laid down that every man had to fulfil himself in three corresponding ways, and therefore it taught three great arts of life: the art of Kama, the care and development of the sensual functions, the art of Artha or citizenship, and the art of Dharma or religion. At the moment we are concerned with the latter, and here again we shall find a threefold division based on just the same principles. For it was recognised that there are, broadly speaking, three types of people who will approach religion best in three different ways, and hence there arose the three forms of yoga: *Karma Yoga*, the way of action in the substantial world; *Bhakti Yoga*, the way of the heart, of feeling and emotion; and *Gñana Yoga*, the way of intellect.[10] And just as the air covers earth, fire and water alike there was another yoga for highly developed people which embraced all three ways, and this was known as the Royal Way of Raja Yoga.

With this foundation it was possible for Hinduism and its offspring, Buddhism, to become the most diverse religions in the world. The many sects of Buddhism can in some ways be fitted into the same threefold division, though this is not altogether the result of any conscious direction. Men are naturally divided in this way, and consquently their ideas will grow accordingly. But we can say that the East has, on the whole, adapted itself more easily than the West to this fundamental principle of human nature because of the ancient Indian tradition of Manu. But human nature so often contradicts itself, for though it is essentially diverse it can seldom agree with good grace to differ. The West is perhaps especially lacking this grace, for once it discovers a 'good idea' it can never rest until the whole world has been induced to find it equally good. The most obvious example of this is our attempt to convert the East to Christianity. Without doubt Christianity is a good religion just as the egg is a good food; but a diet composed entirely of eggs would be decidedly not so good. The rose is admittedly a beautiful flower; some would call it the most beautiful flower, but no-one in his senses would advocate the abolition of all other flowers until positively 'all was roses.'

Another example of our Western horror of diversity is the growth of fascism and communism. Both of these cults insist on uniformity and regimentation, and will tolerate no disagreement, but they do not grasp that uniformity is anything but unity. You can only have unity if you have a number of different things to unite; if everything is the same it is not a unity but a clod – a homogeneous monstrosity. Heraclitus said that life 'is a harmony of opposing tensions, as in the lyre and the bow,' and the one thing that the leveller, the regimentationalist cannot tolerate is tension. He wants everything to go in the same way, just like those who want all pleasure and no pain. Yet here again we meet the old paradox, for it is precisely through trying to avoid tension in this way that he increases tension, for in asserting one opposite he simply aggravates the other. Therefore the East would have us relax, let go, accept the tension, and here again it is not denying life but making it more abundant. For if the strings of your lyre are only to be drawn in one direction, they will remain slack. But there is something holding them at the other end, and we are so intent on getting away from it that we shall soon break the strings. And in either event there will be no music.

We come finally to the second point: that the principles of the Eastern wisdom can be applied on every plane of spiritual development. We would go even further than this and say that they must be applied on the plane of development on which you stand now. So many people in the West imagine that to grow in wisdom they must cast aside all the ties and responsibilities of worldly life, that they must stunt their ordinary, earthly faculties (which they certainly do not know how to use) in order that they may develop new occult and psychic faculties. But it must be recognised that the pursuit of these things has nothing whatever to do with religion; it is purely a question of science. Religion is concerned rather in being faithfully, fully and intelligently what one is. If a wheelbarrow is a good wheelbarrow and serves its purpose to the utmost, then, from a religious point of view, it is just as good as a high-powered car. With a little clever scientific adaptation it may one day be converted into a car, but this can hardly be done while it is still poor as a wheelbarrow. Certainly the car is more effective than the wheelbarrow, but even so it does not follow that it serves its purpose as well. Religious attainment is therefore measured by the extent to which we serve our purpose and understand our purpose, and in this sense an ordinary man with a family and a business may be more enlightened than a great ascetic and magician. If you can fully see into your purpose here and now you may attain the greatest Enlightenment; all that you may add to yourself thereafter by way of powers and faculties will only make you more efficient. But efficiency without understanding is not only useless but dangerous; certainly efficiency is necessary, but please let us have the understanding first.

It is said that Enlightenment is the end of religion. At present we know nothing of the end, but of this we may be sure: that Enlightenment is most decidedly its beginning. And where should we look for that beginning? If Enlightenment is also the end of all experience, let us look for it too in the beginning of experience. Some imagine that it is found in peculiar states of consciousness accessible only to faculties which ordinary people do not possess. But should we be disappointed if we were told that the supreme religious experience is nothing other than our ordinary everyday experience of walking, seeing, eating, breathing, laughing, sleeping and thinking? This, we may feel, is something much too commonplace, too familiar, too dull, too uninspiring. Yet that is only because we are too proud to admit that it mystifies us utterly, that these simple and elementary affairs are much too profound to understand.

Van der Leeuw[11] has said that the mystery of life is not a problem to be solved, but a reality to be experienced. Might it not then be wise to apply again the old Eastern paradox and understand life by *letting* it be a mystery?

MYSTICS OF TODAY (1937/8)
(Series)

•

1 KRISHNAMURTI: THE MESSIAH WHO BECAME A SAGE

Some time ago I received anonymously from South Africa a paper-covered book which I put away among those things which one feels one *might* read eventually but in any case ought to be filed for reference. It was a record of talks given by Krishnamurti[12] while on a visit to Scandinavia, and at that time I knew of him as just one of those many religious teachers who bask in the adoration of frustrated women. But while on holiday last July some people whose intelligence I respect told me that this Krishnamurti, who had once been heralded as a Saviour of the World, was talking uncommon good sense. I remembered the book which had been sent to me, turned it up and read it. Its contents proved so fascinating that I bought another record of his talks.

Almost at the same time a doctor friend wrote me the following rather cryptic message: 'Will you come and have dinner with me on Tuesday; I am trying to get a few people together.' I went. It was a small party of some seven or eight people, most of them old friends, but somehow I had a 'hunch' that we had been asked for a special purpose. It soon appeared that the guest of honour was to be this very Krishnamurti, and after we had been assembled for a few minutes he arrived and was introduced to us. I took the opportunity of having a talk with him and after a time we all asked him questions which resulted in a most profitable discussion. He stayed with us until about 10 o'clock and then took his leave as quietly and as unobtrusively as he had come. And now I doubt if I shall ever open one of his books again, and still less go out of my way to see him again.

Almost every one of Krishnamurti's devotees that I know

constantly uses the phrase, 'Well, I must say this about him although I know he wouldn't approve of it.' That is precisely the trouble. As is well known, Krishnamurti began his career under the auspices of Mrs Annie Besant and others as a modern Messiah. From early childhood he was trained to be a Saviour of the World, and, very naturally, when he attained maturer years he announced that he would rather drive a bus than be a Messiah. But even before he renounced any claim to this 'mission' he had attracted an enormous number of followers, so much so that today his annual camp at Ommen in Holland attracts thousands. Yet somehow, the more he tells them he is not a Messiah, the more he refuses to discuss the whole question, the more he avoids adulation, the more his followers bow down at his feet. This may partly be understood from the fact that he has a most undoubted personal charm; certainly he is the most handsome Indian I have yet seen. But there is a profounder reason than this, and a most disturbing reason. It seems to be that his work defeats itself precisely because he is telling people the naked truth. Now the quickest and easiest way to avoid the truth is to make a god of the man who speaks it. This has the comforting effect of making that truth something inapplicable to 'mere mortals,' something to be worshipped and reverenced but certainly not to be used. Not all his followers regard him frankly as a Messiah. Unfortunately many of them have become victims of something worse than adulation, and that is imitation.

Krishnamurti is always at pains to point out that truth cannot be imitated; it is not yours because you observe a certain spiritual technique or because you think and behave in a certain way of which you have read in a book or seen in the life of another. This is nothing more than a second-hand spiritual experience, which is to say a sham. Religion can no more be learnt from books or lectures than the art of loving one's wife or husband can be learnt from a treatise on matrimony.

But perhaps Krishnamurti is not really a religious teacher. He has nothing to say about God, about the life after death, about the absolute nature of the universe; he teaches no form of meditation, prayer or ceremonial. He says that these things do not matter... more than that – that they are the very means by which we hide the truth from ourselves. At the same time he is no materialist or 'rationalist.' He does not deny God or immortality; he simply says nothing about them, except that if you believe in them in order to shield yourself from suffering they are simply hindrances. For Krishnamurti is interested purely in Life. Here we are on this earth endowed with five senses, with the power of enjoyment, with the capacity to suffer. This, he says, is enough to teach us truth, and yet we exhaust our brains to find means of avoiding them. We want new senses to give us occult experiences; we treasure the hope of immortality to avoid the pain of death; we believe in a loving God to protect ourselves from the unwelcome truth that we stand alone and unaided in a world from which nothing can deliver us. In fact, he wants to show us just how alone and unprotected we are, to bring us back to the foundation of experience, freed from all illusions, all inherited prejudices, all props and crutches. For in everyone there is a conflict, in most of us lying hidden. Our lives are spent in trying to forget this inner struggle, in seeking a thousand and one means of escaping the truth that we are afraid of the world, that we suffer; that, in short, we are unhappy.

It is an old truism that if you seek happiness, you do not find it. For all this seeking, this quest for a spiritual technique which will make life more bearable, is an escape from this fundamental experience. Krishnamurti therefore asks one question: 'You belong to this or that religion; you cherish such and such a belief or ideal; you behave in a certain way in accordance with certain rules or standards. WHY?'

Almost invariably the answer must be that it is because we are afraid and do not like to admit it; because there is a conflict between ourselves and the world, and somehow or other we want to come out 'on top.' Yet the more we oppose the world, the more we look for salvation from it as if it were somehow different from us, the more that conflict is increased. This attempt to escape takes on the most subtle and insidious forms. Krishnamurti says that even trying not to escape may yet be a means of trying to escape, that we may strive to love the world simply because we hate it, believing that this love will in some way deliver us. And so love is made the instrument of hate, and acceptance the tool of fright. The reason is that we make an opposition between love and hate, between acceptance of life and escape from it. If we feel that we hate life and try to counteract that hate with love, we just create another conflict; if we want to run away and try to conquer that desire with an attitude of relaxed acceptance, we thereby oppose the one to the other and become involved in the agony of the struggle between them.

This seems to be a terrible *impasse*. All of us want in some way or other to solve the fundamental problems of life, to make the world more endurable, to attain wisdom, to be happy – even if we can achieve it, paradoxically, by an intensity of suffering. Yet Krishnamurti shows us with unanswerable logic that if we try to overcome the world in any way, even by the indirect means of submission to it, we simply create again the very thing we desire to defeat. For the problem does not lie in the technique, the means, the behaviour we employ to achieve our end; it lies in our motive for employing it. For Krishnamurti always descends with the searching question: WHY? Acceptance of life is just as bad as escape from it if our motive for acceptance is escape. Therefore we shall naturally ask, 'Well, how can we change our motive?' And here Krishnamurti would ask, 'Why do you want to change your motive?' At last, then, we must give the despairing cry, 'Please, what *can* we do about it?' Perhaps we might then ask ourselves why we want to do anything about it. And here, if we are not to fall into the infinite regress of 'motives for motives for motives for motives,' we must simply face the ultimate fact of our utter loneliness and fear. At this point we have no more illusions about ourselves; we have thrown aside every shield and support, every pretence to spirituality. We arrive, as it were, at a complete 'debunking' of our desires, our theories and our ideals. It is not that there is anything wrong with them in themselves; the trouble is that we make them wrong by misuse. There is a Chinese saying that if the wrong man uses the right means, the right means work in the wrong way. The crux of the problem is therefore how to find the right man. But why do we want to find him...?

It appears that Krishnamurti is a spiritual irritant. He is tearing down idols right and left; he is calling in question our holiest treasures and leaving us without a single hope or comfort. His logic drives us like rats into a hole in a rock which comes to a dead end; he makes us feel like the donkey with the carrot dangled before its nose by the man on its back – the more it pursues the faster the carrot slips ahead, and if it stops the carrot remains at the same distance. The mystics of China put it in this way: 'There was a man who kept a goose in a bottle, and in time the goose grew so large that it could not get out. Now he did not want to break the bottle or hurt the goose. How can he get it out?' Why does he want to get it out? Perhaps the solution is therefore to give up wanting the carrot and to leave the goose in the bottle. But why do we want to give up wanting? Why do we want a solution? By no possible means can this searching examination be escaped; we are forced to return to the experience of our helpless solitude, our ultimate despair. And to make that experience even more complete, let us ask, 'Why do we suffer, why this despair, why this fear?' The answer must be that it hurts us because we oppose it, because we do not want it. Then why do we oppose it? Because we fear it, because we suffer. And here we are at last turning round in helpless circles. For our position is just that we do not want to suffer because we suffer, and that we suffer because we do not want to. At this point we must go mad or do something desperate; we can just cry or scream or curse the day we were born into such an idiotic paradox. But no amount of protest can make away with it; the more we fight it, the harder it hits back. It is as maddening as trying to kiss your own lips. When suddenly there comes the moment when we ask, 'Well, what is all this fuss about?' If you try to kiss your own lips you will break your neck; if you *will* pursue the carrot you will tire yourself out; if you don't want to suffer you will go mad with pain. You don't avoid joy, so why avoid sorrow? When you enjoy yourself, you enjoy yourself; when you suffer, you suffer. So why go mad through running round in circles? Walk on[63].

But please don't think that you can save yourself by 'walking on.' Somebody might ask 'WHY?'

——————————— • ———————————

2   CARL GUSTAV JUNG: THE BRIDGE BETWEEN SCIENCE AND RELIGION

It would perhaps be difficult to find another man of science who is more misunderstood by his fellow scientists than Dr. C. G. Jung of Zürich.[13] He is, moreover, in the unfortunate position of standing between two camps, for, on the one hand, scientists accuse him of turning psychology into mysticism, and on the other, men of religion suspect him as one who rejects their most cherished beliefs as mere phantasies of the unconscious mind. This is always the fate of those who tread the Middle Way, of peace-makers, of bridge-builders, of those who try to bring opposites into constructive relationship. Both parties accuse him of favouring the opposite side because they are incapable of appreciating a middle point of view. But the psychologist, whoever he may be, is always in a difficult position. The nineteenth century quarrel between religion and science has, generally speaking, been brought to an end by agreeing that the two are concerned with totally different things. Science is occupied with quantities and their measurements, and religion with qualities and their values; the one corresponds to technique and the other to inspiration; the one is purely descriptive while the other is appreciative. It is concluded that the scientist can no more discuss religion in his own terms than colour can be described in terms of shape, and on this understanding the quarrel has practically ceased, except where certain men of religion still insist that religion implies particular beliefs about the evolution and destiny of the physical world.

But modern psychology stands between science and religion; indeed, it is closely allied to art for it combines both technique and inspiration, measurement and value, intellect and tuition. A mere study of psychology will no more make a good psychologist than mere knowledge of musical theory and suppleness of fingers will make a great pianist. Yet just as the great pianist must have a mastery of technique in order to express his inspiration, so also the psychologist must be a scientist to use rightly his 'mystical' power of healing, to communicate his own innate and indefinable sense of well-being to the sick soul. No amount of study or knowledge will give this particular sense, and yet without it the psychologist is as incapable of healing the mind as a chemist of improving a badly painted picture by 'doctoring' the paint. Psychology extends into both science and religion; there are materialist psychologists such as Pavlov and the late Bernard Hollander,[14] and there are religious psychologists like Lindworsky, Dimnet and Leslie Weatherhead.[15] Yet if psychology as a whole stands between science and religion, Jung stands between these two groups of psychologists.

It is perhaps unfortunate, therefore, that in an appreciation of his work his name should be attached to a term which is used against him by some of his colleagues. But if Jung is to be called a mystic we must take care at the start to understand precisely what, in this connection, we mean by mysticism. For, strictly speaking, Jung is a medical psychologist and as such a scientist. Originally, he was a pupil of Sigmund Freud, but, in the same way as Adler, he eventually differed from his master and founded a 'school' of his own. While the psychology of Freud is known as Psychoanalysis, the psychologies of Adler and Jung are known respectively as Individual Psychology and Analytical Psychology. Now the system of Analytical Psychology can be called mystical if it can be said that mysticism does not necessarily involve belief in the supernatural, if it can be made to include the development of wisdom and peace of mind without any change of physical conditions. The materialist will hold that these things depend on external circumstances and on the physical structure of the brain; the social reformer and the surgeon, he maintains, are the only people who can ultimately change us. The mystic, however, believes that we can change ourselves. But as Jung's particular mysticism can only be understood from his work, let us consider his main contributions to psychology.

The first is his conception of the Unconscious Mind; the second, his division of men into four main psychological types; the third, his study of myths and symbols; and the fourth, his method of 'integration' or achieving a certain mental poise which is similar to some forms of religious experience. For our particular purpose it will only be necessary to consider the first, the third and the fourth. He has made many other contributions besides these, but, generally speaking, they will be found to belong to one of these four headings. Furthermore, it is important to remember that his discoveries are not the result of speculation or simple intuition, but of scientific, clinical experience. The significance of his work is not only in these discoveries, but also in the way in which they have been made, for though many of them have previously been known to mysticism, they have never before been corroborated by science.

In considering his conception of the Unconscious, it must be remembered that the Unconscious is not understood as a definite entity, as having a locality, and no attempt is made to prove its objective reality. It is rather a process or condition of the mind, and its existence is assumed because the assumption has been found of value in the treatment of neurotic people and in the explanation of human behaviour. There are many who stoutly deny its existence, but perhaps it does not occur to them that there are countless organs and processes in their physical bodies of which they have no conscious knowledge whatever, except when they are in some way thrown out of order. It therefore seems reasonable that there are mental factors of which we are as little aware as of our brain cells, kidneys, ventricles and internal glands. It may be that in the past our bodily functions have been consciously evolved just as we consciously learnt the functions of speech and walking. In time they have become habits and so have ceased to occupy our minds; and, in the same way, we would seem to have evolved mental processes which also have grown into unconscious habits. Thus the Unconscious is just the sum total of these mental habits which no longer occupy the field of consciousness, for we are only conscious of those things which need our attention, and these so absorb it that an enormous amount of mental activity goes on unnoticed. According to Jung, the Unconscious contains not only the forgotten experiences and habits of our own lives, but the experience of the whole human race. Buried within us lie the ideas, feelings and impulses of the savage and of the human race at every stage of its evolution. Although they are no longer conscious they are still powerful; more powerful, indeed, for they work without our knowledge and often enough what we assume to be our own conscious decision is just some unconscious impulse in disguise.

This brings us to the third heading, for in the dreams and

phantasies of modern people Jung has found the same myths and images which prevail among primitives and which played so great a part in early civilisations. For when the controlling grasp of the conscious mind is relaxed as in sleep or in day-dreaming, these 'archetypes' or 'collective images' rise to the surface and once more become conscious. In the dreams and 'unconscious drawings' and phantasies of his patients Jung has found images and symbols identical with those of ancient India, China, Tibet, Mexico, Egypt, Greece and Rome. For our minds differ only on the surface; the deeper we penetrate, the more we discover the essential unity of mankind. Thus in the religious belief and symbolism of mediæval and modern times, Jung finds much which he holds to be the product of these deep unconscious factors. Yet it is difficult to understand why this should be called a denial of religion. For, unlike Freud, Jung does not maintain that these 'archetypes' are of purely sexual origin; he does not discuss their origin so much as their very existence and the extent of their power. Their power is great, so much so that they *rule* our conscious activity; they are the fundamental, irrational and ungoverned forces of our being and those who have any understanding of them can see them at work perpetually in the conduct of their fellow men. In politics, religion, war, art, literature and music, the greater part of what we imagine to be reasoned, conscious and autonomous action is in fact determined and shaped by these unknown forces. At times, however, they lead us unwittingly into trouble. Uncontrolled, they sport with our lives, deny our conscious desires and disturb us with moods, impulses and impressions which we fear and suppress. So much do we cherish the belief that we are masters of our own minds that we are perpetually at war with the thousands of unwanted thoughts and desires which never cease to challenge and overwhelm us. And this, according to Jung, is at the root of the greater part of the troubles of civilised man.

The primitive does not believe so much as ourselves in his own self-sufficiency. He is far more aware of these forces, projecting them into the innumerable gods and demons of his mythology. He knows that they are his masters and they rule him to such an extent that they almost entirely eclipse his individuality. What is for us the Unconscious is everyday life for the primitive; for him it has real and objective existence, and he cannot distinguish between ordinary life and what we should call mental phantasy. With the advance of civilisation these mental forces appear to lose their power; they become unconscious through familiarity just as the nose ceases to notice a smell to which it has been accustomed. At the same time our sense of individuality, of personal responsibility, increases and we believe that we are our own masters. But we are not. The old gods and demons live on as before, although our scientists give them more technical and less romantic names.

We come, therefore, to the fourth and last heading, to Jung's method of 'integration,' of bringing about a balance between unconscious impulses and conscious will. He maintains that we should first get rid of the conceit that we are our own masters, and allow our unwanted moods and phantasies to 'speak' to us. We must relax and allow them to come to consciousness, and in this way they will lose much of the power which they gained from remaining unknown. The proverb says that knowledge is power, and again we may say that we must stoop to the Unconscious to conquer it. We must therefore face these powers calmly and quietly, without opposing them and yet at the same time retaining our own sense of awareness.[16] And when we no longer oppose them, they will not oppose us. The mind will become clear just as a muddy pool will clear itself if not interfered with and if allowed to remain still. The mud will sink to its proper place (the bottom) and the surface will reflect the sky in all its splendour.

But when we have so mastered the Unconscious, we must not become puffed up with the pride of victory, imagining ourselves to be gods. For this, says Jung, is only to become the victim of another and deeper force, the archetype of the magician, the man of power. This is just that spiritual pride against which every religion has warned us, and this is the most truly mystical of Jung's teachings. For we gain all by renouncing all, by holding nothing for ourselves, not even the thought of how clever we have been to do it. By this we create what Jung describes as a 'virtual point', a centre of balance, between Conscious and Unconscious which is, as it were, the child of the two – a child which can only be born when the parents know how to love and accept each other. And this child is the reborn man, the Christ-principle, the Bodhisattva, the God-man of which all the religions speak. Jung may say that it is born of the Conscious and the Unconscious, but the Unconscious is only the modern name for the realm of the gods, or the internal counterpart of the external universe.

Thus if his terminology is scientific, his meaning is religious. For what is his purpose other than that reconciliation between man and God, self and the universe, which is the very aim and essence of religion?

———————— • ————————

3 D. T. SUZUKI: THE SCHOLAR WHO MAKES LIGHT OF LEARNING

It is rather startling to be asked by one of the greatest scholars in the world for your candid opinion on his work, and then to be listened to as if you, and not he, were the source of authority. But then Dr D. T. Suzuki[17] is not an ordinary scholar; he seems far more interested in learning than in teaching, for when you go to visit him he has a way of telling you very little, but just enough to 'draw you out' so that you finish by telling him what you wanted to know yourself. And at the same time he learns something from you, for what he learns does not necessarily depend on your intellectual or spiritual insight. He is humble enough and great enough to learn from anything, however mean, for his learning does not consist only in knowledge of books and philosophical systems. Certainly he is a scholar and a philosopher in the true academic sense; yet with his friends he prefers to talk about anything rather than philosophy, and I have seen him absorbed in playing with a cat while all around him raged an intense religious discussion.

For Dr Suzuki's life and work is an intriguing paradox. All his labours are spent in expounding a way of life which, by its very nature, it is impossible to express in words. Upon this way of life he has written a number of weighty volumes, and has translated and annotated a great proportion of its ancient literature. To the great majority of people this literature is wholly unintelligible and so frequently do we find in it references to the futility of relying on words and letters of any kind in one's search for Enlightenment, that it is difficult to see the point of translating such great quantities of even this kind of literature. For Dr Suzuki's work is concerned with a form of Buddhism known in Japan as Zen, and its message has been summed up in these words:

> A special transmission of Enlightenment outside the Scriptures; No dependence on words and letters; Direct pointing to the soul of man; Seeing into one's own nature, and the attainment of Enlightenment.

Originally Zen was developed in China from a contemplative form of Indian Buddhism, but the practical Chinese mind transformed it into a way of *life* rather than a retirement from life. Zen — in Sanskrit *Dhyana* — is said to embody that inexpressible secret which the Buddha discovered when he attained his Supreme Enlightenment, sitting one night under the famous Bo tree over 2000 years ago. This is said to have been passed on through a line of patriarchs until it reached a certain Bodhidharma, who brought it to China in the sixth century AD.

What is that secret? To answer this question Dr Suzuki has written at least six profound and learned books, and he himself would be the last to claim that he has revealed that secret in any one or all of them. For we can explain a number of things *about* that secret but we cannot explain the secret itself. In just the same way we may have ideas *about* life, but if we imagine that life itself consists in these ideas we shall be like a man who mistakes a menu for a banquet. Indeed, this secret is the secret of life, but this is not to say that it is to be found *in* life like a nut is found in a shell; rather we should say that it *is* life, which is to say that it is at once the most obscure and the most obvious thing in the world. Dr Suzuki would say that when we drink a cup of tea or say 'How-do-you-do?' to a friend, or take a walk down the street, in those very things we are participating in that ultimate mystery which is the goal of all philosophy and religion. What, then, is the use of searching in the dim and distant realm of metaphysical speculation and exotic cults for something which lies so immediately under our noses? As the Zen poets themselves express it:

> How wondrous, and how miraculous this,
> I draw water and I carry fuel![18]

Or again:

> This very earth is the Lotus Land of Purity,
> And this very body the body of Buddha.[19]

Undoubtedly Dr Suzuki understands the peculiar humour of his position, of writing so many volumes to explain something so entirely self-evident. At times, perhaps, his sense of humour gets the better of him, for I shall never forget the occasion when he was supposed to speak at the Queen's Hall on 'The Supreme Spiritual Ideal.' He arose and gently announced with an almost imperceptible twinkle in his eyes that he did not know what 'The Supreme Spiritual Ideal' was, and proceeded to give a seemingly irrelevant but very entertaining account of his house and garden in Japan.[20]

In some ways his secret is like the crock of gold said to be buried at the foot of a rainbow, for the more you pursue the rainbow's end, the faster it seems to slip away over the crest of the hill and behind the next clump of trees. It is always just one stage further on, and the moment you think you are about to catch it you suddenly find that you are as far from it as ever.

It would be wrong, however, to suppose that Dr Suzuki's elusiveness is the trick of a charlatan who avoids giving the ultimate answer for fear it may be proved worthless. For he cannot give away the secret of Zen even if he wished; it is something which each must discover for himself. It can no more be passed on from one person to another than you can eat another man's food for him.

Yet one always feels that Dr Suzuki has something of the imp in him for, just as one thinks he is about to reveal the whole tremendous truth, one is met by silence and the most engaging smile. Just the same thing will be found in his books, for in a very special and salutary sense they are unsatisfying books. From the first pages to the last there is something which eludes one the whole time, and its very elusiveness makes the search for it more tantalising, for as soon as the book is finished one feels as if it were a detective story with the last chapter missing. There is something at which he always hints, a mystery which time and time again he *almost* explains, but just at that moment one thinks the solution found, it disappears and the chase begins again. It is rather like trying to cut a ball-bearing with a knife; the harder you press, the faster the ball jumps away to one side.

In Dr Suzuki's own words: 'When Zen commits itself to a definite system of philosophy there is no more Zen. Zen just feels fire warm and ice cold, because when it freezes we shiver and welcome fire. The feeling is all in all, as Faust declares; all our theorisation fails to touch reality. But "the feeling" here must be understood in its deepest sense or in its purest form. Even to say that "This is the feeling", Zen is no more there. Zen defies all concept-making. That is why Zen is difficult to grasp.'

For just because Zen is something essentially living, it is impossible to pin it down to any fixed and rigid formula. It has been said that to define is to kill; and if the wind were to stop for one moment for you to catch hold of it, it would cease to be wind. The same is true of life. Perpetually things and events are moving and changing; we cannot take hold of the present moment and make it stay with us; we cannot call back past time or keep for ever lost sensations. Once we try to do this all we have is a dead memory; the reality is not there, and no satisfaction can be found in it. In the words of a Zen master, we must always 'Walk on',[63] never attempting to turn life into death by grasping at it in order to keep little bits and pieces for ourselves. Hence Dr Suzuki says again: 'The truth is, Zen is extremely elusive so far as its outward aspects are concerned; when you think you have caught a glimpse of it, it is no more there; from afar it looks so approachable, but as soon as you come near it, you see it even further away from you than before. Unless, therefore, you devote some years of earnest study to the understanding of its primary principles, it is not expected that you begin to have a generally fair grasp of Zen.'

In that last sentence is another aspect of Dr Suzuki's character as of Zen itself, and that is the element of severity. For beneath its humorously elusive exterior, there is a terrific and relentless sincerity. For example, Dr Suzuki has a way of ending the chapters of his books which at first sight may seem no more than a joke. He works up his theme to a point where the reader expects the final explanation, and then clinches the argument with a story like this: A disciple asked Zen Master Suibi about the ultimate secret of Zen. 'Wait until there is no one around,' said Suibi, 'and I will tell you.' A little later the two were walking in the garden and the disciple said, 'No one is around now. Please tell me, master, about the secret of Zen.' Pointing to a bamboo Suibi said, 'How tall that bamboo is,' and to another, 'How short that one!' At this point the chapter concludes and we are left 'in the air.'

Is Dr Suzuki pulling our legs? No, he assures us that a story like this is full of the gravest consequences. For if the disciple does not grasp immediately the point of the master's answer he may get a smack on the face or be lifted off his feet and thrown out of the room. Zen literature consists almost entirely of stories like this – stories which baffle the intellect and leave one nonplussed. But that is the very technique of Zen, for its aim is an alertness and spontaneity of being which nothing can upset. In setting these weird conundrums the Master is simply trying to find out whether his disciple is really alive, and if he is not he will not hesitate to knock some life into him with a stick.

A master saw some birds flying overhead and asked his disciple what they were.

'They are wild geese, sir.'

'Where are they flying?'

'They have flown away, sir.'

At that point the disciple received a sharp tweak on his nose. 'You say they have flown away,' shouted the master, 'and yet they have been here from the very beginning!'

We might try to explain this story by saying that the disciple's nose was tweaked because he failed to grasp the eternal moment. The geese are here for a second and then they are gone, but it is no use having regrets about them when they are here no longer. You may look back ruefully at the moment when an opportunity has been missed, feeling that time has flown away. But while you look back it is still flying away from you and leaving you further behind than ever. Hence the tweak on the nose to bring you back to your senses, to make you alive to the moment. For life exists only in the moment, and while we stop to cogitate, to have regrets for the past or fears for the future, we miss it.

Yet here again, the second we stop to explain the story of the geese we lose its essential truth. The geese do not wait in the air to be explained, and unless we can understand them in the moment as they fly and then never look back, we shall have our noses tweaked. For eternity is in the moment just because the infinitely great is the same as the infinitely small. You can never find the moment, for before you can shout 'Now!' it has gone. Yet, paradoxically, you find it by not trying to keep it as it passes, by moving forward spontaneously with it. One might say that the second you stop to find time you lose it; you can only keep it by not stopping to find it. As any musician knows, keeping time is spoilt by any kind of hesitation.

Dr Suzuki explains, therefore, that Buddhism is, as it were, a philosophy of time, giving us another hint of his secret in this way: 'Zen permits no ossification of each moment. It takes hold of each moment as it is born from Emptiness. Momentariness is therefore characteristic of this philosophy. Each moment is absolute, alive and significant. The frog leaps, the cricket sings, a dewdrop glitters on the lotus leaf, a breeze passes through the pine branches, and the moonlight falls on the murmuring mountain stream.'

---

4 THE OXFORD GROUPS: A STUDY IN BAD TASTE

In the past few months several of my friends have written or spoken to me of the new life, the spiritual regeneration, which they have found in an organisation known as the Oxford Groups or Buchmanism.[21] They have kindly supplied me with a number of booklets describing the aims and ideals of this movement, and as there are signs in many parts of the world of its growing strength, it becomes a matter of some importance. This importance, however, does not lie only in strength of numbers; more significant still is the support given to it by people of acknowledged learning and insight. Yet from the literature I have read this support hardly seems possible. It may not be altogether fair to try to understand a movement through its literature alone. But insofar as this literature is the work of its leading minds, it gives an astonishing picture, not so much of their ideas as of the general tone of their thought. It is generally agreed that this tone reveals far more of the real man than mere ideas. People of the poorest spirituality may subscribe, intellectually, to the most lofty creed; but, when they express these ideas, something of their fundamental attitude to life always creeps through. And what is especially interesting about the Oxford Groups is not so much their philosophy but their manner of expression, which so clearly reveals their underlying state of mind.

So far as their philosophy is concerned, this is in the true tradition of Christian mysticism – or nearly so. The central idea is the absolute submission of one's life to the Will of God as expressed in Jesus Christ. This Divine Will they claim to know through silent meditation ('quiet time') in which they listen to the deepest promptings of Conscience. The authenticity of these promptings is tested by their accordance with the standard of 'Absolute Honesty, Absolute Purity, Absolute Selflessness, Absolute Love.' It seems a little curious that the guidance of God should have to be consulted when one not only knows what that standard is but also has the impertinence to say what is and is not the Will of God, but the practice of meditation is altogether to be encouraged. Moreover, the absolute submission to the Divine Will is something closely akin to the surrender of personal desire and the obedience to Dharma found in Buddhism and Vedanta, and to the Taoist practice of *wu-wei* (non-assertion). Yet if one is sufficiently enlightened to be able to say under all circumstances just what this supreme moral standard is, then the consultation of God on the matter seems wholly redundant – and worse, for it is almost an act of condescension, as if to say, 'Although we know very well what is right, we had better ask God.' One must perhaps ask if He would not be a little too bored to answer!

But this is a small point, and mankind is such that we must never exact too much of one another. An especially interesting point of the movement's philosophy is that the political, economic and cultural disease of the world is not the fault of the few but of all. No alteration of laws or systems can heal this disease; the only cure is for each individual to become spiritually 'changed,' and this change they propose to effect in a mass and wholesale way. Just how it comes to pass they do not exactly describe, but its result is apparently that the changed man submits his littlest action to Divine Guidance and is prepared to share with all and sundry, not only his great discovery of the efficacy of Christ but also the worst of his past misdeeds. These are cheerfully confessed in public, and expressions of apology are delivered to all those whom one has knowingly offended. In this manner one becomes free from the burden of sin; the wrong is confessed both to God and man. Is this perhaps another instance of making the latter a check on the former?

There is, however, no doubt whatever that those who follow this way of life do become changed. Just how they become changed is another matter, and this brings us beyond their philosophy to the fundamental Oxford Group attitude to life.

The other evening a friend left me a pamphlet entitled *The New Enlistment,* and in this it was said that when another person takes you on one side and tells you things about himself which he has never told to anyone else, this is chapter one verse one in life changing – 'all the rest is preface.' The pamphlet contains a number of photographs of athletic young men running, walking or just standing together in large numbers, their faces radiant, their arms round each other's necks, so much so that one cannot help connecting their smiles with the sort of smile one sees in advertisements on the face of the man or woman who has used Brown's butter or Smith's soap. A hearty family was shown grouped together in a picture entitled 'This family listens to God every morning' in just the same way as the advertiser shows us the family which has his particular patent food for breakfast. The whole tone of the pamphlet and of their other writings is of the same level. JESUS, we are told, means 'Just Exactly Suits Us Sinners,' while PRAY is 'Powerful Radiograms Always Yours,' and GROW is 'Go Right On Working.' Such remarks are interspersed with little rhymes and long poems which sometimes rhyme and seldom scan. God is discussed just like any other bloke one can ring up on the phone, and the general atmosphere is of immense cheeriness in case one should think that religion is something doleful. Now religion, if it is religion, is essentially humorous, but this is not humour; it is laughing at one's own jokes and putting exclamation marks after them to show they are meant to be funny.

The result is that they are not funny at all; they are

immensely serious. For this is not really a laughing matter. It is the easiest thing in the world to make fun of this kind of movement; it simply asks to be laughed at, and, if the truth were known, rather enjoys it. In truth the Oxford Groups must be considered soberly, not exactly because they are growing in strength but because they are to that extent a symptom of the mind of man in the twentieth century. For the alarming fact is that people whom one considers intelligent can mistake this essential puerility for religion. It is no matter of becoming childlike again, for children are absorbed in deep and important things like the wonder of one's own body, with profound problems about the sun and stars which grown-ups cannot answer with fairy tales and the whole miraculous kingdom of the imagination. But this is rather the state of the boy or girl's 'awkward age,' the adolescent period when children are mercifully sent to school and their parents relieved of an intolerable burden. It is the especially serious time of life, the time of impossible ideals and platitudes. Now an occasional platitude is salutary; it is often an important truth which we try to ignore by calling it ordinary or obvious. But a whole uninterrupted string of platitudes is monstrous, and the more so when they are expressed without any attempt at literary excellence. It is not as if they had been written down with any childlike naïveté, for their style resembles the lower grades of the American press, and their content an effort to 'put across' religion as if it were a new kind of vacuum cleaner.

It will be asked if style and manner are of any account if the thing 'works,' if it does actually make men and women more moral and binds them together in a stronger sense of fellowship. Now morality and fellowship are not names for some definite thing which is one and indivisible; they have as many varying shades as green and blue. Because someone has a green dress which is beautiful it does not follow that all green dresses are beautiful. In the same way, not all morality is beautiful though it may be nonetheless moral, just as an ugly dress may be of an undoubted green. Hence it may certainly be fellowship to share one another's sins, to gather in masses for cheerful 'uplift' and to crack jokes together about God; it may indeed be morality to consider the rights and wrongs of one's littlest actions, during the past day, to follow the teaching of Christ without compromise and tell the whole world about it, and to talk, think and act religion at every possible moment. All this may save civilisation from war and establish the brotherhood of man. But some of us would rather have civilisation perish in blood and fire than have to live on and endure such a brotherhood.

There is an interesting story of a Buddhist teacher named Goso which seems peculiarly applicable to the Oxford Groups. Goso said to one of his disciples, 'You are all right, but you have a trivial fault.' The disciple pressed Goso to tell him what this was, and at last received the answer, 'You have altogether too much of religion.'

'But,' protested the disciple, 'when one is practising religion, don't you think it the most natural thing to be talking of it?'

Goso replied, 'When it is like an ordinary everyday conversation, it is somewhat better.'

'But why do you so especially hate talking about religion?'

'Because it turns one's stomach.'

For in one sense religion is the salt of life, but salt by itself is horrible. If salt is applied by an expert cook, its presence is not noticed, yet it gives savour to the whole dish. But the religion of the Oxford Groups seem not only an overdose of salt, but an overdose of rather crude salt. Compared with other religions it is in no sense a beautiful religion; it has no dignified ritual, no great art, no sublime literature — except the Bible, whose literary merits it does not seek to follow in any respect. And those merits are not mere externals; the restraint, the economy the dignity and the depth of Christ's language are the outward signs of the same virtues in the spirit. That so many young people, possessed of the whole religious and artistic tradition of the world, should follow after this blatant novelty shows a peculiar state of the soul. It is as if the vast and subtle repast of life had lost all its flavour for them, as if in all its varied dishes their tongues sought only the harsh taste of salt. And if they seek wisdom in platitudes, it might be as well to consider the old platitude of Lucretius, *Tantum religio potuit suadere malorum.*[22]

5 THE MYSTERY OF THE TWENTY-FIVE DIVINES

There can no more be religion without mysticism than there can be a human being without life. The moment mysticism dies, its religious form withers and decays in just the same way as the human body, which becomes, instead of a living person, a mere collection of bones, blood, muscles and skin. In every great religion the function of its hierarchy of priests has been to provide this mystical life, this intimate contact with divinity, without which all doctrines and rites are empty. It must be asked, therefore, in our survey of mystics of today how far the priesthood of the Christian Churches is a real priesthood. In other words, we have to ask how far the Church, the mystical body of Christ, has any relation with or understanding of what is mystical, and whether beneath the symbolism of its doctrines and rites there is any widespread practice of mysticism at all.

To an enlightened visitor from another planet a superficial acquaintance with Christianity would be of absorbing interest. For he would find in its creed a collection of thrilling symbols, so much so that he would naturally suppose its initiated priests to be the possessors of a most exalted wisdom. And if he did not stop to enquire further, he would undoubtedly return to his people and say that the outward forms of Christianity indicated the presence of the highest order of mysticism within. It is not only the visitor from another planet who might make this assumption. Even the ordinary 'man-in-the-street' has every reason to believe that among the leaders of the Church there are men of the greatest intelligence; he is sure that no thinking person can accept the doctrines of the Church at their face value as literal truths, and perhaps he begins to wonder if there is not some esoteric body of knowledge known to bishops, cardinals and popes and not revealed to ordinary persons. Because, he would say, if there is not this knowledge, these dignitaries must be either humbugs or slightly lacking in sanity, for to accept Christianity at its face value would not only be an act of stupidity but the rejection of the most precious thing in the world.

An opportunity has now come to hand, however, for us to examine the latest developments of thought among the more intelligent priests of our Church of England. In 1922 the then Archbishop of Canterbury, Dr Davidson, appointed a commission of twenty-five eminent divines to survey the present position of doctrine in the Church,[23] and to discover how far there was agreement or disagreement among the members of the clergy as to the meaning of these doctrines, and to find ways of making such disagreement less acute. After discussions held at fairly frequent periods over a space of some fifteen years, the commission has at last published a report of its findings (*Doctrine in the Church of England*, SPCK, 2s. 6d.).

Perhaps the fact that this report has been published for all to read has made it necessary to exclude more than the mere preliminaries of these discussions. For the inner wisdom which we suppose these initiates to possess has been very thoroughly suppressed, with the sad result that, as it stands, the report has very little to do with religion at all. It has much to do with history and discusses quite a number of things which would better have been left to scientists and experts in psychic research, to philologists and professors of moral philosophy. But of real religious teaching, of mysticism, we have nothing more than the very nicely arranged shell. We learn from an introduction by the Archbishop of York that all the discussions were carried on in the most friendly spirit, that instead of bitterness there was much laughter, and he wisely remarks that theological strife is a worse heresy than theological unorthodoxy. This certainly is a most valuable advance on former times. In fact the whole report shows that a most amicable spirit prevails among the leaders of our Church, and so trifling are the points on which they differ that some have heralded this report as the most vital contribution to Christianity for hundreds of years. Without doubt the report is a very nice piece of work indeed, but it is not easy to see just where the vitality comes in.

It seems as if these learned gentlemen have been indulging in a lofty intellectual pastime of a significance apparently unknown to themselves. It is as if they had been fitting together a jigsaw puzzle with the picture side beneath. It remains now to turn over the finished puzzle and see what is on the other side. Perhaps, in the traditional manner of absent-minded professors, they have just forgotten to turn it over. Or is it that they did not know there *was* a picture on the other side? For the Christian story from the Fall of Adam to the Resurrection is one of the most sublime descriptions of the progress of the individual soul ever known. Therein is shown every detail of the way that each one of us must go to find spiritual enlightenment, concealed under a rather easily grasped series of symbols. This tremendous fact the commission seems to have overlooked altogether, treating this story from a primarily historical point of view as if its significance lay in the fact that it was a series of events which had actually happened – once.

But the whole point is that if these 'events' only happened once they are no more than historical curiosities; unless they can be made to happen over and over again in the souls of men of every time and place they are of no spiritual significance at all. For after all, is there any real spiritual value for us in the knowledge that several thousand years ago in a small area of the Near East some people called Adam and Eve were supposed to have brought a curse on the whole human race through a rather trivial folly? And how many people are really deeply influenced by the knowledge that God was born in human form and suffered the keenest pains of the world in Palestine two thousand years ago? This information is of little use to us unless it is used simply to illustrate the fact that the Fall of Adam is something which happens in the soul of *every* human being who reaches adult manhood, to show that God must be born and crucified in everyone who would become again as a child and inherit the kingdom of heaven. Nothing is to be gained by trying to deny that these things did actually happen in history, but almost everything is lost if it is imagined that their historicity is the most important thing about them. Yet this is undoubtedly the feeling of the Church. Thus the report discusses the various theories of the spiritual state of Adam before the Fall, the various opinions concerning the Virgin Birth and the Resurrection and miracles and of life after death as if the significance of these things lay in their being unique events existing in finite time. This is quite different from the philosophy of St Paul, for in his epistles it is perfectly clear that he is far more interested in Christ as an inward experience than as a historical person, so much so that he hardly ever quotes the words of Christ as recorded in the

Gospels and seldom refers to him by his personal name, Jesus.

Yet so obstinately does the Church cling to history and historical symbols that we can only assume that it has lost the inward meaning, that it lives on the past and embodies the living Christ no longer as a corporate body. For if the Church were truly the 'mystical body of Christ' we should surely hear more of the crucifixion and resurrection of the Incarnate God here and now, and less of the dry bones of history. If the Church were truly alive it would spare no effort to teach man how to attain this mystical union with God above all other things; this would be the central core of its doctrine instead of irrelevant questions of metaphysics and theology. For even morality is beside the point until this mystical understanding is brought to birth. It is a mere code of behaviour forced upon man by fear of external authority until he learns to desire morality for its own sake, through nature instead of through law, and this desire can only arise when Christ is born in the human soul.

And what does this mean? The answer is given in Christ's own words in the Gospel of St John – 'unless a man be born again of water and the spirit he cannot see the kingdom of God.' For these two elements are the symbols of all those things in life which are opposed to one another and yet become creative when they are brought together – positive and negative, male and female, matter and energy, evil and good, rest and activity. In the story, Christ himself was born of these two symbols – the Holy Spirit and the Virgin Mary: spirit and matter. Thus when we accept and lay ourselves open to the wholeness of life with all its pleasant and unpleasant aspects, when we deny nothing and affirm all, when we neither cling to life nor shun death but draw all things to ourselves remembering that 'that which God hath made call not thou common or unclean' – then is Christ born in us, for Christ is the grateful and joyous acceptance of God's universe. The same truth is embodied in the symbol of the Cross, of the Christ figure with both right and left arms outstretched, his body nailed to the symbol of matter and laid open to the entirety of experience.

Yet these are only hints of the depths of meaning which lie

hidden in these ancient symbols. Only when the Church begins to explore those depths will the life of mysticism return to it so that the body of Christ may be saved from becoming a corpse of disintegrated doctrines.

———————————————— • ————————————————

6 THE OLD MAN ON THE DOWNS: A PERSONAL EXPERIENCE

I have often thought that there may be, living among us, mystics as great if not greater than those whose names appear in print. Who, for instance, can say whether or not the man sitting opposite in the bus, looking like a bank manager, is perhaps as great a sage as Socrates, or as great a mystic as Plotinus? If the great teachers of the past came back among us to-day they would probably find the world much too full of talk already, and prefer to live lives of useful anonymity rather than turn again to pen or pulpit. One day last summer my notion that such people exist among us was confirmed by experience. Unfortunately I cannot give the name of this particular 'Mystic of Today' simply because I never knew it. For all I know, he may be someone who writes books and gives lectures, but he told me nothing about it.

I was spending part of my holiday walking in the Berkshire Downs, and early one morning I had left Streatly to climb the hill which you can see from the Thames as you pass through Goring Gap. It was a blazing hot day and I was taking things easily, so it was not until mid-day that I reached the great Ridgeway which runs along the top of the Downs towards Avebury. I had just climbed out of a wood on to the open hills, when about quarter of a mile ahead of me I saw a man sauntering along with his hands in his pockets and a pipe in his mouth. His back was towards me and because of his grey hair I judged him to be about sixty. In spite of the hot sun he wore no hat and was not even carrying a stick. As I came nearer to him I saw that he was wearing a brown tweed coat and grey flannel trousers; his coat was open and flapping about in the breeze, and he seemed to be walking along without any fixed purpose as if he were just following his feet. In about fifteen minutes I came up close behind him, and at the sound of my footsteps he turned round. His head was almost bald in front and a pair of humorous eyes looked at me from beneath large white eyebrows.

'Warm enough?' he asked with a clear, deep voice, removing his pipe from his mouth.

I made some remarks about the gorgeous weather we were having, and we began to wander along together as if it were the most natural thing in the world. He was in no hurry. Occasionally he stopped to kick a stone or look at the view. I had a camera with me and started taking odd photographs. He told me I should come up here when there were some clouds about as clouds always add interest to pictures. Was he fond of clouds? Oh yes, it didn't do to keep one's head in them too long, but they were magnificent things. I suggested that the reason for their beauty was that they never resisted the wind but always adapted themselves to its movement. He looked at me quickly out of the corner of his eye and laughed.

'I believe,' he said, 'you're a philosopher.'

'That's rather a ponderous name for it,' I answered, 'but I suppose you're right in a way.'

'Yes it is. But then, if philosophers wanted to be as beautiful as clouds they would have to learn not to be ponderous. "Philosopher" is a ponderous name for a ponderous person.'

I nodded and quoted Chesterton's remark about angels being able to fly because they took themselves lightly. At that he stopped and looked at me.

'But *how*,' he asked, 'do you take yourself lightly?'

'That,' I said, 'is what I should like to know. Some people can do it, others can't. But how do those who can instruct those who can't?'

'Oh, just by doing it, or rather by not doing.'

'That's an odd remark. What do you mean?'

'Well,' he replied, 'it's the same as the clouds. The clouds don't try to float in the air; they just let themselves go and the wind does the rest.'

'So if we let ourselves go we rise up to heaven?'

'Rise up!' he laughed. 'Good God no, we're already there. The right place for clouds is in the sky, and the right place for humans is on earth, so a human being is really just as much on high as a cloud. If we were heavier than we ought to be we would fall through the earth, and if the clouds were heavier than they ought to be they would come bumping down on the ground.'

'Then,' I went on, 'I suppose you mean that we must let ourselves go and be like earthly clouds, drifting about on the winds of circumstance.'

'It's hardly a question of should or shouldn't, of must or mustn't. Besides, why are you so concerned about what *you* must or mustn't do? When there is must and mustn't there is no freedom, and you want to be free, don't you? Well, who's stopping you? You're already free.'

'For another week, yes. But that's not real freedom. I have to go back then to London, to office work and so on, and if I can't find freedom there it's not much use my looking for it out here, is it?'

'But why look for it?' he answered. 'You've got it now, and when you look for it you forget you've got it. You might as well go about looking for the back of your own neck. You see,' he went on, knocking his pipe out on his heel, 'freedom of spirit belongs to all, but we only have it when we lay no claim to it, like everything else in the world. When you lay claim to anything, that thing claims you and limits your freedom. I love these hills, but if I were to buy them they would keep me so busy that I should never be able to get away from them. At least, that's true in one sense. A rich man is only a slave if he ties himself to his wealth. But he needn't. He can use it as if it belonged to someone else. And so it does in reality. After all, this pipe does not really belong to me any more than the sun or the stars. Yet in another sense all of them are mine just because I lay claim to none of them.'

And at that he began to roar with laughter, and when I pressed him for an explanation he continued: 'You see, the joke is that I have just laid claim to the fact that I do not lay claim, and so I am claimed by my no claiming! I suppose I should never have talked about this, for the moment one opens one's mouth one falls into traps. The point is that if you try to gain all things by renouncing all things you get into a vicious circle. It's an elusive business, like chasing your own shadow. The faster you run after it, the faster it runs away from you, but if you run away from it you can never escape it. So why worry? If we can't find heaven by looking for it or escape it by running away from it, then we're already in it.'

'Is that so?' I asked. 'Is this world really a heaven? Your remark might apply equally well to hell.'

'True enough,' he answered, 'but hell could only disturb you if you had a body and a self to be disturbed.'

'Yes, that may be. But aren't those also things you've just got, which you can't catch by chasing or escape by running away?'

'Quite so, but in that they're like anything else; if you don't claim them, they don't claim you.'

'I'm afraid,' I said, 'you talk me to pieces. This is all very well, but the fact remains that there are some things which give us pleasure and others which give us pain. At one time we're in heaven and at another in hell, and what every man wants to know is how to get rid of hell.'

'To do that you must also get rid of heaven. You must do without either heaven or hell, pleasure or misery.'

'And how,' I asked, 'do you to that?'

'Just this,' he replied, 'when you are in heaven go to the palaces of the angels, and when you are in hell go down into the furnace with the devils. But do not hang about in either place.'

The day was hastening on and I felt it was time to be getting back. What was more, clouds were appearing away in the West and it looked as though a thunder storm might be blowing up after the hot weather. So I made my excuses, said I must be going home and asked my companion where he was staying.

'Well, nowhere just at present,' was his reply. 'As a matter of fact I have a small flat in London, but I shan't be going back for a week or two yet. For a time I shall just go on walking, eating when I'm hungry and sleeping when I'm tired. I carry a razor in my pocket and get some hot water from a cottage when I want a shave, and that's about all my luggage.'

I looked at the black clouds in the distance.

'If you're going that way,' I said, 'you'll have to find shelter soon and I don't see a house for miles.'

He looked towards the storm and smiled.

'Yes,' he said, 'and beyond that storm is the sun again, and beyond that yet another storm. But the rain doesn't matter – so long as you keep moving.'

*　　*　　*　　*

I have never seen him again. He went sauntering on along the Ridgeway while I hurried back to Streatly. The last I saw of him was as I went down behind the crest of a hill. From the moment I had left him he never looked behind, but just went on his way with the wind blowing about in his coat and his pipe stuck in the corner of his mouth. He carried nothing with him, yet somehow he looked as if he owned the place, for he was so much at ease, even with a total stranger. Perhaps he was one of those whom St Paul described 'as having nothing but possessing all things.'

And again he reminded me of that strangely beautiful passage from the Gospel of St John: 'The wind bloweth where it listeth and thou hearest the voice thereof, but canst not tell whence it cometh nor whither it goeth. Even so is everyone that is born of the spirit.'

——————————— • ———————————

7 G. K. CHESTERTON: THE 'JONGLEUR DE DIEU'

Although I am anything but a Roman Catholic, the recent death of G. K. Chesterton [24] felt almost like a personal loss. For with no writer of today did I find myself in deeper sympathy. It was not that I agreed with all his ideas, but rather that I felt myself in complete accord with his basic attitude to life. If I could believe that that attitude really reflected the mind and heart of the Roman Church, I should have become a Catholic long ago. But it must be remembered that Chesterton 'went to Rome' very late in his life, and one may suspect that his view of reality had become a little dulled and that in his love for romance he had been captured by an institution which knows more about the power of glamour than any other community in the world. This was, perhaps, unfortunate but, nevertheless, I should be the last to quarrel with anyone for his love of romance, because it indicates a certain childlike attitude to life which is the passport to the kingdom of heaven. It is, in fact, the sense of wonder, the sense which transforms every littlest thing in the universe into a divine mystery.

A very remarkable person once told me that the greatest

wisdom was to be surprised at everything, and I believe Chesterton would have shared this opinion. That he possessed this sense of wonder to a degree can be seen from even the briefest glance at his poems. As I turn over their pages my eyes fall upon the lines:

> In heaven I shall stand on gold and glass,
> Still brooding earth's arithmetic to spell;
> Or see the fading of the fires of hell
> Ere I have thanked my God for all the grass.

And again in *The Holy of Holies*:

> Speller of the stones and weeds,
> Skilled in Nature's crafts and creeds,
> Tell me what is in the heart
> Of the smallest of the seeds.

And the answer:

> God Almighty, and with Him
> Cherubim and Seraphim,
> Filling all Eternity –
> Adonai Elohim.

The sense of wonder expresses itself in gratitude, and I know of no finer exposition of the mysticism of gratitude than the concluding pages of Chesterton's *Autobiography*.

'The aim of life,' he says, 'is appreciation; there is no sense in not appreciating things; and there is no sense in having more of them if you have less appreciation of them.'

And he takes the modern optimist to task for despising humble and elementary things because man, in his scientific omnipotence, can create such 'superior' varieties. Chesterton takes ordinary dandelions as his illustration of this, and remarks of such optimists, 'They were not in touch with this particular notion, of having a great deal of gratitude even for a very little good. And as I began to believe more and more that the clue was to be found in such a principle, even if it was a paradox, I was more and more disposed to seek out those who specialised in humility, though for them it was the door of heaven and for me the door of earth. For nobody else *specialises* in that mystical mood in which the yellow star of the dandelion is startling, being something unexpected and undeserved.'

That Chesterton was not wholly in accord with the mind of the Church of Rome may be seen in what may be called his 'spiritual worldliness.' For he was in no sense a world-denier in the manner of ascetic monks who shun the beauties of this world in order to inherit the glories of the next. Indeed, he seemed to worry little about the life beyond death, for to him even this world was heaven, seen with opened eyes and alert senses. For one does not have to leave the world to find divinity, either in thought or through bodily death.

> There is one sin: to call a green leaf grey,
> Whereat the sun in heaven shuddereth.
> There is one blasphemy: for death to pray,
> For God alone knoweth the praise of death.
>
> There is one creed: 'neath no world terror's wing
> Apples forget to grow on apple-trees.
> There is one thing needful — everything —
> The rest is vanity of vanities.

In other words, ordinary experience, if you look at it in the right way, is nothing other than the supreme religious experience which is the goal of all mystical endeavour. You may look beyond the stars for God and search for knowledge of Him in all the philosophical and theological treatises in the world. Yet we are standing face to face with Him at every moment of our lives.

> In youth I sought the prince of men,
> Captain in cosmic wars ...
> But now a great thing in the street
> Seems any human nod,
> Where shift in strange democracy
> The million masks of God.

For in truth there is nothing more surprising and mysterious than perfectly ordinary objects. There is nothing more wonderful than the astonishing fact that we are alive, that we breathe, eat, sleep, walk, laugh, cry, and the danger of scientific investigation is that in attempting to explain these mysteries it may imagine that it has explained them away. When I read the rationalist books of Haeckel,[25] the Dialectical Materialists and of all who try to make out that life is nothing but this or nothing but that, my reaction is just that though such ideas are very logical they are also very dull. Nothing is more deathly to the soul than the imagination that one has solved all mysteries or even that one stands a chance of so doing. And a person who thinks he has reduced the universe to nothing but matter or nothing but a conglomeration of electric waves becomes as uninteresting as if he were nothing but matter himself. As may be expected, he becomes an intensely proud and serious person. The world no longer intrigues him, because there is nothing left for him to explain; his knowledge acts as a great weight upon his soul which drags him down to hell. But if he were a true scientist he would understand the paradox that the more you know, the more mysterious everything becomes until you are forced to roar with laughter at your own efforts to make yourself the equal of God.

Chesterton never tired of making fun of this kind of spiritual pride; seriousness was to him a heresy, and especially the seriousness of scientific logicians. Thus in *Orthodoxy* he writes: 'To accept everything is an exercise, to understand everything a strain. The poet only desires exaltation and expansion, a world to stretch himself in. The poet only asks to get his head into the heavens. It is the logician who seeks to get the heavens into his head. And it is his head that splits.'

We have said that the sense of wonder expresses itself in gratitude; it also expresses itself in humility, not to mention humour. For the essence of humour lies not in seeing what is funny about other people and things, but what is funny about oneself. It is the art of seeing oneself in correct proportion with the universe, and laughter is the reaction which follows the realisation of the insignificance of human knowledge and strength before the might and mystery of the cosmos. And I do not refer only to the great, vast cosmos which the astronomers explore; I mean also the equally mysterious cosmos which is vast in its littleness, which may be discovered in drops of muddy water and insects invisible to the eye. Our lives are surrounded with such mysteries, and the least that can be asked of us is that we should be boundlessly grateful for such a feast of entertainment. What we have done to deserve it I cannot imagine, but it surely behoves us to use it with infinite reverence, to explore it with the same sense of having been honoured as if we had been invited by the Almighty to come and sit at His right hand by the throne of judgement, and to regard it with the same awe as if we were looking upon the ultimate glory of His face.

It is often denied that mystery has any connection with mysticism, but personally I feel that mysticism is in fact the keenest appreciation of mystery. It is as if the world suddenly ceased to be just the world, as if trees, stars, and so forth were no longer just trees, stars and so forth, but instead had become TREES, STARS, MEN, ANIMALS, STONES and HILLS, each one of them as eternally mysterious as God Himself. In the face of this mystery man would tread softly and take his own importance very lightly. To quote *Orthodoxy* again: 'A bird is active, because a bird is soft. A stone is helpless, because a stone is hard. The stone must by its own nature go downwards, because hardness is weakness. The bird can of its nature go upwards, because fragility is force. In perfect force there is a kind of frivolity, an airiness that can maintain itself in the air... Angles can fly because they can take themselves lightly.' In other words, he who takes his own importance seriously cannot rise up to heaven.

It is in this capacity to take himself lightly and in his inexhaustible sense of wonder that I feel Chesterton's real greatness lies. Volumes more might be written about the other aspects of his life and work, but this seems to me the core of his mysticism and the most important thing he has to say to us. For if we could feel something like his tremendous interest in ordinary life, if we could know how really extraordinary it is, we should never fall into the boredom which breeds sin. For sin, which so often seems to us terrific, is in truth a minute thing, a dirty little corner of the universe in which men hide their heads, into which I believe they would never even glance if they had any idea of the vast number of infinitely more interesting and entertaining things that lie outside. But Chesterton came as one of St Francis' 'Jongleurs de Dieu' (God's Merry Men) and blew aside this pettiness with 'a great, rollicking wind of elemental and essential laughter,' with *joie de vivre* perhaps a little like the feeling which God had when he looked at His universe and 'saw that it was good.' I do not think that he forgot or tried to ignore the many terrible things that man can suffer; what surprised and excited him was that a moment's contemplation of even the smallest piece of God's handiwork could make hours of pain worth while, and so he learnt the art of 'having a great deal of gratitude even for a very little good.' For it is this sense of wonder which sets us free, which opens up for us the gates of a great, wide universe in which we have the tremendous privilege of being able to explore and enjoy, to look this way and that as we will and see on every side a divine mystery, and to wander on and on therein without ever being able to come to its end. In such a world who but a lunatic would seek after sin?

> Like emptied idiot masks, sin's loves and wars
> Stare at me now: for in the night I broke
> The bubble of a great world's jest, and woke
> Laughing with laughter such as shakes the stars.

———————————— • ————————————

8 CRANMER-BYNG: THE APOSTLE OF PERSONALITY

Many of the most interesting mystics of our time are those who do not set up schools and surround themselves with cliques of disciples. Even more interesting are those who do not so absorb themselves in their mysticism that they become, of all the useless creatures, mystical specialists. We have heard much of the evils of those who keep their religion separate from their ordinary life; it is perhaps time we heard something about the evils of those who carry this separation to such lengths that they have no ordinary life at all. For in so doing they make religion the one thing it was never meant to be – an end in itself.

Presumably this failing is born of the old error that the things of the spirit are in some way higher than and preferable to the things of the earth. This, however, is a form of materialism, being an abortive attempt to understand the spiritual world by the analogy of the material world, which is to say, imagining that there is such a thing or state as the spiritual world which can be known and entered apart from the material world. It is a 'philosophical' version of the old dualism of earth and heaven, of the natural realm of men and things and the supernatural world of gods and angels, considered as two distinct localities or planes of being. To primitive minds they are localities and to more advanced minds states of existence, and it is thought that the destiny of man is to pass from one to the other, freeing his soul from the dross of matter with the winnowing fan of religion. Of such loose thinking there is always one sure test, which is to enquire of the believer the nature of the spiritual state to which he aspires. The answers will be diverse in all respects but one, namely that they will be very dull. I do not mean that they will be uninterestingly expressed; most of them will be highly ingenious, and many will be flights of poetic fancy which will entirely deceive the uncritical mind. But all of them will come under one or more of the following headings:

1 The desire to abolish the material world as we know it;
2 The desire to attain a state of unity wherein all differences cease to exist;
3 The desire to abolish the pairs of opposites and attain a state wherein death, pain, darkness and travail vanish utterly away.

Nowadays few have any particular longing for the traditional tinsel heaven of misunderstood Christianity, where people live for ever and ever, singing the praises of God and walking about with harps on streets of gold. Most of us will admit that after a few months of this we should be frankly bored. The popular Mohammedan heaven of houris and good things to eat is perhaps more attractive, but even this would shortly become too much of a good thing. Rather than face an eternity of this, most of us would prefer to go to another place.

But the tinsel heaven is going, and in its place comes a conception of supposedly Eastern origin, to wit a state in which the individual is so merged into 'the Divine' or absorbed in the contemplation thereof that to all intents and purposes he ceases to exist. This Divine is never very attractively portrayed, for in all descriptions of it one thing is common: that it is not spiced, as is life, with variety. It is certainly infinite, immortal, unconditioned and so forth, but by themselves none of these terms have any meaning.

Someone has wisely said that there is nothing infinite apart from finite things, and Chesterton expressed the same truth when he said that God was the synthesis of infinity and boundary. Yet even supposing that these things could exist by themselves and did actually constitute a something to be known as pure, unadulterated Spirit, we must admit after a little thought that they would be abysmally dull. No doubt when we had reached the state of being one with them we should have left behind that finite mind which alone can feel dullness. But it is only this mind which can feel interested, and if we are to give up being bored on the one hand or amused on the other, the resulting condition is hardly distinguishable from pure oblivion. With such an ideal it is not surprising that many of our mystics become mystical specialists, and in this they are at least consistent. They wish to pass beyond ordinary life and enter into the purely spiritual. Religion for them becomes an end in itself, something to which ordinary life must be subordinated rather than something whereby ordinary life may be transformed.

There are, however, others who hold the view that ordinary life is our main business and religion a spice to give it zest. They ask for no greater miracles than trees, clouds, plants and men, and no more lofty occupations than the employment of the many astonishing faculties which Nature has given us. Being true mystics, they want to be like God, or in harmony with God. God we assume to be a sensible person; as such He did not waste His time in contemplating vast eternities of unruffled Divine Essence. He created a universe, a surprising, diverse, miraculous and fascinating multitude of things – and why? Because He is an artist, a creator, who *abhors a vacuum*. In the same way, every child feels the urge to throw a stone into a smooth pond, to create interesting waves and splashes on the intolerable smoothness. This, I believe, is the real meaning of 'divine discontent.'

It is therefore something of a treat to find in an age when

102

mystics seek pure unity and politicians pure uniformity, a mystic who is an artist in the sense I have described. His name will be familiar to many as the founding editor of *The Wisdom of the East Series* – a collection of more than fifty popular books on Eastern mysticism whose aim is 'to unite the old world of Thought with the new world of Action.' He has not pushed himself much before the public eye. Early in life he deserted the literary and philosophical cliques of his time, dissatisfied with their isolation from ordinary life and their tendency to revolve in a world of pure ideas of no great consequence to any but themselves. He decided instead to live in the country, to interest himself in local government, considering that no mystic is of any value unless he is at the same time a proper citizen, doing his share in the world's work. And now, in the ripeness of age, he has written a book which everyone should read and keep by his bedside.* It is not an easy book. It is written and printed so beautifully that at times the delights of the form obscure the sense of the substance, but from every point of view it repays many readings. It does not matter much where you open it, for it is one of those pleasant rambling books which in the old days were called 'Meditations.' It is an autobiography of the author's mind, and contains a message which bears endless repetition.

In a time when the world is slowly being forced to choose between one or another form of totalitarianism, which is the creed of the anthill and the hive, it is good to hear Mr Cranmer-Byng[26] extol the ideal of Personality. For this is an ideal quite foreign to the mysticism of absolute unity, on the one hand, and the politics of uniformity on the other. The one uses religion to destroy and supersede the workaday world of nature and man, to deny the very creation which God has troubled to make; the other employs politics to sink human personality into the social mass, wherein man becomes as dead and dull as his own machines. Mr Cranmer-Byng shows that these doctrines must fail because they do not recognise that man is essentially an artist, and that the artist is nothing if he is not a *person*. This does not mean that man fulfils his being only by becoming what a specialised world calls an

* *Tomorrow's Star*. By L. Cranmer-Byng. Golden Cockerel Press. 7s. 6d.

artist, that is to say, a painter, a musician or a poet. On the contrary, ordinary life is itself the supreme art.

> When every act (he writes) is charged with significance, when the everyday routine is changed into ritual, when the commonplace becomes the miraculous, when joy comes to us through the adventure of creation ... then personality is recognised for what it has become, a light that moves forward, a radiation from the soul of man on the pathway of his destiny.

True, personality is only the creative instrument and not the creator himself, but its importance lies in being the bridge between God and the individual. By himself, the individual sinks to the undifferentiated mass, and by Himself God becomes a formless infinitude. But Mr Cranmer-Byng shows that when the two are joined by personality they are given a meaning, for the individual ceases to be a mere empty mask, becoming instead a being through whom sounds the voice of God, for what is personality but a compound of *per* and *sonare*, 'to sound through'? By itself a flame will not burn, by itself a lamp is an empty thing; but put them together and something lives. In the same way, air by itself scatters aimlessly, and a trumpet by itself is just a piece of brass; yet combine them, and we have personality – a 'sounding through'. Therefore all talk of the 'Brotherhood of Man' and the sanctity of the social mass is empty jargon, 'for brotherhood is not in flesh or blood or type, things that distinguish the closely related from the distant kin, but in the sacred bond that unites us with equal nearness to the Maker of divine image limited in form.' For without that relation of the unity of God to the diversity of individuals we have abstraction on the one hand and empty masks on the other. But 'the achievement of personality is the end of masquerade.'

Is there, then, any hope for a world where the forces of uniformity threaten to eclipse that variety which is the spice of life? One of the finest things in Mr Cranmer-Byng's book is his faith in the power of Nature to assert herself above human stupidity, to make us realise that we are her children in spite of ourselves.

> And lastly (he writes) there is the old *Genius Loci*, slowly

obliterated and submerged by the creeping tide of civilisation, the valley spirit, the mountain spirit, the spirits of the cornlands, pastures, woods and streams, the Home Spirit of man in daily contact with his Mother Nature. Yet though we bury her she is not dead, but sleeping; her seeds are hoarded in each barren wilderness of bricks and mortar, and her dreams of paradise regained, hidden in the hearts of her children, are waiting to break through that the cycle of the four seasons may be restored.

SEPARATE ARTICLES

·

ZEN (1937)

Although Zen is a word of only three letters, three volumes would not explain it, nor even three libraries of volumes. If one were to compile books on the subject to the end of time, they would not explain it, for all that could be written would only be ideas *about* Zen, not Zen itself. Indeed, whoever imagines that he has explained Zen has in fact only explained it away; it can no more be bound by a definition than the wind can be shut in a box without ceasing to be wind. Thus any attempt to write on Zen may seem an absurdity from the beginning, but that is only so if either reader or writer imagines that Zen can be contained in a set of ideas. A book about London is in no sense London itself, and no sane person would dream of thinking that it is. Yet apparently intelligent people often make the equally ridiculous mistake of identifying a philosophical system, a dogma, a creed, with Ultimate Truth, imagining that they have found that Truth embraced in a set of propositions which appeals to their reason. There are thousands of men and women searching through volume after volume, visiting religious societies, and attending the lectures of famous teachers, in the vain hope that they will one day come upon some explanation of the mysteries of life: some saying, some idea, which will contain the solution to the Infinite Riddle. Some continue the search till they die, others imagine that in various ideologies they have found what they desire, and a few penetrate beyond ideas about Truth to Truth itself.

There are some religions and philosophies which lend themselves more easily than others to the error of mistaking the idea for the reality, religions in which the creed and the symbol are emphasised at the expense of the spiritual experience which they are intended to embody. This, however, is less a reflection on those religions than on the

106

ignorance of their devotees. But there is at least one cult in which this error is almost impossible, precisely because it has no creed, no philosophical system, no canon of scriptures, no intellectually comprehensible doctrine. So far as it can be called a definite cult at all, it consists of devices for freeing the soul from its fetters, devices which are picturesquely described as fingers pointing at the moon – and he is a fool who mistakes the finger for the moon. This cult is Zen, a form of Buddhism which developed in China and now flourishes principally in Japan. Zen is itself a Japanese word, derived from the Chinese *Ch'an* or *Ch'an-na*, a form of the Sanskrit *dhyana*, which is usually rendered in English as 'meditation' or 'contemplation.' This, however, is a misleading translation, for although in yoga terminology *dhyana* signifies a certain state of contemplation, a state of what we should somewhat inaccurately call 'trance,' Zen is a far more inclusive term. We come nearer to its meaning if we remember that the word *dhyana* is related to *gñana* (the Greek *gnosis*) or Knowledge in the very highest sense of that word, which is to say supreme spiritual Enlightenment. *Gñana* (another form of which is sometimes spelt *dzyan*) is very close to Zen, the more so when we remember that Zen is said to have come into the world at the moment when Gautama the Buddha found Enlightenment when sitting one night under the famous Bodhi Tree at Bodh Gaya in northern India. There, according to the teachers of Zen, he found something which cannot be expressed in any form of words; an experience which every man must undergo for himself; which can no more be passed on from one man to another than you can eat another person's food for him.

Zen, however, as a specific cult, is mainly a product of the Chinese mind. Buddhism developed in India as a highly subtle and abstract system of philosophy, a cult of sublime other-worldliness perfectly suited to the inhabitants of a hot climate where life is able to flourish with little labour. The Chinese and Japanese, on the other hand, have a climate nearer to our own and have the same practical bent as the peoples of northern Europe. Perhaps the greatest triumph of Buddhism is that it was able to adapt itself to a mentality so far removed from the Indian. Thus Zen has been described as the Chinese revolt against Buddhism. It would be nearer the truth to call it the Chinese interpretation of Buddhism, although the term 'revolt' certainly conveys the fierce, almost iconoclastic character of Zen – a cult which has no patience with any practice or formula which has not immediate relationship with the one thing of importance: Enlightenment. To understand this revolt or interpretation (or better, 'revolutionary interpretation') some of the fundamental principles of Buddhism must be borne in mind.

The Buddha, who lived some 600 years BC,[27] taught that life, as we live it, is necessarily unharmonious because of the selfish, possessive attitude we adopt towards it. In Sanskrit this attitude is called *trishna* (often mistranslated 'desire'), and though there is no one word for it in English, it may be understood as the craving to resist change, to 'save our own skins' at all costs, to possess those whom we love; in fact, to hold on to life 'like grim death.' And that particular phrase has its moral. If anything that lives and moves is held, it dies just like a plucked flower. Egotism is a fierce holding on to oneself; it is building oneself up in a haughty stronghold, refusing to join in the play of life, refusing to accept the eternal laws of change of movement to which all are subject. But that refusal can only be illusion. Whether we like it or not, change comes, and the greater the resistance, the greater the pain. Buddhism perceives the beauty of change, for life is like music in this: if any note or phrase is held for longer than its appointed time, the melody is lost. Thus Buddhism may be summed up in two phrases: 'Let go!' and 'Walk on!' Drop the craving for self, for permanence, for particular circumstances, and go straight ahead with the movement of life. The state of mind thereby attained is called Nirvana. But this is a teaching easy to misunderstand, for it is so easy to represent the doctrine of 'letting go' as an utter denial of life and the world, and Nirvana as a state infinitely removed from all earthly concerns.

Zen, however, corrected this error in the most surprising and unique manner. So much so that a great part of the Zen teachings may appear at first to be mere buffoonery or nonsense.

A disciple came to Zen Master Chao-chou and asked, 'I have just come to this monastery. Would you mind giving me some instruction, please?'

The master replied, 'Have you eaten your breakfast yet, or not?'

'Yes, I have, sir.'

'Then wash your dishes.'

It is said that as a result of this remark the disciple was suddenly enlightened as to the whole meaning of Zen.

On another occasion a master was about to address an assembly of students when a bird began to sing in a nearby tree. The master remained silent until the bird had finished, and then, announcing that his address had been given, went away.

Another master set a pitcher before two of his disciples. 'Do not call it a pitcher,' he said, 'but tell me what it is.'

One replied, 'It cannot be called a piece of wood.'

The master, however, was not satisfied with this answer, and he turned to the other disciple who simply knocked the pitcher over and walked away.

This action had the master's full approval.

It will be asked whether these antics have the least connection with religion, even with ordinary sanity. They are regarded by the exponents of Zen as full of the deepest significance, and when we remember that Zen has been, beyond question, one of the most powerful influences in shaping the art and culture of the Far East, such behaviour is entitled to respect. Has it some symbolic meaning? What is it about? The answer is that it has no symbolic meaning, and that it is *about* nothing. But it *is* something, and that something is that very obvious but much ignored thing – *life*. The Zen master is in fact demonstrating life in its actuality; without words or ideas he is teaching his disciples to know life directly.[28] Sometimes in answer to a religious question he will give a smack on the face, returning a reality for an abstraction. If he gave a reasoned answer, the disciple would be able to analyse it, to subject it to intellectual dissection, and to imagine a mere lifeless formula as a living truth. But with a smack, a bird, a pitcher, a heap of dishes there can be no mistake. A smack is here one moment and gone the next. There is nothing you can catch hold of, nothing other than a most lively fact, as much alive as the passing moment which can never be made to stay. And a bird is a bird; you hear its song, but you cannot seize the notes to make them continue.

It just *is*, and is gone, and you feel the beauty of its song precisely because the notes do *not* wait for you to analyse them. Therefore the Zen master is not trying to give you ideas *about* life; he is trying to give you life itself, to make you realise life in and around you, to make you live it instead of being a mere spectator, a mere pedant absorbed in the dry bones of something which the life has long deserted. A symphony is not explained by a mathematical analysis of its notes; the mystery of a woman's beauty is not revealed by a post-mortem dissection; and no-one ever understood the wonder of a bird on the wing by stuffing it and putting it in a glass case. To understand these things, you must live and move with them as they are alive. The same is true of the universe: no amount of intellectual analysis will explain it, for philosophy and science can only reveal its mechanism, never its meaning or, as the Chinese say, its Tao.

'What is the Tao?'

A Zen master answers, 'Usual life is the very Tao.'

'How does one bring oneself into accord with it?'

'If you try to accord with it, you will get away from it.'

For to imagine that there is a 'you' separate from life which somehow has to accord with life is to fall straight into the trap. If you *try* to find the Tao, you are at once presupposing a difference between yourself and the Tao. Therefore the Zen masters say nothing about the means for becoming Enlightened, for understanding the Tao. They simply concentrate on Tao itself. When you are reading a book you defeat your purpose altogether if you think about yourself trying to concentrate on it; instead of thinking about what is written, your attention is absorbed in your efforts to concentrate. The secret is to think of the book and forget yourself.[29] But that is not all. The book is of little use to you if you go to the other extreme and simply let it 'run away with you.' On the contrary, you must bring your own understanding and intelligence to it, and then through the union of your own thoughts and the thoughts in the book, something new is born. This union is the important task; you must just do it, and not waste energy in thinking about doing it. The same is true in Zen. It does not ask that we should so submit ourselves to life that the world altogether masters us and blots us out. There are some who never live, who are always having thoughts about life and feelings about life; others are swept away on the tides of circumstance, so overwhelmed by events that they have nothing of their own.

Buddhism, however, is the Middle Way, and this is not compromise but a union between opposites to produce a 'higher third'; just as man and woman unite to produce a child. The same process is found in almost every religion, in some deeply hidden, in others plainly revealed. In Christianity man must be born anew of water and the spirit, symbols of substance and energy, concrete life and the mind of man. Thus the prayer to Christ to be 'born in us' is the hope for the same Enlightenment that we find in Buddhism, and the story of Christ's birth is its allegory. For the Holy Ghost is spirit, and Mary (Lat. *mare* – sea, water) is the world, called in Sanskrit *maya*. And the mother of the Buddha was also called Maya, and he too was supposed to have been miraculously conceived. Thus the realisation of the Christ within, the Buddha within, the Tao within, or the Krishna within is in each instance the result of a process which Zen presents to us in this unique and almost startling manner. It is the understanding of the One which lies behind the Many; the bringing together of opposites, of subject and object, the ego and the universe, to create the Holy Child.

And yet we must beware of that definition, of that convenient summary of religious endeavour. It so easily becomes a mere catchphrase, a truth so fastened in a nutshell that it ceases to be of the least use. In its prison it withers away and dies. Therefore Zen comes at this stage with a most inconvenient question, 'When the Many are reduced to the One, to what is the One to be reduced?' Only he who knows what that is understands Zen. It would be futile to try to explain any further, for to do so would be to defeat the very purpose of Zen, which is to make everyone find out for himself. It is like a detective story with the last chapter missing; it remains a mystery, a thing like a beam of light which can be seen and used, but never caught – loved, but never possessed. And by that we may know that Zen is life.

———————— • ————————

IS RELIGION NECESSARY? (1938)

At the end of July 1937, the Second World Congress of Faiths was held at Oxford[30] to discuss 'The World's Need of Religion' – a subject which has of late been given considerable publicity throught the Archbishop of Canterbury's 'Recall to Religion.'

Many have wondered at the word 'Recall,' for it must be asked whether any but the very few have at any time in history been religious in the true sense of the word. Certainly there was a time when people went to church more than they do today, and there may have been times when society was more righteous. There are, indeed, a host of definitions of the word 'religion,' but no serious thinker would ever identify it with the mere observance of precepts. For such observance may be anything but religious; it is an outward activity which may be undertaken for a whole variety of inner motives. It may be the result of true religious feeling, yet at the same time it may simply be the expression of pride and selfishness. Almost everyone agrees that a certain measure of morality is at this time one of our most important needs, and the World Congress of Faiths was agreed that no amount of political expedients could bring fellowship among the peoples of the world unless individuals paid more attention to the moral law. We can be certain, however, that no morality is going to be truly effective unless it is emphatically *desired*. Actions performed purely from a sense of duty are performed grudgingly, and morality which is a means to a selfish end soon loses its sheep's clothing.

Hence the world is in need of something more than right conduct. Everyone will admit that morality is reasonable and that it would be a 'good thing' if we could have it; we admit it both of society and of ourselves. But between seeing its reasonableness and its actual realisation there is a vast gap. For the important question is, do we want it? And the answer is most assuredly that we do not – otherwise we should undoubtedly have it.

So many people say loosely that they want a greater social fellowship when what they really mean is that they feel it to be necessary and reasonable. But no-one who knows anything of his own human nature would identify this feeling with an ardent desire, for constantly we are acting against conscience and reason just because there is a divergence between desire and duty which no amount of reason can prevent. Therefore we have to find something which has more power than reason over human desire. But here we are faced with the difficulty that, unless we desire to change our desires absolutely, nothing can change them short of pure terror or the offer of some particularly attractive reward. Yet neither of these can really alter the position, for in each instance the desire remains essentially selfish. It is not surprising, therefore, that Christianity insists on the essential sinfulness of human desire by reason of the Fall, maintaining that it can only be redeemed by the Grace of God. For according to this doctrine we are utterly unable to help ourselves; to try to make oneself good without taking into account the Grace of God is like trying to lift oneself up by one's own belt. Christianity therefore counsels that we should confess our own wretchedness, our inability to change our desires, and humbly call upon God to enter our souls and cleanse them. This doctrine contains a profound truth, but before we can go into this we must ask ourselves whether moral perfection is after all a desirable end.

And this raises the even deeper question of whether religion is not in fact an absolute denial of all that we understand as life. There appear to be two aspects of religion; in some faiths, such as Christianity, they are found together, whereas in others, such as Buddhism, there seems only to be one. The first is the feeling of reverence, wonder and gratitude for God and His universe – a feeling which is expressed in the worship of thanksgiving and adoration. The second is the culture of the soul, by prayer or meditation or action: the attempt to bring the individual into some kind of unity and accord with the ideal purpose of which the universe is at present the somewhat imperfect expression. In Christianity this purpose is called the Will of God, while in Buddhism and Vedanta it is known as Dharma or the Absolute Law of Life. There can be no question of the first of these aspects being in any way a denial of life, for it is founded essentially on the love of life, on boundless gratitude to the Creator for having given us such a delightful world. Yet it is hard for those whom the world treats roughly to share in this feeling, though Christianity holds that we should be thankful even for adversity seeing that this world is not given to us for mere enjoyment. We are here to work out a purpose, and our gratitude should be not only for the pleasant things of life but for the privilege, the opportunity, of being allowed to share in the fulfilment of this divine purpose. It is here that the first aspect leads on to the second; gratitude for the opportunity presupposes an attempt to make use of the opportunity, and this use is the culture of the soul.

But what is this purpose? How do we know that there *is* a purpose? And if the purpose is what the teachers of religion declare it to be, is it a good purpose? At the World Congress of Faiths Dr Maude Royden gave a most eloquent address on the necessity and the efficacy of working out this purpose in our lives. But somehow she forgot the most important thing – she never said what this purpose was, and one seldom finds a teacher who has any clear ideas on this matter at all. Some will say that it is to bring the universe to perfect peace and harmony. But here we must ask the awkward questions – would not this amount to the cessation of the universe; and did God create the world simply for its abolition? Life exists because of conflict and tension, and music can only be produced when there is a tension of the strings. A pendulum can only swing if it swings in two opposite directions; otherwise it must come to rest. If there were only joy and goodness we should cease to appreciate them just as the eyes become blind through too much light, for if light is to be known as light there must be periods of darkness. Mystics explain that the divine purpose is the union of the soul with God, the return of the manifold universe to its original unity. Yet if this be true, we must ask why it ever came forth from this original unity and what is the point of just going round in circles. Furthermore, we only know life as life because it consists of a multitude of separate things. Some of these things are pleasant, others painful, but we must admit that all of them are wonderful and profoundly interesting. Would life not be rather dull if they were all merged into a homogeneous lump of pure matter or pure energy where nothing was the matter and there was nothing to be energetic about? Perhaps we may therefore say that periods of uniformity are necessary in order that we may appreciate diversity; death is to prevent us from becoming tired of life. Yet if this be so we must change our ideas about the divine purpose.

It would seem that the purpose is not to achieve this

absolute unity any more than the purpose of life is death. This is only a part of God's Will. He has not made a diverse world of good and evil in order that it may progress towards a particular end, for in His omnipotence He might easily have created that end at once, even before He had said, 'Let there be light!' Thus to imagine that the aim of religion is just to expedite man's return to his original source, his primordial unity with God and the loss of his separate identity, is wholly beside the point. This may be just as necessary a stage in the movement of life as death and sleep; but it is a stage and not an end, not in any sense the final achievement of a purpose. Furthermore, no-one in his senses tries to expedite his death or to hurry through the day in order that he may get back to bed as quickly as possible. For this would indeed be a denial of life. If we are made as separate beings involved in a tension of opposites, of good and evil, joy and sorrow, light and darkness, it is absurd to imagine that the purpose of this is just to end the separateness and the tension. This may have to end (for a time) and this end will come in the natural course of things. But to try to achieve that end quickly is actually to blaspheme against the Will of God, for His purpose is not fulfilled in the future but in the present. We do not achieve it by running forward to some future state, for this is in fact simply running away; it is playing out of time with the orchestra of the universe. For the strange truth is that we are fulfilling the divine purpose at *this* moment, whether we know it or not, simply by being what we are. With all our peculiar desires and imperfections and limitations we are fulfilling it in spite of ourselves, for try as we may we cannot get away from it. For the ultimate paradise, the ideal state, the great fulfilment, or whatever we may call it, is neither in the past nor in the future; it is *now*. Pursuing, we cannot catch it; fleeing, we cannot escape it; and the reason that we do not understand it is that all the time we are engaged in running away from it or after it.

This brings us to the seemingly dreadful conclusion that all our strivings for a better and more moral world, our conception of religion as an improving process, a sort of glorified scientific progress towards ultimate perfection, are beside the point; that, indeed, they are quite useless. But what else is this than the confession of our own sinfulness and helplessness? And what else is that than admitting that we are what we are?

Yet here is the peculiar and paradoxical mystery: that in admitting that we are what we are, in being what we are, in humbly and reverently accepting our condition and, as it were, laying it open before the eyes of God, we at once begin to accord with the divine purpose. And at this moment we are transfigured and redeemed. For the paradox is that in the effort of trying to lift ourselves up by our own belts we do not see that we are already up! In Christian terms, God is filling us with His love and His Grace all the time, for by reason of this alone are we able to exist. But we do not realise this because of our self-preoccupation, our perpetual attempt to save ourselves without His help. Yet by His love we are already saved, and damnation consists simply in shutting our eyes to this astonishing fact.

For this reason it is said that religion is contained in the phrase, 'Become what you are.' Or in the words of the Indian mystics, *'Tat tvam asi!'* — 'That (Brahman) art thou!' — at this very moment in being what you are, in thinking what you think, in doing what you do. All that separates you from God's purpose is your own proud effort to achieve what you imagine to be that purpose by your own power. And therein is our blindness, and the tragi-comedy of our lives, for the purpose is already achieved in every moment.

'So,' you will ask, 'are we then just to make no effort, to sit down under evil and do nothing?'

But remember, if you think you can save yourself by making no effort, sitting down under evil and doing nothing, you deceive yourself again. It is not a question of what *you* do, but of what God does, and you cannot save *yourself* by any means, either by doing or not doing.

God is always saving you, but this is not easy to understand.

———————————— • ————————————

SPEAKING PERSONALLY (1938)

The Development of a Theme, in response to Mrs Eleanor C. Merry's Article 'The Threshold of a New Age'

I am very glad that Mrs. Merry'[31] in her article 'The Threshold of a New Age' [*Modern Mystic*, July 1938 – see Appendices, pp275–82], has given me the opportunity to clarify some of the points raised in my own article 'Is Religion Necessary?' For I had expressed a point of view which may easily be misunderstood if the terms and phrases employed are insufficiently defined. However, allowing for this, and having read both my own article and Mrs Merry's again several times, I am still not quite sure what the difference of opinion is about. There is so much in her article with which I find myself in perfect agreement, that I can only assume that one of two things has happened: either that she has assumed my ideas to belong to a specifically Oriental background, or else that I have not made myself sufficiently clear.

Both of these eventualities require some personal explanation and I ask readers to bear with me if I make something rather like a confession of faith. The words I used which appear to have been the chief cause of the difficulty were these: 'It is not a question of what *you* do, but of what God does, and you cannot save yourself by any means, either by doing or not doing. God is always saving you, but this is not easy to understand.'

Here, as Mrs Merry points out, we have the elusive Eastern doctrine of non-action (a better term is 'non-assertion'); but it is not, as her subsequent remarks seem to imply, a doctrine of utter renunciation and denial of the world. That is to say, not as I understand it. My interpretation of this doctrine is derived from Chinese sources, and unfortunately these are less well-known in the West than the Indian. The Indian approach to religion is, generally speaking, world-denying; Indian Buddhism is an outstanding example of this tendency, and is avowedly no more than a means of escaping from the world as we know it to a state where all diversity is merged into an infinite one-ness, sometimes called No-thing-ness because it is a 'something' in which there are no separate things. Being a confirmed Westerner, I cannot find sympathy with this point of view, simply because the ideal state in question seems abysmally uninteresting. I tried to make this very plain in my article, saying that this state of uniformity seemed the very antithesis of life, and that there was no purpose in living if this denial of life was to be the end. I suggested that this state might bear the same relation to universal life as death to individual life, but in that case it is not an ideal state but a passing stage, and certainly not the fulfilment of the divine purpose.

The Chinese, however, are much nearer to Westerners in mentality than the Indians, and their interpretation of Buddhism is utterly different, the principal reason being that their native mysticism in Taoism evolved a doctrine of 'non-action' (*wu-wei*) wholly its own. Taoism is based on the concept of the Tao, which means something like the Way or Meaning of life as it is – a term which should be held synonymous with God in the sense I wished it to have in the above quotation from my article. Life expresses itself in a multitude of pairs of opposites: I and thou, living and dying, pleasure and pain, man and woman, day and night. None of these things can exist without its opposite; man is meaningless without woman, but in man *and* woman there is meaning, and this meaning is Tao, whose symbol is the child. But Tao is not some abstract, formless essence which can be conceived as existing apart from these pairs of opposites; it is less an entity than a condition, the condition of relationship between opposites. In fact it IS the opposites considered together. Take them apart and Tao vanishes, but this taking apart is something which we can only suggest for the sake of argument; in fact it cannot happen. People do try to make it happen, however. They desire pleasure without pain, life without death, and so on, and this desire is life-denying because, if it were attainable, the world would vanish into nothingness.

Therefore when I asked 'Is Religion Necessary?' I was referring to those forms of religion whose logical conclusion is the dissolution of the world. Certain Indian religions state in plain terms that that is indeed their aim. But there are others which unintentionally work towards that goal, though they would be the last to admit it. These are the religions which strive for earthly perfection – and by earthly I do not mean only material. In this sense the phrase 'earthly perfection' should be understood as the final, eternal and total achievement of a state which is in fact one of a pair of opposites. Immortality is an example. Life as a whole is immortal, but the forms of life are not. A person is a form of life, and thus personal immortality is to my mind not only unattainable but undesirable. It may be, however, that in each of us there is a more-than-personal consciousness which survives bodily death, but I feel that this is a scientific and metaphysical question, not a religious one.

Admittedly I have got myself into trouble through using the term 'true religion' in rather a limited sense. For I feel that spiritual life and endeavour are not concerned at all with many of the things which figure so prominently in religion. Cosmogony, morality, theology, eschatology (the study of the life after death) and metaphysics are, in my judgement, material rather than spiritual questions. And this is coming near to the crux of the whole matter. To put it in another form, I believe that occultism and ethics belong to science rather than religion, for they are primarily matters of knowledge, behaviour and faculty. You may have vast knowledge, admirable behaviour towards your fellow men, and the capacity to attain states of consciousness and perception unknown to ordinary men. But these things are only tools, and man has to learn the lesson that they are not necessarily the keys to happiness. Yes, happiness is the word. Do not confuse it with pleasure. Call it rather the love of life in all its aspects; call it spiritual freedom. No-one can deny, however, that it is the thing which all men desire. The word has certain unfortunate associations but, so long as the quest for happiness is not identified with so-called hedonism, we must admit that all human striving and all religion arises from the desire to be happy. In other words, man wants to be so adapted to life, to pleasure and to pain, that he can say, 'I love it.'

Knowledge as such does not necessarily bring happiness, and by knowledge we must understand not only book-knowledge but also first-hand experience. You may have an occult experience which proves to you beyond all doubt that you will live for ever, but if you do not love life as pleasure and as pain, you will be thoroughly depressed by this knowledge. The reason that knowledge does not necessarily bring happiness is that happiness depends not on what you know or do, but on what you desire. It is a question of motive. It is a truism that if you search for happiness you never find it. Less of a truism, but also true, is the fact that if you search for happiness by a studied not-searching for it, you still fail, because the latter is only an indirect form of the former, its first cousin once removed. Then how are we to find it? That is the problem, for we have to get it neither by looking for it nor by not looking for it. We cannot get it by doing something about it, nor by not doing, because both methods arise from the same desire – which is to *do* something about it by direct or indirect means. But the Chinese sages teach a way of not-doing which is above and beyond these pairs of opposites, but which yet exists in them! Before we consider this, however, let me return once more to Mrs Merry's article.

The attainment of happiness is not in any way analogous to walking from Bloomsbury to Westminster.[32] I do not think Mrs Merry was implying that Westminster is a nicer place than Bloomsbury, but this is what she unintentionally suggests, the point being that if one is not happy in Bloomsbury, one will certainly not be happy in Westminster. For happiness belongs to the man who walks; not to the places to which he goes. Her actual intention was to point out that the two places are some distance apart and that you do not make the whole journey by taking the first step. Quite so; this applies to science, occultism and all other means of increasing one's knowledge and developing one's faculties; in fact to all things about which one must DO something if one is to make progress. But happiness is not like that, for there is nothing one can *do* about it in the same sense. And yet it is the thing we want most of all.

None of this must be taken to imply that science and occultism are a waste of time. They are perfectly legitimate activities so long as it is recognised (and this is most important) that *they are not the means by which happiness is found but the field wherein it is found.* And this may be said of anything else, such as bootmaking, painting, housekeeping, farming or going for a walk. Then what are the means? The answer is that the means are the same as those one would adopt in turning round to look at one's own eyes.

Let us examine more closely what is meant by happiness. It is, I believe, love of life in all its aspects arising from a sense of spiritual freedom. For in this sense love and freedom are one because real freedom is not what the world supposes it to be. It is not just fooling about as you like without any regard to the rules of life and without any hindrance. The difference is this: that the false concept of freedom is freedom to do as one likes. True freedom is freedom to do as one likes and also as one doesn't like. In fact it consists in doing absolutely anything, whether you like it or not, the point being that if your freedom excludes certain actions or circumstances which you don't like, it is no longer free. It is limited by your own whims. Yet it is not really limited; it is only limited to your knowledge. In truth you cannot limit this freedom, for it belongs to the universe which includes all things pleasant and painful, great and small. If anything is excluded the freedom is not genuine, for God excludes no creature however sinful or humble from His love and grace. Therefore spiritual freedom in this sense cannot be had by going anywhere particular or by doing anything particular, for this implies that the person who goes or does is under the impression that he has not got that freedom already. But the stupendous truth is that he has, and what is more, that however much he may deceive himself to the contrary, he cannot get away from it. By no possible means can you limit or deprive yourself of your spiritual freedom, for all that you think or do and all that comes to you from outside yourself is the free activity of the universe which excludes nothing. And when you realise that by no possible action, by no desperate crime, by no folly, by no calamity, can you exclude yourself from that freedom, then you will realise the meaning of love.

You say this is a dangerous doctrine? – that whatever you do and whatever is done to you partakes of God and His omnipotent freedom? Yes, and no. For once realised it has a strange effect on one's mind. The knowledge that one has this freedom is a responsibility, but having it one does not desire to abuse it. For vicious actions are all mistaken attempts to achieve happiness, which this realisation has given in such abundance that one need ask for no more. Furthermore, it releases a mighty energy in the depths of the soul so that one almost 'walks on air', as the saying goes. For you feel the power of the universe at work in all that you do, and without any effort, for you know that nothing you can do can cut off that power. And with such force in one's hands one learns the meaning of responsibility as never before!

This, to my mind, is the main business of religion, for, as I pointed out in my previous article, it is a matter of 'becoming what you are.' And so far from implying any denial of the world of opposites, of the ego and of the transient forms of life, it is a tremendous affirmation of them; all things, however they behave, are the Tao and cannot be anything else, and by this they are redeemed in spite of themselves. But although this redemption, this spiritual freedom, is something quite independent of morality, it is not an escape from the moral law. There is still a price to be paid for folly. But in this sense immorality is not a spiritual sin – it is a material, mental, emotional or psychic error which produces its results in accordance with the laws of those planes of existence.

If a sage carelessly drops a match on a pile of gunpowder he cannot escape being blown up; the explosion, however, does not limit or invalidate his spiritual attainment. In just the same way, a moral error will have its painful consequences, but it cannot detract from one's spiritual stature. For the highest in spiritual attainment are those who realise that in this realm there is no such thing as attainment, that spiritually we are redeemed as we are in spite of ourselves, through no virtue of our own. Those who imagine that before they can enter into the love and freedom of God they must make themselves great by their own efforts suffer from spiritual pride. This is a hard truth for the ambitious to swallow, but Christianity has taught it for two thousand years (rather blindly) and the Chinese knew it even earlier.

In conclusion I must say that this is not intended as a direct 'answer' to Mrs Merry, but an attempt to state my position in such a way that the issue between us (if one really exists) may be clarified. For people cannot discuss things with one another to any purpose until they are quite sure that they understand one another's languages.

———————— • ————————

THE ONE (1939)

The doctrines of religion are symbols used by saints and sages to describe spiritual experiences, just as ordinary men use words to describe mental and physical experiences. Students of religion recognise two kinds of spiritual experience, of which the first resembles what we call a state of mind, such as happiness, love or fear, and the second an experience of something outside ourselves, as when we see stars, trees or hills. In the language of religion, the first kind of experience may be called the sense of freedom, salvation or deliverance, and the second a beatific vision. The doctrines of religion have their origin in attempts to convey these experiences to others by enshrining a state of mind within an idea about the universe or by recording a vision as the basis of an article of faith. Visions are somewhat more spectacular and sensational than states of mind and, because they have form, colour and motion, they are easier to describe. Thus they are common in all religions, but they do not necessarily carry with them the sense of freedom, salvation or deliverance which is the most profound, the most satisfying and the most lasting of religious experiences. There are few who would not rather thave this sense than a thousand visions.

Many attempts have been made to describe the feeling of salvation which the Buddhists call *Nirvana* and the Hindus call *Moksha*.[33] Where these descriptions are in the form of doctrines we notice that among such doctrines there is a wide variety of differences whereby students of religion are often misled. If the doctrines of Christianity are different from those of Hinduism, it does not necessarily follow that the religions are different, for more than one doctrine may describe a single state of mind, and without this state of mind the religion, as a mere collection of doctrines, has no meaning whatever; it is just as if it were a babble of unintelligible words. But doctrines differ because people have different mental backgrounds and traditions; an Englishman and a Chinese may have the same feeling but they will speak of it in different ways because they are relating it to different mental contexts. It is therefore most unwise to study religion from the standpoint of doctrine *as* doctrine, for this is the purest superficiality. Doctrines and conceptual ideas vary as languages vary, but one and the same meaning may be conveyed by both English and French. Christians believe in a personal God and Buddhists do not, but as regards the true essentials of religion this difference is as superficial as the fact that in French every noun has a gender, whereas this is not so in English.

Therefore to extract the true meaning of a religious doctrine we must ask, 'What does this doctrine mean in terms of a state of mind? What sort of feeling towards life and the universe would have caused a man to think in this way?' For religious experience is like the experience of beauty; indeed, it is something closely akin to feeling beauty in the whole of life instead of in a single picture, scene, image or melody. Beethoven and Stravinsky may both arouse the sense of beauty, and they are quite as different in their own ways as Christianity and Buddhism. The important thing, however, is that they arouse that sense; we may discuss and argue over their respective 'merits' till all is blue without coming to any conclusion. It would be more profitable, however, if we could take one who feels beauty in Beethoven and one who feels beauty in Stravinsky, and then consider the varying degrees of profundity in their respective feelings. But here we should be dealing with such intangible and imponderable factors that ordinary methods of criticism and discussion would be useless, and we could only judge by intuition. The same principle applies in religion, for the feeling of beauty in art or music is here the feeling of salvation. By this I do not mean freedom of moral conscience nor even the certainty of an everlasting life of bliss after death, although such things may be attained by any number of different religious systems. These elementary forms of 'salvation' have much the same relation to the deeper forms as mere sensuous thrill has to the perception of beauty.

What, then, is a truly deep feeling of salvation?

Insofar as this question can be answered at all, perhaps it is best to consider one of the greatest doctrines in all religion in terms of a state of mind. For this purpose the best choice is probably the Hindu or Vedantist conception of Brahman, because this is at once the simplest and the most subtle of doctrines – subtle just because it is so simple. The same doctrine is found in other systems, but Vedanta gives it the best philosophical expression. It is that all possible things, events, thoughts and qualities are aspects of a single Reality which is sometimes called the Self of the universe. In themselves these many aspects have no reality; they are real only in that each one of them is a manifestation of Brahman or the Self. To put it in another way, the true self of any given thing is Brahman and not something that belongs exclusively to the thing in question. Each individual is therefore an aspect of Brahman, and no two aspects are the same. But man's self is much more than what he considers to be his ego, his personality called John Smith or William Jones. The ego is a device or trick (*maya*) employed so that Brahman may manifest itself, and man's innermost self is therefore identical with the Self of all things.

Thus if anyone wants to know what Brahman is he has just to look around, to think, to act, to be aware, to live, for all that is known by the senses, thought in the mind or felt in the heart *is* Brahman.

In other systems of thought Brahman has many other names – *Tao* in Chinese, and mystics the world over find similar meaning in the words 'God', 'Allah', 'Infinite Life', '*élan vital*', 'the Absolute', or whatever other term may be used. In fact, the intuition of the One Reality is the essence of all mystical religion, but few people understand clearly what it is to feel this intuition in oneself. We are perhaps more apt to think of this idea just as a metaphysical speculation, a more or less reasonable theory about the fundamental structure of life. Someday, we think, it might be possible for us to delve down into the deepest recesses of our souls, lay our fingers on this mysterious universal Essence and avail ourselves of its tremendous powers. This, however, does not seem quite the right way to look at it. For one thing, it is not to be found only 'in the deepest recesses of our souls,' and for another, the word 'essence' makes it sound as if it were a highly refined, somewhat gaseous or electric and wholly formless potency that somehow dwells 'inside' things. But in relation to Brahman there is neither inside nor outside; sometimes it is called the principle of 'non-duality' because nothing else exists beside it and nothing is excluded from it. It is to be found on the surface as much as in the depths and in the finite as much as in the infinite, for it has wisely been said that 'there is nothing infinite apart from finite things.' Thus it can neither be lost nor found and you cannot avail yourself of its powers any more than you can dispense with them, for all these conceptions of having and not having, of gain and loss, finite and infinite, belong to the principle of duality. Every dualism is exclusive; it is this and not that, that and not this. But Brahman as the One Reality is all-inclusive, for the Upanishads say:*

---

* *Himalayas of the Soul*. Translations of the principal Upanishads. By Juan Mascaro. London, 1938. p. 89.

It is made of consciousness and mind: It is made of life and vision. It is made of the earth and the waters: It is made of air and space. It is made of light and darkness: It is made of desire and peace. It is made of anger and love: It is made of virtue and vice. It is made of all that is near: It is made of all that is afar. It is made of all.

What, then, is non-duality in terms of a state of mind? How does the mystic who has realised his identity with the One Reality think and feel? Does his consciousness expand from out of his body and enter into all other things, so that he sees with others' eyes, and thinks with others' brains?

Only figuratively, for the Self which is in him and in all others does not necessarily communicate to the physical brain of John Smith, mystic, what is seen by the eyes of Pei-wang, coolie, on the other side of the earth. I do not believe that spiritual illumination is to be understood in quite this sensational way. We shall answer the question sufficiently if we can discover what is a non-dualistic state of mind. Does it mean a mind in so intense a state of concentration that it contains only one thought? Strictly speaking, the mind never contains more than one thought at a time; such is the nature of thinking. But if spirituality means thinking only and always of one particular thing, then other things are excluded and this is still duality. Does it mean, then, a mind which is thinking of everything at once? Even if this were possible, it would exclude the convenient faculty of thinking of one thing at a time and would still be dualistic. Clearly these two interpretations are absurd, but there is another way of approach.

Spiritual illumination is often described as absolute freedom of the soul, and we have seen that the One Reality is all-inclusive. Is the mind of the mystic similarly free and all-inclusive? If so, it would seem that his spirituality does not depend on thinking any special kinds of thoughts, on having a particular feeling ever in the background of his soul. He is free to think of anything and nothing, to love and to fear, to be joyful or sad, to set his mind on philosophy or on the trivial concerns of the world; he is free to be both a sage and a fool, to feel both compassion and anger, to experience both bliss and agony. And in all this he never breaks his identity with the One Reality – God, 'whose service is perfect freedom. 'For he knows that in whatever direction he goes and in whichever of these many opposites he is engaged, he is still in perfect harmony with the One that includes all directions and all opposites. In this sense, serving God is just living; it is not a question of the way in which you live, because all ways are included in God. To understand this is to wake up to your freedom to be alive.

But is that *all*? Is it possible that spirituality can be anything so absurdly simple? It seems to mean that to attain spirituality you have just to go on living as you have always lived; all life being God, any kind of life is spiritual. You say that if the idea were not so ludicrous it would be exceedingly dangerous. First we might remind ourselves of a saying of the Chinese sage, Lao-tzu:

> When the wise man hears of the Tao, he puts it into practice . . .
> When the fool hears of it, he laughs at it;
> Indeed, it would not be worthy to be called Tao if he did not laugh at it.

The idea that any kind of life is spiritual is a terrible blow to man's pride; from the spiritual point of view it puts us on the same level as stones, vegetables, worms and beetles; it makes the righteous man no nearer to salvation than the criminal and the sage no nearer than the lunatic. Thus if all else about the idea is folly, it is at least a powerful antidote to spiritual pride and self-reward for being a good boy; indeed, it is not something which you can *get* at all, however fierce your efforts, however great your learning and however tireless your virtue. In the spiritual world there is no top and bottom of the class; here all men and all things are equal and whatever they do can go neither up nor down. The only difference between sage or mystic and ordinary, unenlightened man is that the one realises his identity with God or Brahman, whereas the other does not. But the lack of realisation does not alter the fact.

How, then, does one attain this realisation? Is it just a matter of going on living as one has lived before, knowing that one is free to do just exactly as one likes? Beware of the false freedom of doing as you like; to be really free you must also be free to do as you don't like, for if you are only free to do as you like you are still tied up in dualism, being bound by your own whims. A better way of attaining realisation is to let

127

yourself be free to be ignorant, for fools also are one with God. If you strive to attain realisation and try to make yourself God, you simply become an intense egotist. But if you allow yourself freedom to be yourself, you will discover that God is not what you have to *become*, but what you *are* – in spite of yourself. For have we not heard it said a thousand times that God is always found in humble places?

'The Tao,' said Lao-tzu, 'is like water; it seeks the lowly level which men abhor.' And while we are busy trying to add cubits to our stature so that we may reach up to heaven, we forget that we are getting no nearer to it and no further away. For 'the kingdom of heaven is within you'.

———————— • ————————

THE CROSS OF CARDS (1939)

It is said that playing-cards were devised by the ancients to hide a secret where those not 'in the know' would never think of looking for it. For heresy-hunters are serious-minded people who would never think of looking for religion in a game. It is curious to think how men have gambled, fought and slain one another over these unknown symbols, and it is interesting to wonder whether the most accomplished 'poker face' would fall a little on discovering that he was playing for lucre with emblems just as holy as the cross, the chalice and the crown of thorns. Probably not, for men have done things just as terrible in the name of symbols whose holiness they recognised. However, it is no less strange that the puritanic mind should see in diamonds, spades, hearts and clubs the signs of vice, to be avoided at all times and more especially on Sundays.

Today the forms of playing-cards are very different from the original Tarot, but an ordinary modern pack is not without significance, even though it may not be quite the same significance that was originally intended. What that was I do not know, but the *living* meaning of a symbol is what it means for each man personally. Therefore my interpretation of this particular symbol is not the result of research but of my own intuition and has no claim to be *the* interpretation. Like the often-quoted Topsy, the idea 'just growed' when I laid out the four suits of the pack and began to wonder what it was all about. It is said that 'the ways to the One are as many as the lives of men,' and as I worked at the symbol this became obvious not only from the symbol itself but also from the many possible interpretations that might be given it. However, we begin by laying out the cards in the form of a cross, thus:

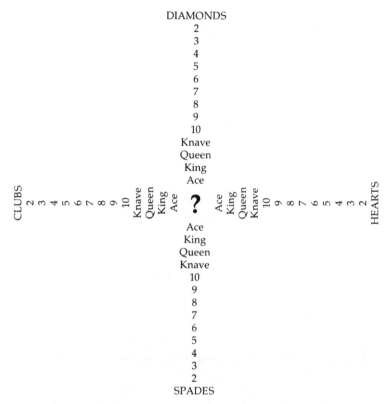

To the North are Diamonds, to the South Spades, to the East Hearts and to the West Clubs, running inwards to the centre from the two to the Ace. The first question was to decide the meaning of the four suits, and at once the four elements of Fire, Earth, Water and Air suggested themselves together with the four faculties of the human mind, Intuition, Sensation, Feeling and Intellect[34]. But which belonged to which? It was at once obvious that Spades belonged to Earth and Hearts to Feeling. Sensation is the avenue whereby we

129

receive our impressions of material things, and so this was accorded to Earth and Spades. Feeling is a passive, feminine faculty, not usually well developed in men; we talk about 'feminine intuition' but as a rule we generally mean feminine feeling – a certain sensitivity to emotional values, to psychological 'atmospheres' and feeling-situations where men are apt to be 'slow in the uptake.' It was thus decided to place Hearts and Feeling under the feminine element of Water – that passive substance that always yields but can never be defeated. Opposite Hearts we have Clubs, and it was not at once easy to decide whether Fire or Air should be called the opposite of Water. Fire and Water are hostile, but Air and Water are creative, for in the beginning 'the spirit of God moved upon the face of the waters,' and, 'except a man be born of water and of the spirit, he cannot enter into the kingdom of God.' It was therefore decided to make the figure harmonious instead of hostile, regarding the four suits as complements rather than opposites. Thus as Air complements Water, being the active agent which shapes the passive substance into the forms of waves, Thought or Intellect, as Air, was put opposite Feeling, as Water. Feeling is passive but Intellect — a masculine quality* — is active and often aggressive, and so belongs appropriately to Clubs. Intuition and Fire remain to be classed with Diamonds, for Intuition is the spiritual faculty which complements Sensation, the sensual or material faculty. Fire is not hostile to Earth, but its lightness (in both senses) complements the soil's darkness and heaviness. To Buddhist philosophers the diamond (*vajra*) is the symbol of spiritual consciousness because of its strength and luminous clarity.[35] It has been said that 'a diamond is a piece of coal which has stuck to its job,' being that which results from intense fire working upon black carbon. Therefore the four suits are understood as follows:

Diamonds (Fire & Intuition) – Spades (Earth & Sensation)
Hearts (Water & Feeling) – Clubs (Air & Intellect)

But what about the rest of the figure? We see that there is a

---

* Philosophy, metaphysics and mathematics, intellectual sciences *par excellence*, are scarcely ever pursued by women. In all history there are not more than two women who have excelled in these sciences. Innumerable women, however, have been great mystics.

progression of numbers and court cards from the extremity of each arm of the cross to the centre – four ways of approach to the Divinity at present represented by a question mark as He is unknown. Corresponding to the four faculties, the Hindus devised four kinds of yoga for awakening man's understanding of his union with Brahman, the Self of the Universe: *karma yoga*, the way of Action; *bhakti yoga*, the way of Devotion; *gñana yoga*, the way of Intellect[36], and *raja yoga*, the way of developing the higher faculties of Intuition. But it will be seen that in our figure each path is of a like pattern, running:

2 3 4 5 6 7 8 9 10 Knave Queen King Ace

This progression shows, among other things, each stage of man's path to supreme Enlightenment from the child and the primitive to the sage. From 2 to 10 the path seems to be going backwards, as will shortly be apparent, because it often seems that civilised man is further from spirituality than the child and the primitive. Actually this is not true, for in the parable of the Prodigal Son it is the prodigal for whom the fatted calf is slain and not the faithful son who had always stayed at home. Civilised man is the prodigal and primitive man the faithful son, for one has to be divided from union with the Father before one can truly appreciate it. To adapt a line of Kipling's, 'He does not know Union who only Union knows.'

We begin with the 2, for with every one of our four faculties the first thing of which we are aware, the very foundation of our experience, is the difference between that which we call our self and that which is not the self, between the thing which we call 'I' and the outer universe. This is the first of all the pairs of opposites of which life is composed, the subjective and the objective. But these two things do not exist in our consciousness without a third factor, namely the relationship between them, which is shown by the 3. That relationship may be attraction or repulsion, of love or fear, or of a balance between the two which is called indifference. Without trinity, duality has no more meaning than man and woman without child, and unless there is a relationship between ourselves and the universe we can have no consciousness of our existence – indeed, we could not even exist. To some things in the universe we react with love or attraction, and to others with fear or repulsion, and this is as natural as that fire should make us warm and ice make us cold.

But here the difficulties begin, because man does not stop with that basic reaction to life. It is not that he just likes some things and dislikes others; he has also decided feelings about the state of liking and disliking, and so from 3 we proceed to 4. This stage marks the beginning of self-consciousness and civilisation, for man becomes attached to loving or liking and wishes to have about him only those things in the universe which arouse attraction. At the same time he becomes afraid of fear because it makes him ashamed, being a menace to his pride and self-esteem. But this does not get rid of his fear; it only adds one fear on top of another. Thus as soon as man becomes self-conscious and self-esteeming and fully aware of his reactions to things, he starts trying to interfere with the processes of his soul. And this is called civilisation. He is not content to be the primitive who just loves and fears things without shame, thinking no more about it. He must now control his reactions and shape them in accordance with some preconceived pattern of character development. Fear must not exist in his vocabulary and so-called 'love' must be cultivated under such names as ambition and happiness. But this interference with the natural processes of the soul (psychologists call it repression) removes us further and further from basic realities, precipitating us into a sort of tail-chasing procedure. Like dogs trying to catch their tails, cats running after their own shadows and lunatics trying to lift themselves up by their own belts, men try to make themselves what they think they *ought* to be – a form of self-deception which receives rude shocks when the surface of civilisation is removed. This regression from basic realities is represented by the cards from 4 to 10, the latter being the point where man has completely forgotten his union with life, where his self-consciousness has reached the stage of utter isolation and where he is hopelessly bewildered by what the Chinese call 'the ten thousand things' – or the manifold and apparently separate and chaotic objects and events of the universe.

This is the moment of crisis in human evolution. Man becomes acutely aware of his unhappiness and insufficiency, and realises, appropriately enough, that he is a Knave. What is he to do about it? Look at the next card, the Queen — the feminine, passive principle — and if you look carefully at the card you will see that each of the four Queens holds an open flower. The Knaves hold swords, spears and daggers, emblems of their hostility to the life from which they have so estranged themselves, but the flower which is open to sun and rain alike is the symbol of acceptance. The Knave has estranged himself from life by his pride and false morality, by fighting the natural processes of the soul and trying to make out that he is greater than he is. ('Which of you by taking thought can add one cubit to his stature!') But the Queen accepts those processes, both the love and the fear and all the other opposites by which those feelings are aroused – life and death, pleasure and pain, good and evil. She knows that man must accept all the aspects of life if he is to be happy, and that if he would see the god in himself he must not deny the demon. *'Demon,'* runs the Hermetic aphorism, *'est deus inversus'* – the demon is a god upside-down. Therefore the Queen stands for that acceptance and spiritual love which, like His sun, God 'maketh to shine both upon the just and the unjust.' As yet, however, this acceptance is incomplete, for the Queen is only the female or passive aspect of acceptance. The complete union and harmony with life which is the goal of all these four paths is not simply a quietistic state of spiritual *laisser-faire* in which man just allows life to live him. This is, indeed, a step on the way, but the very idea of allowing life to live you, of submitting to your destiny, to the will of God, or whatever it may be called, still implies a distinction between yourself and life, nature or God.

When this distinction is overcome there is no longer any question of yourself being ruled by life and destiny or of yourself ruling your life and destiny; the problem of fate or free will then disappears, for the ruler and the ruled are united, and you do not know whether you are living life or whether life is living you. It is as if two dancers were dancing together in such perfect accord that the lead of one and the response of the other were one and the same movement, as if action and passivity became a single act. In our figure this is symbolised by the King. In their hands the Kings hold swords and axes like the Knaves; in fact, the Kings *are* Knaves but

133

with this difference: that the Knaves are compelled to be Knaves and cannot help themselves, whereas the Kings are free to be Knaves. This is the difference between the man who is moral (who fights the dark side of life) because he fears evil, and the man who is moral because he knows he is perfectly free to be immoral. In the stage of the Queen we discover our *freedom* to be moral instead of our *compulsion*. For when you feel that you are free to be as evil as you like you will find the idea rather tedious.

Thus in the Queen and the King we have the free, royal pair, symbols of spiritual liberty – liberty to love and to fear, to fight and to yield, to resist and to accept and — yes — to be free and to be compelled, for freedom is not absolutely free unless it is also free to be bound! Therefore the combination of these two is represented in the Ace, symbol of the union between oneself and life which arises from this complete acceptance of life. Here the four paths meet, but an uncomfortable empty space is left in the middle of the cross and something seems to be needed to tie the whole figure together – shall we say to make it holy? We have reduced the many, represented by the 2, to the One, represented by the Ace, but the Buddhist problem asks, 'When the many are reduced to the One, to what shall the One be reduced?' For as the figure stands it would seem that there is a difference between the many and the One, that in going along the path from the 2 to the Ace you have actually acquired something which you did not have before. Spirituality, however, is not *acquired*; it is only *realised*, because union with life is something we have all the time even though we do not know it. Our seeming loss of union in the civilised, self-conscious stage is only apparent, only something which occurs in Time but not in Eternity. From the standpoint of Eternity, every stage in the path is both beginning and end and middle; there is neither coming nor going, gain nor loss, ignorance nor enlightenment.

What shall we put in the middle? I think we have forgotten a card – the one we usually leave in the box. What about the Joker?

A profane symbol? Not at all. For the joke about the whole thing is that, wherever we stand on the paths, we are really at the Goal – only we do not know it. It is like looking all over the house for your keys only to find that you are carrying them in your hand, whereat you sit down and laugh at yourself.

But the Joker makes an appropriate centre for another reason: in games he is allowed to represent any other card in the pack. So also in this figure he is the 2 and the Ace and all that lies between – Alpha and Omega, the beginning and the ending . . . the first and the last.

Indeed, as Chesterton said, there is a closer connection between 'cosmic' and 'comic' than the mere similarity of the words!

———————————— • ————————————

IS THERE AN 'UNCONSCIOUS'? (1939)

When we say that the chief contribution of modern psychology to human knowledge is the concept of the unconscious mind, we have to be careful of our terms. For the idea of the unconscious does not belong by any means to all modern psychology, and those schools to which it does belong have somewhat different views on the subject. The concept is associated principally with the names of Freud, Jung and Adler, but there is no one name which covers their three schools. Freud's system is psycho-analysis; Jung's is analytical psychology; Adler's is individual psychology. There is no real reason, however, why they should not all be called psycho-analysis, because if, as is frequently done, we group them under the name 'modern psychology' we thereby group them with such important systems as gestalt psychology in which the concept of the unconscious plays no part. Popularly it is believed that psycho-analysis teaches that man has *an* unconscious mind; this is not strictly true, for the unconscious is not to be understood as an entity or mental organism having definite location and identity. There is no actual division between the unconscious and the rest of the human organism, for it bears somewhat the same relation to the mind as the glands, liver, kidneys, etc., bear to the body: they are integral parts of the body, but we are not ordinarily conscious of them. The only difference is that the unconscious has no specific boundaries. It consists rather of the *condition* of being unaware of certain desires, impulses, tendencies, reactions and phantasies in our mental and emotional make-up. It has its physical parallel in the condition of being unaware of various bodily organs and processes.

There appears, however, to be little or no mention of the unconscious in the world's religious, mystical and occult philosophy. Indeed, to many students of these matters the idea is distasteful, and Freud, the father of psycho-analysis, has never been forgiven for regarding religion as a neurosis. In fact, the majority of religious people, whether of orthodox or heterodox persuasion, regard psycho-analysis in all its forms as an upstart science whose avowed object is to 'debunk' all the noble impulses of humanity by ascribing them to repressed sexuality. Much of the contempt in which psycho-analysis is held is well deserved, but this should not blind us to a certain amount of gold among the dross. The trouble with this new science is not so much psycho-analysis as psycho-analysts. We might mention the professor in charge of a certain well-known clinic who devotes his life to the study of ink-blots. The patient is made to drop a blot of ink on a piece of paper and is suddenly asked what he thinks it looks like. Being rather puzzled and humorous the patient usually grins and says something like, 'Oh, it might be an elephant with warts,' whereat the professor assumes a far-away expression and murmurs, 'Very significant. *Most* interesting. An elephant, yes. With warts. Exceedingly interesting.'

This case is not unusual, for the strange ways of psycho-analysts and psychiatrists would fill many volumes. I have heard fully qualified MDs discuss the case of a small boy whose propensity to bed-wetting was undoubtedly due to his unconscious identification of himself with Jupiter Pluvius. Still more significant are the gatherings of doctors and patients for summer schools where people take you by the hand, look into your eyes and ask you whether you are an extravert or an introvert. Indeed, such forms of psychology have swiftly acquired all the symptoms of crank religions. But just as there are half-wits and charlatans as well as true students in mysticism and occultism, psychology also has its heights and depths, both as to its ideas and its practitioners. There are, too, the same internal conflicts, the same bigotry, the same dogmatism, the same personal idolatry, but one could hardly expect otherwise and the mutual contempt of religion and psychology is but 'the pot calling the kettle black.'

In spite of all, however, psycho-analysis has a definite and valuable contribution for students of religion *in our time*. I say 'in our time' because psycho-analysis is essentially a modern remedy for a modern ill; it exists for that period in human history for which the unconscious is a problem, and a problem it has been since man began to imagine that all his difficulties of soul and circumstance could be solved by the unaided power of human reason. The ancient paths of mysticism and occultism resolved the problem of the unconscious from the very beginning, even before it became a problem, for their first requirement was that man should *know himself*. Whereat he very quickly found that the huge, brute forces of nature had their counterparts in his soul, that his being was not a simple unit but a pantheon of gods and demons. In fact, all the deities of the ancient theologies were known to the initiated as the inhabitants not of Olympus but of the human soul. They were not mere products of man's imagination any more than his heart, lungs and stomach are products of his imagination. On the contrary, they were very real forces belonging both to nature, the macrocosm, and man, the microcosm. Occultism was thus the art of living with one's gods and demons, and you had to know how to deal with them in yourself before you could deal with them in the universe. The ancients understood the laws which man must follow in order to live with them, how by love the gods would become your friends and the demons your servants. In every initiation rite it was necessary to pass through that valley of the shadow where the neophyte comes face to face with the Dweller on the Threshold and all the most terrible powers of the psyche. But the rite could only be successful if he faced them with love, recognising them as manifestations of the same Divinity which was his own true Self. By this love he broke their spell and became a true initiate.

But man became over-rational and forgot the gods and demons, relegating them to the realm of outworn superstitions. He looked for them in the skies and found only infinite spaces, dead rocks and orbs of burning gas. He looked for them in thunder and wind and found only unintelligent forces of atmosphere. He looked for them in woods and caverns and found only scuttling animals, creaking branches, shadows and draughts. He thought that the gods were dead but in fact they became much more alive and dangerous because they were able to work unrecognised. For whereas the old occultists began with the principle *know thyself*, the rationalists began with *rule thyself*. They chose what they considered to be a reasonable pattern of character and strove to impose it on their lives without any preliminary exploration. They forgot that it is impossible for man to behave like a sage until he has first come to terms with his inner pantheon; as a result he could only achieve a poor imitation of the sage's behaviour because he had not done the necessary groundwork. For this reason the rationalist, puritanic mind is a veneer above a muck-heap, an attempt to copy greatness by wearing its clothes.

But when psychologists began to have the idea of the unconscious this was simply man's fumbling rediscovery of the lost gods and demons. Naturally experienced occultists of both East and West were inclined to smile, for to them this new force called the unconscious had never existed as such. And when people started talking about the unconscious as if it were just a repository of repressed sexuality, the occultists laughed outright, knowing that it contained far more powerful divinities than libido, who was just a little imp dancing upon the surface. It must have seemed funnier still to hear the unconscious discussed as if it were a sort of individual with secret, dark designs and an unfortunate habit of wanting and thinking in direct opposition to the conscious. For the unconscious is not an individual; it is simply that about himself which man does not know. As such it is a purely relative term, because some people know more about themselves than others. Symbolically it may be represented as an individual, for in dreams the unknown aspect of men presents itself as a woman and *vice versa* with women. But actually when it is said that the unconscious does this or that, it means that certain particular aspects of your internal universe are on the move without your conscious knowledge.

The concept of the unconscious is nevertheless important to *modern* students of religion and occultism in that it is a reminder of the forgotten gods and of the place where they are to be found. Too many would-be mystics and occultists try to follow the rationalist technique of imposing a discipline upon themselves without first understanding the nature of the thing to be disciplined. You have to come to terms with the gods before you can ignore them, and those who jump straight from ordinary ways of living into the complex disciplines of occultism are inviting trouble. For until those terms have been made, the gods rule us although we have a way of persuading ourselves that their often unreasonable dictates are our own free and considered choice. Thus imitation of the sage is often a device put up by the demons for our own destruction, for modern man simply does not realise that until he has been through the Valley of the Shadow his life is not his own. Until he looks within himself, seeks out his hidden pantheon and overcomes it by love (or what psychologists call 'acceptance'), he remains its unwitting tool.

In all the old philosophies — Yoga, Buddhism, the Greek Mysteries, the Egyptian Mysteries — this exploring of the unknown self was the essential first step, and now the same thing is attempted by the psycho-analyst, using a different technique and terminology. That there are failures and mistakes is only to be expected, for here are men trying to work out the divine science on their own with little recourse to the experience of the ages, though to this there are a few notable exeptions. And though students of religion may be offended when religion is ascribed to repressed sexuality, it must be remembered that in many cases this may actually be true and that psychologists have had insufficient opportunities to study that comparatively rare phenomenon, the genuine mystic or occultist. For what would such a person want with psycho-analysis? The warning to the beginner, however, still stands, for unless you really know yourself, how can you say that your apparently noble aspirations are what they seem to be? Thoughts are often wolves in sheep's clothing.

Then is the first step on the path a visit to a psycho-analyst? Unfortunately the matter is not quite so easy. If you can find a *competent* analyst, perhaps, but the profession of analyst attracts many who need their own medicine more than any of their patients. The reason is that psycho-analysis has not yet had sufficient profundity of experience to judge its own results, to institute a hierarchy of 'initiates' who can be trusted to say who is and is not fit to take up the profession. There is another alternative, though the professional analyst usually regards it with horror: that is to analyse yourself. It needs care and a pair of feet planted firmly on the earth, but if due regard is paid to the rules it can be done. You can follow the age-old techniques of meditation and you will often be safer in your own hands than in those of an analyst. Of course it is risky, but in these days so many people expect a 'safe' way to wisdom. The way to wisdom is, however, a great deal less 'safe' than the way to making a fortune; it is perhaps the riskiest and most worthwhile thing in the world, but you should not start out on it unless you are prepared to break your neck.

———————— • ————————

THAT FAR-OFF, DIVINE EVENT (1939)

What is it that Tennyson described as that 'far-off divine event to which all creation moves'?

In mystical and occult philosophy it is the return of all individual things to the divine source from which they originally came – an event which Hindu cosmology places at the end of a stupendous period of time called a *mahamanvantara*, or a 'great manifestation' of Brahman. For according to Hindu and Theosophical teachings, universal activity is a succession of the days and nights of Brahman, the outbreathings and inbreathings of the One Reality of Life, whose name is derived from the Sanskrit *brih-*, from which our own word 'breath' is also descended.

Modern science has now begun to think of time in somewhat the same terms as the ancient Hindus, for they measured these days and nights of Brahman by groups of *kalpas*, a *kalpa* being a mere 4,320,000,000 years. If these things be true, the ordinary man or woman has to accept them rather much on faith; and because it is difficult, if not impossible, for ordinary people to test their verity, and because the periods of time involved are past imagining, it will be asked whether such ideas are of the remotest practical value. For the events of which we are speaking are certainly divine and undoubtedly far off, and it may seem that the ancient Hindus were indulging in idle speculations for want of anything better to do.

The difficulty of this Hindu conception of the 'far-off, divine event' when all things shall again become one with Brahman is that, taken at its face value, it makes the soul despair. For not only does so terrifying a period of time lie between now and the final resting of the universe in Divine Bliss, but the doctrine also goes on to say that eventually the universe will return again into manifestation, to another, and another, and another repetition of the whole process *ad infinitum*. It is important to remember, however, that the ancient teachers of these doctrines often described cosmological processes in terms of time simply for the sake of explanation, whereas they should actually be understood in terms of eternity. In this sense eternity is not just everlasting time; eternity is beyond time; it is *now*. The days and nights of Brahman are spread out in time in rather the same way as a ball of thread an inch in diameter is unrolled to the length of a hundred yards. Its real state resembles the ball, but to be presented to the human mind it has to be unrolled. For our idea of time is spatial; it has length, which is a spatial dimension. But eternity has no length, and the nearest thing to it in our experience is what we call the present moment. It cannot be measured, but it is always here.

The value of this Hindu idea becomes apparent when we think of it in this way. For it means that the 'far-off, divine event' is not just millions of years in the future; it is now. At this moment the universe is both manifested as a collection of separate individual things, and at the same time each of these things retains absolute unity and identity with its divine source. The object of Hindu and for that matter of almost all Oriental religion is to awaken in man the realisation of this unity and identity. In Hinduism this realisation is called *Moksha* or *Kaivalya*, and in Buddhism *Nirvana* and it is astonishing how seldom the West achieves any real understanding of what this condition of the spirit involves. The old nineteenth century idea that *Nirvana* meant simply Oblivion is now generally discredited, but some of the conceptions which have taken its place are almost as fantastic. Certain allowances for this misunderstanding must be made, for just as in the West there are mature and immature

141

conceptions of Christianity, so in the East there are mature and immature conceptions of Hinduism and Buddhism. Even some of the canonical scriptures of the East are just as overlaid with the interpolated comments of scribes as the Bible, even more so in the Buddhist scriptures.

It is therefore quite common to find *Moksha* or *Nirvana* described as a type of trance condition in which all sense of the separate forms and objects of the universe has vanished, to be replaced by a state of 'infinite consciousness' into which the individual becomes absorbed even though his physical body may continue to live on. If he ever returns out of this trance condition it remains always in the back of his mind; the things around him seem like the insubstantial shadows of a dream, for:

> Life, like a dome of many-coloured glass,
> Stains the white radiance of eternity
> Till death tramples it to fragments. . . .[37]

At death he merges his individuality forever into infinitude unless he wishes to return again to the earth in order to teach the Law to men. But one of the principal mistakes of Western interpretations of Oriental thought is to equate Brahman with the infinite and the realisation of one's identity with Brahman as a change from finite to infinite consciousness. It is well to remember the pertinent words of the *Isa Upanishad*:

> In darkness are they who worship the world alone, but in greatest darkness they who worship the infinite alone. By a knowledge of the former we are saved from death, and by a knowledge of the latter we are preserved to immortality.

The highest Hindu philosophy bears the name *advaita*, which is the principle of 'non-duality,' meaning that Brahman is that to which nothing can be opposed as long is opposed to short, light to dark, pleasure to pain, positive to negative and infinite to finite. This also is a cardinal principle of Mayhayana Buddhism, from which it is clear that neither in Hinduism or Buddhism can it be said that the highest spiritual attainment is to become merged into any kind of infinitude.

Just as Brahman is beyond duality, so also is the state of mind or consciousness in which man realises his identity with Brahman. In other words, one cannot say that *Nirvana* is infinite and not finite, or *vice versa*, or even that it is a consciousness of unity and not diversity. Here again is an Oriental conception which is little understood in the West, for it is often thought that the supreme Universal Reality of Hinduism and Buddhism has the quality of one-ness as distinct from many-ness, and that realisation is the knowledge that the forms and objects of the universe are in fact one, even though they appear to be many. Their seeming diversity is said to be an illusion (*maya*) which the wise man will overcome. But this Reality is not quite one in the sense we give to the word; to use a Vedantist expression, Reality is 'one-without-a-second.' In the ordinary way the idea of *one* immediately suggests the idea of *many* or of *none*, for the moment you have the concept of nothing you also have the concept of something, while in the same way we could not entertain the idea of many things without that of one thing. The reason for this is that the idea of one-ness belongs to the multitudinous 'pairs of opposites' (*dvandva*) of which life is composed, for one suggests many just as long suggests short; the two concepts are mutually essential and the one can only be known by means of the other. But Brahman or Reality is beyond opposites, being that which does not require distinction for its existence. For Brahman *is* all things, this world we see around us, together with our consciousness and the thoughts in our minds and the feelings in our hearts. To see Brahman we have just to look with our eyes, for Brahman is nothing other than what we are beholding at this moment.

'So what?' you ask. 'At the moment I am beholding a magazine. Is that anything to get excited about? Should I feel uplifted and spiritually enlightened just because this magazine is Brahman? I don't see anything divine and mighty about this collection of paper and printer's ink.'

In view of this it will also be asked what is the difference between a sage and an ordinary ignorant man. We are accustomed to believe that a sage or mystic is one who beholds God or Brahman in all things; but if Brahman *is* all things, surely an ordinary man in seeing them is doing no less than the sage? This is perfectly true, but the difference between the sage and the ordinary man is that the latter fails to realise it. The reason is that because there is nothing apart from Brahman, Brahman cannot be seen in quite the ordinary way. To see things we must be able to *distinguish* them, which

143

means that we must be able to separate them from other things or from ourselves. But with Brahman this cannot be done, for when you look at this magazine Brahman is looking at Brahman. We have therefore to consider how the sage comes to understand this and in what way this understanding is of practical value.

Naturally the sage does not understand it only conceptually; for him it is not just an intellectual idea, as that space is curved. A mathematician may be able to prove, in theory, that space is curved, but he cannot see it curved with his eyes, and thus the knowledge is for him purely conceptual and makes no difference to his ordinary behaviour. He does not start to walk in curves; and unless he is absent-minded in the way of some of his kind he does not find it impossible to go from San Francisco to New York without going through Mexico City. But for the sage the knowledge of his identity with Brahman is of immense practical importance; he knows it as well and as fully as he knows that he is alive. But this certainly does not mean that in place of himself, other people, houses, stars, hills and trees he sees a formless, all-pervasive and infinite luminosity, which seems to be some people's idea of the Divine Reality. If such a state of consciousness were possible, it would still be dualistic, involving an utter difference between Reality and the ordinary world. It should rather be said that he feels Brahman, the force of the universe, at work in everything he does, thinks and feels, and this gives a powerful and liberating impulse to his spirit. For he feels free and delivered, which is the precise meaning of *Kaivalya*. He is freed from himself, which is the only thing that ever bound anyone, because he has let himself go. The unenlightened man keeps a tight hold on himself because he is afraid of losing himself; he can trust neither circumstances nor his own human nature; he is terrified of being genuine, of accepting himself as he is and tries to deceive himself into the belief that he is as he wishes to be. But these are the wishes, the desires that bind him, and it was such desires as these that the Buddha described as the cause of human misery.

People imagine that letting themselves go would have disastrous results; trusting neither circumstances nor themselves, which together make up life, they are forever interfering and trying to make their own souls and the world conform with preconceived patterns. This interference is simply the attempt of the ego to dominate life. But when you see that all such attempts are fruitless and when you relax the fear-born resistance to life in yourself and around you which is called egoism, you realise the freedom of union with Brahman. In fact you have always had this freedom, for the state of union with Brahman can neither be attained nor lost; all men and all things have it, in spite of themselves. It can only be realised, which is to say made real to you, by letting life live you for a while instead of trying to make yourself live life. You will soon reach the point where you will be unable to tell whether your thoughts and feelings are your own or whether life put them into you, for the distinction between yourself and life will have disappeared. If the truth be known, there never was any distinction, save in our imaginations. This is called union with Brahman, for 'he that loseth his life shall find it.'

.

PART TWO:

Writings for

The
New
Britain Movement

ARTICLES FOR THE
ELEVENTH HOUR

———————— • ————————

HAVE YOU HEARD THIS ONE? (1934)

Mr G. K. Chesterton[24] once observed that there was a closer connection between 'cosmic' and 'comic' than the mere similarity of the words. For if we trace the idea of the comic right down to its roots, we find a process which might well be called a universal law. A well-known definition of the comic was provided in Mr Wyndham Lewis's[38] essay on 'The Meaning of the Wild Body,' where it was suggested that it was the part of an inhuman thing pretending the intelligence of a human being, as a sack of potatoes running down the street or a lamp-post in a bowler hat.

But it seems that there is a more fundamental definition than this, for it occurs to me that the lamp-post is not amusing so much because it is behaving as if it had the intelligence to wear a hat, but because it is taking on the airs of something greater than itself, namely, a man. In the same way it would be humorous to see a bicycle pretending to be a pantechnicon by being wheeled along with a grand-piano on its saddle. Conversely it would be humorous to see an important and dignified policeman on point-duty in Piccadilly Circus rolling over on the ground like an unbalanced beer barrel. For the root of the comic lies in small things pretending that they are great, and great things pretending that they are small. And the universe is comic as well as cosmic in the sense that we have the Great Creative Energy which we call God manifesting itself in cabbages, flies, taxi-cabs and lobsters, while on the other hand we have small things (such as men) believing that they are the most magnificent things under the sun.

Yet the paradox is that from one point of view man is not

comic enough, while from another he is much too comic. That is to say, on the one hand he has little conception of his true greatness, while on the other he conceives as his greatness attributes which are essentially his most infantile. This is especially noticeable when we come to review, quite objectively, the present condition of the world, and we have to realise that changing that condition is less a matter of utopian idealism than a matter of seeing a joke.

For here we have nature-conquering man (*homo sapiens*), made in the image of God, still discussing with extreme seriousness the possibility of dropping such dangerous toys as bombs on to other people's houses, dressing up in *shirts and worshipping a new mechanical deity called the State, and starving in the midst of unparalleled abundance. The fooling of himself by such infantile pranks constitutes the greatest problem of the age. There is no doubt that this joke is somewhat grim, but in spite of the tragedies which arise from it, it is good that there is a joke to see; otherwise we might never remove ourselves from the alarming and incredible condition of modern society.

Hence one of the most important tasks of the leaders of a New Order is to show people just where the old is funny, since the virtue of laughter is that it 'bears no malice' and the louder and more genuine it becomes the more it puts the cause of it to confusion. In this way, too, they will be infinitely more welcome to society than the austere moralist who warns it gravely of impending doom. For if these leaders can become, in the phrase which St Francis gave to his followers, 'God's Merry Men,' we can be sure that the old order will not come to its end in the blood and destruction of the class war, but in the creative and revitalising atmosphere of a Gargantuan guffaw!

———————————— • ————————————

ON TEACHING ONE'S GRANDMOTHER (1935)

So much is being talked about Indian politics just now that the moment seems opportune to say something of the real significance of India to the British Commonwealth of Nations

* [brown – Ed.]

lest anyone should imagine that it has something to do with Mr Randolph Churchill, [39a] cotton, the White Paper, or Foreign Missions to the Heathen. The calamity is that Grandmother India has left us a legacy for which we do not seem to be at all grateful, since we have stolidly ignored it and tried to make out that it was the portion set aside for her own starving children – her gigantic material wealth. For the legacy intended for us was her even more gigantic spiritual wealth, and so far from being grateful for it we have tried to pretend that its value was merely as a museum curiosity and have had the impertinence to offer a misunderstood version of our own spiritual heritage as a substitute. Serious interest in the philosophical and religious legacy of India is, for the most part, confined to academicians, to a certain species of scientist whose practice it is to kill everything he touches by dissecting, analysing, and classifying it – and then putting it away on a shelf for the use of specialists only. As Dr Jung has remarked:

> This, in fact, is the Western way of hiding one's own heart under the cloak of so-called scientific understanding. We do it partly because of the *misérable vanité des savants* which fears and rejects with horror any sign of living sympathy, and partly because an understanding that reaches the feelings might allow contact with the foreign spirit to become a serious experience.

At the present time the British Empire has a special significance since, potentially, it is not only the best instrument for the introduction of the New Order of man into the world, but it is indeed the only instrument. What Voltaire said of God is also true of this Empire – that if it didn't exist it would have to be invented, for if it were dissolved the only possible basis for a federation of nations would have disappeared. Yet the suitability of the Empire as an instrument for creating the New Order lies not only in the fact that it has some sort of unity; it lies equally in the fact that within that unity there are so many diversities, so many religions, races, and traditions – that it includes the spiritual legacies of Christendom and India. The task of creating this New Order is principally one of realising — of making real — an order which already exists unknown to all but a few. For just as there are certain fundamental principles upon which the bodily organism works whether we know it or not, so are there similar principles for the social organism. These

151

principles we might call the Twofold Basis and the Threefold Structure.[39b]

The Twofold Basis is best seen, so far as it can be seen anywhere, in the Empire – in this *unity* containing so many *diversities*. In a certain sense it can be demonstrated by a comparison of the Empire's two great religions – Vedanta and Christianity. For what, essentially, is the meaning of Vedanta? 'They who see but One in all the changing manifoldness of this universe, unto them belongs Eternal Truth – unto none else, unto none else!' And of Christianity? 'Are not two sparrows sold for a farthing? and not one of them shall fall on the ground without your Father knows: but the very hairs of your head are all numbered. Fear not therefore; ye are of more value than many sparrows.' For while the theme of Vedanta is the fundamental *identity* of all things, the theme of Christianity is rather their fundamental *value* as individual entities, and the synthesis of these two themes is an essential of the New Order. In short, the Twofold Basis is the fact that while every part of an organism is in essence identical with the others, each has a distinct and important uniqueness which must be fulfilled to the greatest extent if the whole is to be completely expressed in its parts. Thus, while the European consciousness has been chiefly occupied with the assertion of individuality, with the value of individual men and things, the Indian consciousness has been occupied with the Unity that lies behind the *maya* or illusion of separateness. And it is just because *both* are right that it is absurd to speak of converting India to Christianity or the West to Vedanta. What is necessary is that Western man should accept the contribution which India has to make in this profound intuition of Unity, and in return he should offer Christianity to the Indian, not as a substitute for his own religion, but as its essential complement.

In the Threefold Structure India has another contribution to make to the New Albion, for it was in the ancient Code of Manu that the Threefold Order of Society was first expressed and eventually grew into the modern conception of the Threefold State. Just as there are three principal functions in the body — stomach, heart, and head — so are there three corresponding functions in society – economics, politics, and culture. In the Indian conception these functions were based on the three qualities (*gunas*) of man — *Tamas, Rajas* and *Sattva* — instinctive desire, ambition, and the balancing quality of reason. On the *gunas* were established the three great castes: the Vaishya (traders and producers), the Kshattrya (warriors and statesmen), and the Brahmana (counsellors and spiritual guardians). Outside the social organism was another caste, the Sudra, the 'hewers of wood and drawers of water', who, in modern civilisation, have been replaced by the machine. That conception is thousands of years old and it is valid, with certain adaptations, today because it is founded on the laws of man's own being to which he must conform or perish, and the particular work of India has been to discover and understand those laws. It is just in this way that we have much to learn from India, and there can never be a New Albion if Almighty Britain continues to imagine that her dependencies have no other contributions to make than material wealth. Britain's gift to Albion is the culture and tradition of Europe — Christianity — but if her gift is to be of any use it must not be given from a desire to dominate; it must be given in the recognition that the contributions of India and the rest are likewise of essential value to new Albion as the forerunner of the New Order.

BOOK REVIEWS FOR THE ELEVENTH HOUR

———————— • ————————

THE WORLD OF MAN (1935)

The World of Man, by Georg Groddeck (The C. W. Daniel Co.)

The World of Man is a selection from the writings of the late Georg Groddeck[40] based on his last work *Der Mensch Als Symbol*, published in 1932, although some of the most interesting chapters were written as far back as 1911. The central theme is a discussion of the true greatness of man. Groddeck contends that almost the entire culture of modern Europe has grown up under a misconception of this greatness, the misconception that 'the proper study of mankind is man', that the human being can be isolated from the rest of nature, that the depiction and dramatisation of his character, his passions and his desires can, in itself, be a worthy *motif* for art, music and literature. Such a culture Groddeck describes as mere 'psychologisation', and Shakespeare, Beethoven, Balzac, Ibsen, Dickens and Dostoievski are described, in spite of their admitted powers of inspiration, as 'psychologisers' rather than great artists. Goethe and Bach are alone excepted, while the height of this misconception is detected in Nietzsche, the apostle of man's tremendous egoism, of the conceit that he is lord over nature, that he is the centre of the universe, and that he can be the object of admiration and interest for his humanity alone.

Over against this conceit Groddeck sets the fact that we are no more than the tools of nature, and that our consciousness, our Ego, is no more than a device conceived by our unknown self, 'the It', to further its own ends irrespective of what we imagine to be our own wishes. We may boast of what we have achieved by the power of our wills, but it remains that:

154

> the assertion 'I live' only expresses a small and superficial part of
> the total experience 'I am lived by the It' (which is) ... the sum
> total of an individual human being, physical, mental, and
> spiritual, the organism with all its forces, the universe which is
> man – a self unknown, and for ever unknowable, and I call this
> the It as the most indefinite term available without either
> emotional or intellectual associations.

For far from being the conqueror of nature and of himself,
man is part and parcel of nature and cannot be understood as
separate from her, while it is only in the realisation of his
identity with her that he can produce any great artistic work.

> Men lose their chance of cultural development if they turn away
> from nature, cease to recognise their dependence upon the
> universal whole, and direct their love, their fear, their reverence
> only upon the strivings and sufferings of their fellow men.

Yet there is truth in both these apparently opposite points of
view, for it is just in the recognition of the fact that he is
utterly dependent upon the universe that man achieves his
true Godlikeness. In an introductory note to this volume,
Count Keyserling makes a singularly apt comparison between
Groddeck and Lao-tzu, the Chinese philosopher who realised
that the highest form of man was he who made himself a
perfect instrument for the forces of nature, adapting himself
continually to Tao – the stream of life. For the final solution to
the problem lies, I believe in the ancient precept,

> Help nature and work on with her, and nature will acknowledge
> thee as one of her creators and make obeisance.

———————————— • ————————————

THREE BLIND EYES (1935)

Conservatism and the Future. A Symposium. (Heinemann.)
The Liberal Way. Published under the authority of the National
Liberal Council, with a Foreword by Ramsay Muir. (Allen &
Unwin.)
Marxism. Murry, Macmurray, Holdaway & Cole. (Chapman
& Hall.)

It is unfortunate that some confusion exists between the word
'imagination' and the phrase 'building castles in the air'. For

imagination is the forerunner of creation, the possession of vision for the future, and, disastrously, the bug-bear of modern politics. It is distinguished from building castles in the air by the fact that those who possess it recognise immediacy of thought and action as the essential without which ideals become ways of escape from reality. Yet truly imaginative persons cannot in fact be said to have ideals in the usual sense of the word, for the essence of an ideal is that it is unattainable. In short, it might be said that while the space between an ideal and its realisation is infinite, the space between imagination and creation is infinitesimal. For those who have any vital vision for the future do not make any absolute distinction between the vision and the act of bringing it into being. The calamity of present-day politics is the absence of such a vision, and a perusal of these three books, *Marxism, Conservatism and the Future*, and *The Liberal Way*, has led me to the conclusion that while Marxists have a big vision of little quality and Conservatives have a little vision of big quality, Liberals have a little vision of little quality.

In *The Liberal Way* the only ghost of a vision (respectable and platitudinous as it is) appears in the last chapter where we are informed that Liberalism hopes:

> to create a nation ... of free, responsible, law-abiding, and self-reliant men and women, free from the grinding servitude of poverty ... with healthy bodies and trained minds; enjoying a real opportunity to make the most and best of their powers for their own advantage and that of the community ... and secure of sufficient leisure to live a full life and to enjoy the delights of nature, letters, and the arts.

This they aim at achieving on the basis of good old nineteenth-century political methods complete with gold standard, free trade, non-functional democracy and an unfederated Empire, adapted to the needs of the twentieth century by a few superficial reforms or, rather, adjustments. The Liberal Party is conscious that it has been deserted by the Great British Public, and now it asks us to believe that this desertion and the world crisis are cause and effect. About as much so as the desertion of hansom cabs!

On the other hand, *Conservatism and the Future* shows a somewhat more intelligent grasp of the situation, especially in the essay by Lord Eustace Percy on 'The Conservative

Attitude and Social Policy'. The book has been compiled to present the public with a positive Conservative policy instead of a mere refutation of Socialism, and to this extent the compilers have done useful work. But in actual substance it shows little imagination other than a hint by Mr Hugh Molson at the desirability of some sort of House of Industry and Lord Eustace Percy's treatment of the true function of the State. In the field of Economics, Mr W. S. Morrison, KC, has certainly understood the paradox of poverty amid plenty, but he can see no solution for this beyond an increase of purchasing power as a result of absorbing the unemployed in agricultural work which has great possibilities of development in this country, if the landowners can be kept from going bankrupt. The idea of a National Dividend he dismisses with the remark that 'no means of dividing up the nation's wealth has yet been discovered to work satisfactorily for long except the method of distributing it in profits, salaries, and wages'. It appears that neither Liberals nor Conservatives have the imagination to see the real significance of labour-saving machinery and unemployment; perhaps the 'utopian' belief that it must mean the liberation of man's energies for something better than just keeping himself alive is too true to be good.

Finally we come to *Marxism* where we do indeed find vision, but it is the vision of a 'depersonalised' society. In a chapter on 'The New Man' Mr Murry writes:

> It would be utterly wrong to mitigate the impact of Marx's discovery, not merely that the 'individual' is an illusion, but that his sole concrete reality is that of a cell of a social organism, governed by unconscious laws ... At the heart of Marxism lies a grim effort at 'depersonalisation', which, unless a man has undergone, I do not believe he will ever be a Marxist save in name.

'Grim' is the right word, for the Marxist has only seen half of a truth; the truth that society is based on two fundamental principles, the one of unity and identity, the other of diversity, uniqueness, and function. If the unity which is the social organism is to be fully expressed through its parts, then it is essential that each part, each person, should be true to its function, that there should be mutual fulfilment of this uniqueness.

If modern society with its spiritual isolation is the denial of unity, Marxism is the denial of diversity, while in the New Order of Man we must affirm both principles and relate them to one another in the knowledge that the individual's concrete reality is both that of a cell in the social organism and that of a person, free and unique.

———————— • ————————

A FACE WITH A WINK (1935)

The Communist Answer to the World's Needs. By Julius F. Hecker, Ph.D. (Chapman & Hall)
Life and Money. By Eimar O'Duffy. Revised and enlarged edition. (Putnam.)

Last week we had 'Three Blind Eyes'; this week we have a face with a wink, for one eye (Dr Hecker) is almost closed (just a little bit is open), while the other (Mr Eimar O'Duffy) is open, but not absolutely comfortable: it is a trifle strained through having too much to do.

The Communist Answer is the sequel to Dr Hecker's *Moscow Dialogues* and takes the form of a series of discussions between a Church of England Canon, an economist, a Nationalist, a Labour MP, a Quaker, a Douglasite, a Revolutionary Socialist, an American, and Socratov – the mouthpiece of Communist opinion. It is so attractively bound and printed that I was disappointed to find its contents so unworthy of its appearance, for Dr Hecker has not only tried to cover too much ground in one volume, but in Comrade Socratov he has given us a philosopher with plenty of intellect and little humour, which is worse than disappointing; it is unconvincing.

The discussions range over a great variety of subjects, including the Five-Year Plans, Social Credit, technocracy, the New Deal, world peace, Fascism and cultural development, but the number of subjects is so large and the space allowed to each so small that one is always left with the feeling that questions have never been properly answered. Indeed, they are not always properly asked, and invariably the author's catholicity is marred by his superficiality. But letting alone such obvious demerits, and apart from some effective

158

criticisms of rival policies, the constructive part of *The Communist Answer* is the old tale about the class war, the necessity of a temporary proletarian dictatorship, and the vision of an over-planned society – efficient, strictly logical and scrupulously hygienic. Some of the ideas put forward remind me of the lovers who would never kiss without using antiseptics, for fear of catching a cold which one of them might be developing. Special scientifically organised breeding farms for human beings are advocated with a seriousness that has to be seen to be believed, while inconvenient propositions are dismissed with a liberal application of that doubtful label 'bourgeois':

> Liberty, justice, the pursuit of happiness, and all the other so-called 'inalienable' rights are the products of the conditions of the seventeenth and eighteenth centuries, which marked the ascent to power of the bourgeoisie.

Yet unless my knowledge of history is very confused I seem to have heard of some people called Plato, Aristotle, Confucius, and Ashoka who lived quite a long time before the beginning of the eighteenth century. Of course, it depends upon the ends for which liberty, justice and the pursuit of happiness are used, and while it is true that during the last three centuries these principles have been used for very questionable ends, Dr Hecker should note the important distinction between a principle and its application.

Revolutionaries who reject the idea of the class war are charged, as usual, with refusing to face up to realities, with trying to heal a leg when the only possible remedy is amputation. Yet such an attitude can only result from a profound misunderstanding of the nature of society, for if a particular part of society is out of order, nothing is solved by sending that part out of society. If a certain set of people exploit another set, we must accept the fact that the only remedy is that it should learn to recognise the value of the exploited set to the total organism. To exploit it is to deteriorate its value, while for the exploited to massacre the exploiters is to destroy the totality. The Communist society dooms itself to go about maimed, for the class war is a form of attempted suicide.

In Mr Eimar O'Duffy we have a philosopher with intellect and humour – a past-master in the art of *reductio ad absurdum*.

Both in his analysis of the present economic muddle and in his constructive proposals he shows the happy faculty of making things so clear that one must laugh at the lunacy of nothing being done about them. An outstanding merit of *Life and Money* is that he interprets the Age of Plenty from the human as well as from the technical point of view, visualising the cultural possibilities which it holds for mankind. And although he relies too much on Social Credit alone for the fulfilment of his vision, his book remains as one of the most excellent and *the* most entertaining introduction to an understanding of the significance of money in the Age of Plenty.

———————— • ————————

UNDERTONES OF PEACE (1935)

Time to Spare. A Symposium with an Introduction by S. P. B. Mais. (George Allen & Unwin.)
The Challenge to Democracy. By C. Delisle Burns. (George Allen & Unwin.)

The argument is sometimes advanced against advocates of social change that 'things are a lot better than they were' or 'you wouldn't grumble at modern conditions if you'd been alive seventy years ago... When *I* was a boy', etc. But it is just the fact of *not* having been alive seventy years ago that makes all the difference, for human nature is such that one's reactions to privation depend on the standard of living to which one has been accustomed – not the standard of some other period of history. I suppose that according to this argument the unemployed should consider themselves lucky not to be hauled off as galley-slaves. But while it is true that, *for us*, the sufferings of a galley-slave would be greater than those of a man trying to support a family of seven on 30 shillings [£1.50] a week, galley-slavery bears the same relation to the standard of life four hundred years ago as unemployment bears to that of today. And I'm not at all sure that the condition today is not even more absurd than four hundred years ago, when there were no machines to propel ships, for now we have machines to make all the wealth that men desire and yet we keep several millions starving and burn the surplus wealth because we cannot sell it to them at a profit. And the result?

> Thousands like myself (writes John Evans) are condemned to live in despair and slow starvation, watching our wives and children rot before our eyes. Neither Fascism nor Communism nor any other 'ism' holds any terror for us. *Nothing* can be worse than what we've got at present.

John Evans is a contributor to *Time to Spare*, the published broadcast talks on unemployment given by unemployed men and women from various parts of the country. It is a strange and terrible book, for besides the contributions by the unemployed there are several by such well-meaning persons as Mr S. P. B. Mais, the Rev. Cecil Northcott, and Professor V. H. Mottram on the various types of welfare work that can be done for 'these unfortunates'. These very orthodox commentators are so sadly lacking in imagination that, side by side with the contributions of the unemployed, their own efforts appear merely futile. That it should be thought necessary to have to organise welfare centres for the starving unemployed in a world overflowing with abundance is an absurdity for which every man and woman in the country is partly responsible, for until we get rid of the Age of Scarcity mentality, imagining that Plenty is remote and Utopian, we shall still be condemning millions to live in conditions which are a disgrace to every member of the nation.

If you haven't made up your mind about social change, read *Time to Spare*. It may give you a turn!

Mr Delisle Burns's *Challenge to Democracy* is an analysis of the present conditions of civilisation, of the breakdown of old democratic principles, of 'free trade' and 'individualism', from the point of view of social psychology rather than politics or economics, which, in his view, play only a secondary part. He sees no possible development of society through dictatorship, for throughout his book he asserts his faith in the good sense of ordinary people, provided that they realise among themselves a sense of community – that is, a sense that social services, and political and economic reforms cannot rightly be for the benefit of any one section of society alone. For he has understood that society is an organism wherein 'if one member suffers, all members suffer with it', and, leaving aside specific technical improvements, he has concentrated on the problem of a change of the individual's attitude to the community.

———————————— • ————————————

IN BLACK AND WHITE (1935)

Jesus Wept. By Arthur Wragg, with an introduction by Vernon Bartlett. (Selwyn & Blount.)
Sex and Revolution. By Alec Craig. (George Allen & Unwin.)

The significance of Mr Arthur Wragg's[41] technique is not only artistic, for it is a technique of contrasts, of black and white, peculiarly suited to the most paradoxical age of the ages. Of course, contrasts may be all very well when the lion and the lamb lie down together, but it is a different matter when people starve in the midst of abundance and lunatics are left in charge of the inventions of wise men. Yet though it may require a stretch of the imagination to see the lamb at peace in the lion-house, this would not seem to be nearly such a miracle as what we have got at present – the sages at peace in the madhouse. For with all our knowledge and skill we cannot solve the problem of how to get rid of the madness, the reason being that the doctors in our asylum seem to have forgotten that it is an asylum, and instead of trying to cure the patients are comforting themselves with the thought that their insanity is not so bad after all. 'Trade is looking up, you know, and prosperity is on the return. Sixpence [2.5p] off the income tax', etc.

But while the doctors are consoling themselves with such sedatives, Mr Wragg comes along with a bucket of icy water. He depicts the hideous contrasts of the modern world with a sense of reality which shows him to be one of the few doctors who can make a true diagnosis, and his drawings reveal hysteria, isolation, obsession, and depravity. Drawings from *Jesus Wept* will be reproduced in *The Eleventh Hour*, and it will be seen that an attempt to describe the contents of this book would be a hopeless task. It is a book worth buying for yourself and even more worth giving to your friends. In subject matter it is very similar to *The Psalms for Modern Life*, for there is a certain monotony about all Mr Wragg's work – but not the sort of monotony that would soothe anyone to sleep. It is the monotony of the untiring insistence of a man who will spare no one any pains in revealing a monotonous nightmare in stark black and white.

Yet what are the underlying causes of all this madness? In *Sex and Revolution* Mr Alec Craig suggests that 'a democracy where sexual disharmony and maladjustment are rife is not likely to come to wise political decisions. The sex-repressed and the sex-obsessed are easy victims to intellectual charlatans of all kinds'. It cannot be denied that he has put his finger on one of the major causes, for lack of understanding this most vital of the functions of life is bound to reflect itself in every department of man's activity. It is strange that while savages give their children a most careful education in sexual conduct, civilised races generally neglect it, allowing the whole subject to be monopolised by pornographers, while the majority of men and women are left in abysmal ignorance. When communities have no more than odds and ends of information about the very motive-force of their lives, it is not surprising that they resemble madhouses. Mr Craig covers the whole field of modern sex-life, from the political, economic, religious, legal, and scientific viewpoints, and though his insistence on the subject may seem to some the result of a bee in his bonnet, we may be sure that the bee will not be buzzing to no effect.

———————— • ————————

FOLLOW MY LEADER – OR BLIND MAN'S BLUFF (1935)

Britain's Political Future. A Plea for Liberty and Leadership. By Lord Allen of Hurtwood. (Longmans.)
The Prevention of War by Collective Action. By Lord Howard of Penrith. ('Friends of Europe' Publications. No. 8)

It is all very well to talk about a new technique of leadership, but where are the leaders? I turned to Lord Allen's book as a member of the generation whose fathers were killed or spiritually paralysed in the War, and I found no answer. It is a generation which has come into the world with no hope of the 'spacious days' of its nineteenth century ancestors, into a world surpassingly rich in the basic necessities of life, in scientific knowledge, in the cultural heritage of the ages, but alarmingly poor in the capacity to make use of its wealth. This poverty arises from the lack of leaders with an understanding of the social organism as a whole, for in spite of the abundance of 'raw materials' at our disposal, those who are responsible for their use have no sense of proportion, no conception of the relationship between the various aspects of our communal life or of the relationship of those aspects to the destiny of man. One often hears people speaking of the virtue of 'seeing life whole', but in a time when learning more and more about less and less is the order of the day, this virtue becomes increasingly difficult; and when the social organism is taken with a sickness, a legion of economic, political, religious, ethical, psychological, dietetical and educational panaceas are offered by specialists who can see little further than the confines of their own 'subject'.

Yet, so far as he goes, Lord Allen is generally right. He appeals for a technique of leadership based neither on violence nor, as has been the custom in most democratic countries, on fear of the mob, and he makes out a convincing case for the use of reason, which has been made possible by the spread of scientific understanding and that new and effective means of propaganda – broadcasting. That is well, but until we can find statesmen of wide vision and a sense of proportion, even one who is so sweetly reasonable as Lord Allen will fail to convince the nation that society is an organism, to be administered as such, and not a process of going round in small circles and patching things up here and there. I do not believe we can hope for any wide vision from those who can offer us nothing better than Fascist hysteria, Communist suicide, Labour sentimentality and Conservative plodding, since the adherents of all these policies are like short-sighted men without a map, on a journey to nowhere in particular, pushing a 50 h.p. Rolls-Royce, not for lack of petrol, but for fear they would get lost if they drove it.

There are some sensible people who call themselves the Friends of Europe. For some time these people have been publishing a series of realistic pamphlets, and now we have an excellent contribution to this series by Lord Howard of Penrith on the vexed problems of 'sanctions', the 'aggressor nation' and collective security. It is a pamphlet that should be widely read in this country in particular, for it will be remembered that after the War, France was agitating for some definite scheme for collective security (even an international police force was suggested), while Britain believed that disarmament was possible without it, and hung up all proposals by making absurd difficulties about defining the 'aggressor nation'. As Lord Howard points out:

> I look upon the adoption of some plan for collective action against an aggressor as the only real key to the problems of reduction of armaments, and of genuine economic recovery, because by such a measure alone, as it seems, can we re-establish a sense of security throughout the world, a true feeling of confidence that our whole economic life will not again be completely upset by another world war.

And again, on the problem of defining the aggressor:

> It is clear that every country which wishes to play the aggressor will always proclaim its own innocence of any aggressive intention, and that it will require a long process of law to decide which is really the aggressor ... Any nation should be considered an aggressor which, on being summoned to agree to an immediate armistice pending investigation of the causes of the dispute and their submission to arbitration or to the Hague Court for final settlement, refused to sign such an armistice or, if signed, to abide by it.

On the question of what sanctions should be applied to bring an aggressor to heel, Lord Howard contends that economic and financial boycott is, as a general rule, perfectly sufficient and that the idea of military sanctions need not enter into practical politics. The financial boycott would prevent an aggressor:

> from buying from or selling to the rest of the civilised world, until it agreed to the armistice pending a settlement of the dispute by peaceful methods. It does not require much imagination to grasp how impossible it would be for any country to carry on war in such circumstances for more than a few months or even weeks, it being a fortunate dispensation of Providence that no country is, or can be, wholly independent of the outside world.

———————————————— • ————————————————

THE THREE WORLDS OF MAN (1935)

Between Two Worlds. An Autobiography, by John Middleton Murry. (Jonathan Cape).

One Light Burning. A Story, by R. C. Hutchinson. (Cassell.)

To say that a man is well balanced must mean that he is equally well developed in each of his three worlds — the world of things, the world of people and the world of culture — and there must be something unbalanced in a pre-occupation with any one of these three to the exclusion of the others. For this reason I should call Mr Middleton Murry's autobiography unbalanced since it is concerned almost entirely with the story of his relationships with other people, so much so that one wonders whether he has any interest in things and culture. It is true that culture is not so much hidden as things, for the author is a man of letters and his wife, Katherine Mansfield, was a poetess, but the 490 odd pages of this book are so filled with the story of the personal reactions of a small number of people to one another that anyone who is not a keen student of social psychology would soon find it rather wearisome. This is not a reflection on the unbalanced mentality of a social psychologist, for social psychology is an excellent science so long as it does not claim to be the most important science and so long as it does not try to make us believe that nothing in the world is of so much consequence as relationships between people. It is true that these relationships are important, and what is even more important is that just at this time we need a new kind of relationship between people, but for that matter it is just as essential that we should have a new kind of relationship to things and to culture. But Mr Middleton Murry's autobiography is pre-occupied almost to the extent of obsession with the reactions between himself and a group of people amongst whom Katherine Mansfield, and D. H. Lawrence and his wife Frieda play the most prominent parts. In fact a better title for the book than *Between Two Worlds* would have been 'Very Much in One World', for his isolation from people into his 'other' world of impersonal and almost mystical visions seems to have come more from his reactions to them than from an absorbing interest in anything beyond.

To illustrate this point further let us compare Mr Middleton Murry's autobiography with Mr R. C. Hutchinson's latest novel, *One Light Burning*. Here is a book in every sense more evenly balanced, although it inclines to go in the opposite direction – towards a pre-occupation with things. It is the story of the behaviour of another small group of people to one another in the face of tremendous physical difficulties, with the highly improbable plot of a professor's search in Northern Russia and Siberia for a lost theologian. Yet though the plot is improbable it is seldom that one finds a novel which is more worth reading. It tells of the feelings which grew up between the party of five men completely cut off from the civilised world in illimitable wastes of snow and tundra, of the professor's fight against sleep until he drove sleep altogether away from him, and of his transformation from a pedant into a being capable of human emotions. It is just in Mr Hutchinson's understanding of man's relation to things, to violent physical realities, that he contrasts with Mr Murry, and, although reviewers are infamous for saying this sort of thing, I must say that I have found nothing in recent literature to equal his description of man's struggle with nature in her most terrible aspects.

> The storm broke just as they were starting... A spatter of flakes broke loose from the main flood to attack them on the flank; a sudden reflex drove snow into their mouths and nostrils. The snow half froze as it wrapped about their bodies, turning them to pillars of crystal. They held to each other with arms interlinked, without speaking, hardly thinking except to hope desperately for their release.

But read it; one quotation can only give a slight hint.

————————— • —————————

INVERSION OF INVENTION (1935)

The Frustration of Science. A Symposium, with a Foreword by Professor Frederick Soddy, FRS (Allen & Unwin.)
The Secret War for Oil. BY Hanighen and Zischka. (Routledge.)

Perhaps it is too much to expect the human race to understand the implications of what has happened during the last hundred years, for it has come into the possession of a power which up till now it has regarded as a sort of glorified plaything. But science is a dangerous toy when its function is misunderstood, and if we refuse much longer to grasp the significance of this tremendous instrument for human evolution we shall be faced with alarming consequences. More than ever that 'great orphan, humanity,' is in need of a large band of capable mothers to show the poor infant how to play with its toys, which it has been solemnly picking to pieces to see the wheels go round. This may be a rather superior attitude to take, but I have been wondering during the last few days how anyone can help feeling superior when the members of this advanced and civilised continent of Europe are fooling about with this mysterious mumbo-jumbo which consists of sending diplomatic notes, entering dignified protests, being endlessly tactful at Geneva, and telling people at home that no stone has been left unturned to find a solution to the grave economic problems which baffle the best minds of the day. The one rule in this game seems to be that you may never say what you mean, which would be a shame because it would spoil the mystery.

Thus it is not surprising that some of the benevolent uncles who went to such pains to provide all these ingenious and very excellent toys are getting disturbed for fear that the dear child will either take them completely to pieces or blow itself up, and in *The Frustration of Science* some of the leading scientists of today, including Sir Daniel Hall and Professor P. M. S. Blackett, have expressed their concern in no uncertain terms:

> It used to be said (writes Sir Daniel Hall) that the greatest public benefactor was the man who could make two blades of grass grow where one grew before. Not so today, when the nations are considering agreements to restrict output and even destroying the products of the soil... For two generations the scientist has been entreated to make the land more productive and to reduce costs; but as an American professor of agriculture writes to me: 'Ten million acres of cotton and some thousands of tobacco have been ploughed under. The latest move is the killing of some 5 million pigs weighing under 100 lb. and the slaughter of some 200,000 prospective mother sows. *If this will bring national prosperity I have wasted my life.*'

The italics are mine. For besides being sheer economic lunacy, this state of affairs is an insult to the thousands of highly skilled men and women who have made possible an Age of Plenty; instead of being honoured as the greatest benefactors of mankind, their work is destroyed in the interests of a folly called business, while the place of honour is taken by politicians whose chief skill seems to be an infinite capacity for saying what they do not mean. Sir Daniel Hall speaks for agriculture, and the same story is told for industry by J. D. Bernal, for Medicine by Professor V. H. Mottram, and for aviation by J. G. Crowther.

But scientists must be careful not to spoil their case. Someone has wisely said that the expert should not be on top but on tap, and there are indications in *The Frustration of Science* of the scientist's desire to make the world a little too efficient and hygienic. Personally I strongly object to being told what sort of a world I ought to want to live in; like others I have my own tastes in these matters, and however healthy, or advanced, or scientific it may be, I do not want to live in Mr Bernal's city:

> under one roof, a roof which could be transparent glass without visible support. Inside, the weather need not be left to the changes of nature. It could be provided with all its varied characters of wind and rain and sunshine, according to what people liked ... each section of the town could have its own weather ... With large rooms, hundreds of feet high and square miles in extent, the normal noise of human beings would be heard not more than in the open country. For a long time people would probably be conventional enough to cling to the old habits, particularly the desire for privacy, but in the long run the greater convenience and freedom of the new environment would be bound to lead to a new social life.

Of course, the line between the artificial and the natural is difficult to draw, but however efficient these artificialities may be, they all lead in the direction of synthetic babies, tabloid food, laboratory flowers, gramophone birds, and other horrors of the social hot-house. It may be a resistance to 'progress' on my part, but who is the authority on what progress is? The scientist has no more right to say that this is progress than I have to say that it lies towards the abolition of bowler hats, gold clocks under glass cases, and by-laws apparently made up by people with nothing to do on wet afternoons, all of which happen to be particular fads of my own.

But even worse than the frustration of science is the

deliberate abuse of science. *The Secret War for Oil* — a collection of revelations so sensational that they are hard to believe — is an exposure of the exploitation, bloodshed, and misery caused by the fight for markets and fields between the world's great oil concerns - Standard, Dutch-Shell, Anglo-Persian, Mexican Eagle. The book is rather spoilt by the use of the peculiar journalese which the modern press uses to ensure that a sensation shall be made as sensational as possible.

> In Mesopotamia (Deterding) rubbed his magic lamp and the genie of oil appeared on the deserts of the Arabian nights. Deterding's drillers started to bore the historic sands.

Apart from this, *The Secret War* is an informative study of the powers behind modern politics, but I feel that Messrs. Hanighen and Zischka would have made a considerably better case if they had relied upon a cold, objective and detailed statement of facts, instead of dressing up their allegations in the worst tawdrinesses of present-day journalism. If the charges which they have made are true, our oil magnates must be creatures without morals or humanity; but to say so in too many words will only make people laugh. It doesn't do to squash a wasp with a steam-hammer.

———————— • ————————

ABOLISH THE ORDINARY MAN! (1935)

Plain Ordinary Man. By Arthur Radford. (Routledge.)
Education and the Citizen. By Col. E. A. Loftus. (Routledge.)

A few months ago I suggested at a small political meeting that there was no such thing as an ordinary man. This rather sweeping statement provoked a subsequent speaker to get up and say, as if he had been offended: 'I am responsible for running a group of young fellows connected with the Movement which I represent here this evening. We are, I suppose, more or less ordinary people, although [getting a bit nasty here] we've just been told that we don't exist.'

I am sure that no one, if he is honest, likes to believe that he is an ordinary person, but through false modesty or fear of being thought eccentric, we take refuge from being conspicuous by claiming to be that hypothesis, the plain man-in-the-street. But the phrase 'ordinary person' is a contradiction in terms, for the whole point about a person is that he has personality, which my dictionary defines as 'distinctive character', and a civilisation where people can humbug themselves into the belief that they are ordinary and that it is good to be ordinary seems to me as dull as a meal in which all four courses are semolina pudding.

While the greatest joy of life is the fact that everything is different, here we have a world in which thousands of people almost pride themselves on being ordinary, of a pattern, like the others. But just because each person is unique whether he likes it or not, the ordinary man is a sham and a denial of the personal principle. Thus a New Order of society is necessary, not for any particular class or group, not for the justification of any idea, but simply for the sake of Personality. As Mr Radford points out in *Plain Ordinary Man*:

> Society must be so organised that men are allowed to develop their personalities: in this way they attain freedom of the spirit ... There will be those who imagine that they know the character of this personality which lies awaiting development and will set out to produce the organisation which will develop it... (But) the personalities of men are infinite in variety and all 'organisations' that are at all thorough-going savour of the 'parade ground', whether those in command are saints or sinners, and anything in the nature of enforced uniformity produces repressions and tendencies to disruption.

While we have, in this country, escaped so far the 'parade ground' methods of Fascism, forces are at work which stifle the development of personality and make it possible for there to be such a thing as an ordinary man, and Mr Radford has written a remarkably interesting study of these forces and of the lives of their victims. He does not merely confine himself to a highly informative description of present conditions, of the family life, education, occupations, and amusements of working people, but at the same time traces their historical background and suggests ways and means of reconstruction, chief among these being the realisation of the Age of Plenty made possible by mechanised production. Mr Radford is nowhere guilty of exaggeration or sensationalism, and in this readable, sane and thoroughly comprehensive book he shows a civilisation which can be summed up in the one word 'Frustration'.

A more specialised work which throws additional light on the origins of ordinariness is Col. Loftus' *Education and the Citizen*. For too long the aim of education, both in 'Public'[42] and National schools, has been the production of a type, and the training of the mind has been subordinated to the accumulation of large numbers of facts of which a knowledge is necessary for the purpose of passing certain examinations. Col. Loftus describes the methods of instruction and discipline used in all the various kinds of schools existing in this country today, and, while recognising the valuable work that has been done to improve education in the last fifty years, shows their inadequacy to prepare citizens capable of taking part in the life of a modern community. But in suggesting the necessary changes he gives too much emphasis to change of subjects taught. Surely it is true to say that what children are taught is of secondary importance compared with the effect that teaching has upon their mental powers – powers of concentration, rational thought, adaptability, appreciation of values, sense of proportion, and the capacity to 'take things in'. In short, the purpose of education should be to train the mind to master any subject rather than to master the mind with a few selected subjects, for facts are useless without the ability to understand and use them.

—————————— • ——————————

'GREAT ARGUMENT ABOUT IT AND ABOUT' (1935)

Science and Religion. By N. Bishop Harman, FRCS (George Allen & Unwin.)

If it is true that dirt is matter in the wrong place, it is also true that nonsense is sense in the wrong place. Thus the conduct of a chicken is in every way excellent in the hen-house, but there would be something a little ludicrous in laying eggs on the drawing-room chairs and scratching for worms in the carpet. For the same reason we should feel rather anxious about the mental state of a chemist who insisted on discussing embroidery in terms of Boyle's Law and the freezing point of sulphuric acid, but it is rarely that anyone notices a similar confusion when a scientist talks about religion in terms of science. Now science operates entirely with the intellect – the faculty which deals with separate, individual things and the relationships between them, which asserts that two and two make four, denies that the moon is made of cheese, classifies groups of objects, observes the movements of bodies in relation to other bodies, and discriminates between the pairs of opposites such as hot and cold, light and darkness, pleasant and unpleasant. Intellect is concerned, therefore, with the world of separateness and relativity; it can appreciate the existence of a given thing only by reason of its non-existence in another place, and its movement only by reason of the fact that it changes its position in relation to something else which appears to be still. But intellect has nothing to do with religion, for whereas science can only exist in the world of diversity, religion can only exist in the world of unity, where affirmation and negation disappear along with all the other pairs of opposites. That is to say, religion is concerned with the 'unknown quantity' which lies behind contraries, which gives rise to existence and non-existence, stillness and motion, good and evil, light and darkness – with the *tertium quid*, which is neither the two extremes taken together, but that which makes them possible and gives them their meaning. For example, space is the *tertium quid* of 'far' and 'far ['near'? – Ed.]', and space in itself, as apart from things existing in it, can neither be measured nor intellectually understood; nothing can be asserted or denied concerning it, and in this it is like the 'mysteries' of religion.

So it is that whenever intellectualists like Dr Harman approach the subject of religion and God (the *Magnum Tertium Quid*) with their scientific affirmations and negations they involve themselves in innumerable contradictions. Dr Harman attempts to use science to support the existence of a personal God and the immortality of the soul, and he advances the old argument that because the scientist finds order in every part of the universe and that indeed we are 'fearfully and wonderfully made', therefore there must be behind the universe a Personality. Man's mind enables him to construct things in an ordered way, with purpose and design, and hence it follows that because there is clearly purpose and design throughout the universe, therefore there is sustaining and directing it a Being who plans, orders and constructs after the manner of persons, for, he writes, 'a well-designed piece of mechanism compels us to conclude, from our previous experience of such things, that there is a mind behind it, some person devised it'. Order presupposes Personality.

But does it? Where is there chaos in the world, where is there lack of design and absence of plan? Certainly not in unconscious and inanimate things. Whoever saw a stone floating on water contrary to the law of gravity? Do the planets turn round and go backwards on their orbits and upset the solar system? Do cabbages sprout out of daffodil bulbs? No, there is only chaos when man comes along and performs strange irregularities such as starving when there is plenty of food or eating so much that he makes himself sick. Thus it is equally arguable that purpose is the blind reaction to necessity, that man copies order from the impersonal world because pain arises when he does not, but that since he is personal, irresponsible and capricious, since he is self-moving in a far greater degree than other things, therefore he takes every opportunity of breaking away from the restraint of order. It might just as well be true that order presupposes helpless Impersonality which must always move in ruts, while Chaos presupposes something with a wild will of its own, which gets ideas into its head, hates too much repetition, upsets things for fun, indulges in illogical stunts and insists on asserting its independence, freedom, and right to do what it likes, always liking the extraordinary, the novel and the absurd.

The argument could be carried on for ever, simply because there is no solution to it that can be expressed in scientific (i.e. intellectual) terms, since it concerns something which has as much to do with science as ping-pong with poetry. When Dr Harman asserts that belief in God is 'arguable, reasonable, logical, demonstrable', he falls into the old error of scholastic philosophy which Bacon described as 'working upon itself, as the spider worketh its web, bringing forth cobwebs of learning, admirable for its fineness of thread and work, but of no substance or profit'. For religion can only be approached through the intuition, and the things that are found there can no more be described in terms of intellect than colour in terms of shape. But that is another story.

———————————— • ————————————

WAR AND PEACE (1935)

War: Its Curse and Cure. By William Leighton Grane, with an Introduction by Wickham Steed. (George Allen & Unwin.) *An Impossible Parson.* By Basil Martin. (George Allen & Unwin.)

The only fault of Canon Grane's otherwise excellent book is that he pays militarism the compliment of taking it seriously. In every other respect *War: Its Curse and Cure* is a sane and realistic study of the international situation. The author draws a striking parallel between the war mentality of the present day and of the years before 1914, and shows the necessity for some definite lead in foreign policy from Great Britain. In 1914 such a policy might well have prevented war, but then as now the excuse is advanced that statesmen in a democratic country cannot afford to disregard public opinion, and it is notorious that many people in this country still regard Britain as a fortress defended by the silver sea whose policy should be to close her doors to the troubles of the continent and remain in 'splendid isolation'. But Canon Grane points out that this excuse:

> ignores the undoubted fact that sound and resolute political leadership may easily prove a considerable factor in forming public opinion. Indeed, it is probably an instinctive desire for this kind of initiative which accounts for the popularity of modern dictatorship.

The responsibility, however, does not lie with statesmen alone, and Canon Grane shows that one of the most urgent tasks of the present time is to ensure that the right side shall win in the mental conflict between the philosophers of war and peace; false philosophies which encourage the war mentality must be stripped of their glamour. But I do not believe that this can be achieved either by argument or invective, for these are methods effective only when used against sane opponents.

175

The same is true of Christian Pacifism, which Mr Martin advocates in his *Impossible Parson* – a fascinating autobiography which describes his fight against the absurd conventions which pass for institutional religion. It is often that 'turning the other cheek' inflicts a moral defeat on an aggressor, but when the aggressor is mad and incapable of feeling a moral defeat, this method is like beating the air. But Mr Martin's book is not only concerned with war; it is the story of an intellectual adventure in which the author suffered much abuse and unpopularity, but just because he does not make a martyr of himself and shows a keen sense of humour, the book is not only of value as a spiritual challenge; it is at the same time highly entertaining and very readable.

But so far as questions of war and peace are involved, let us remember that modern militarists are infantile lunatics, and in the conflict of ideas they can only be defeated if they are treated as such. Logic is useless, because if anyone excels in logic it is the lunatic; but ridicule is the sharpest weapon since the madman, unless his madness is pathological, can only be brought to sanity if he is made to realise that he is making a fool of himself.

————————— • —————————

JAPAN ON THE WARPATH (1935)

L'Espirit du Japon. By Dr Alphonse Gaudier. (Editions Brouard, Paris.)
Samurai. By Ivan Molotoff. (Baker, Jameson & Price, New York.)

Japanese militarism has a unique history, for in no other country has there been so close an association between philosophy and the art of fighting. But with the introduction of the modern technique of warfare it was inevitable that this association should lose its strength, except in so far as militarism is connected with the patriotic religion of Shinto, which could hardly be dignified with the name of philosophy. Strange as it may seem, the various methods of fighting in feudal Japan (i.e., before the introduction of Western civilisation) were based on the highest principles of Chinese thought as set forward by Taoist and Buddhist sages. Perhaps the most striking example of this is, as M Molotoff shows, in the art of ju-jutsu – a well known method of self-defence in which one's opponent is defeated by the use of his own strength. Translated literally, *ju-jutsu* means 'the gentle art' and the legend goes that it originated through watching the branches of trees in a heavy fall of snow. Supple branches simply gave way under the weight and sent the snow to the ground, while on thick and rigid branches it accumulated until they cracked. Relating the early history of this art, M Molotoff points out that this legend:

> is none other than the Chinese doctrine of *wu wei*, or 'action in inaction'. To illustrate this doctrine we may take the example of water: if a knife is thrust into it, it will yield with the greatest of ease, but as soon as the knife is withdrawn it will close up so that no trace of the thrust remains. Thus the invulnerability of water is due to its liquidity, its non-resistance, its capacity to adapt itself to all circumstances.

He goes on to show that this was the attitude to life taught by the Taoist philosophers. Man must not resist any impression that comes into his mind, for the highest form of man 'employs his mind as a mirror: it grasps nothing; it refuses nothing; it receives, but does not keep'. Thus in ju-jutsu a blow is never resisted, for the defender merely steps to one side, grasps the attacker's wrist and encourages the force of the blow to continue in the same direction until it oversteps itself, sending the attacker off his balance. Then it is an easy task to upset him! Together with this non-resistance there is another aspect of this 'mirror-like' attitude of mind, and that is the focusing of attention wholly on the immediate circumstances.

In ju-jutsu, as in kendo (fencing), you must never think out what your opponent is going to do next, and you must never let your mind be occupied with what he has just done. If you are listening to music, you must follow the tune as it flows, for by trying to imagine what is coming and in thinking over what has passed, you miss the continuity of the melody. In the same way it is necessary to be constantly aware of your opponent's movements, since the slightest mental wavering will give him an opportunity to catch you off your guard.

Dr Gaudier, in his *Esprit du Japon*, shows that this attitude of mind is what is known in Zen Buddhism as 'straightforwardness'. Zen was by far the highest product of Chinese thought, and the main theme of Dr Gaudier's work is its tremendous influence on Japanese culture.

> Zen (he writes) has been described as a religion of 'dyanamic immediacy'. One of its exponents once answered the simple question, 'What is Zen?' by saying, 'Walk on!' For this is what it calls 'straightforwardness' or 'going right ahead'; it teaches that we should accept things as they come to us, preserving always a vital awareness of the moment.

This is precisely the state of mind one is taught to adopt in ju-jutsu and kendo, and it is not surprising that in feudal Japan the samurai (the warrior class) were the principal devotees of Zen.

Dr Gaudier also points out the relationship between this 'straightforwardness' and the great Sumiye school of painting. The artists of this school used a peculiar rough and brittle paper for their work, which made it necessary to use the brush swiftly and deftly. Once a line was drawn there could be no going back to touch it up, and in this is seen the influence of Zen with its insistence of going right ahead with life, never turning back to regret past mistakes, never stopping to 'perfect'. For perfection means symmetry, rigidity, death – three things never found in the finest Japanese or Chinese art.

——————————— • ———————————

DIE NEUE GEMEINSCHAFT! (1935)

Deutschland zwischen Nacht und Tag. By Friedrich Heiss. (Volk und Reich Verlag, Berlin.)
Richelieu's Political Testament. Three Centuries of European Insecurity. By Walter Hagemann. (Editions Politiques et Sociales, Geneva.)

A friend of mine who is a keen supporter of the new régime in Germany has presented me with an interesting collection of Nazi propaganda. From this collection I have selected *Deutschland zwischen Nacht und Tag* (Germany between Night and Day) and *Richelieu's Political Testament* as the two most significant specimens. The former is one of those productions in which the Germans excel – a beautifully arranged book of highly artistic photographs, while the latter (written in English) is an interpretation of European history in which an important truth is given an important kink.

The book of photographs is clearly meant for home consumption; as propaganda it would hardly appeal to foreigners, for no attempt is made to hide military pomp and glamour, while the Fascist ideal of 'depersonalisation', of merging the human person into the mass, is only too clear. In the first half we are shown pictures of the devastation wrought by the War (the devastated objects being chiefly guns and fortresses), while these are followed by scenes of the suffering and 'decadent' Germany of pre-Hitler days. There are destitute men and women sleeping on benches and tottering about the streets, people dancing and drinking at bars, beauty-queens in bathing costumes, Communist demonstrations and street riots. Then, with a section entitled *Die Neue Gemeinschaft* (The New Community), there comes the change, and we are shown the triumphant and splendid Germany of the Third Reich. The impression given is one of vastness, of gigantic crowds of people saluting or parading in uniform, of huge factories, tremendous blocks of tenements, of enormous works of engineering, while the individuals photographed are shown, not as human persons, but rather as types; as typical workers, children, soldiers, and women. One figure alone is allowed to stand out from the mechanised crowd as a human being, and that is Herr Hitler who is seen playing with children and shaking hands with a group of adoring young men.

Herr Hitler assures us, 'No war can become the permanent condition of human life. No peace can be the perpetuation of war. Sooner or later, victors and vanquished must find the way back to the community of mutual understanding and trust.' These words from his great speech of October 14, 1933 are quoted on the first page of Herr Hagemann's *Richelieu's Political Testament*, yet it would be surprising to find 'mutual understanding and trust' advanced by attempts such as this to lay all the blame for the Germano-Gallic conflict on France. It is, of course, true that the Cardinal de Richelieu did more than any other man to effect the final break up of the unity of Catholic Christendom by supporting Protestants in Germany against the armies of the Catholic Wallenstein in the interests of French acquisitiveness and nationalism. But at the same time it is a perversion of history to say that 'France in the course of the last three hundred years has, with the single exception of the Crimean War, waged only aggressive wars'. She may have been the first actually to declare war in 1870, but it was Bismarck's policy of Prussian Imperialism culminating in his falsification of the Ems telegram that provided the *casus belli*, for war with France was an essential step in his scheme for uniting North and South Germany. And the New Germany would do well to consider Bismarck's own bitter words spoken only a short time before his death as he sat before the fire on a winter's evening, when a friend suggested that he had made Germany a great and glorious nation:

> Yes; but the misfortune of how many? But for me three great wars would not have taken place, eighty thousand men would not have perished, fathers, mothers, brothers, sisters, widows, would not have been plunged into mourning. I have settled all that with my Creator; but I have gained little or no joy from all my work.

FROM THE ARCHIVES OF THE NEW ATLANTIS FOUNDATION[43]

————————————— • —————————————

THE NEW ORDER (probably 1934)

The Two-fold Basis

The precept 'Become what you are' is the key to the New Order, for to become actual the New Order must exist in its totality even while it is potential. That is to say, the task of creating the New Order in the future is a matter of realizing (of making real) what exists as a seed in the present.

Speaking generally the New Order has two aspects: the first of unity and identity, the second of diversity and function. These two are complementary.

Fundamentally, the many selves of mankind are not separate but One, for behind all differences is the Common Source, the Self, the Creator as distinguished from the instruments of creation. Without this there could be no coherence, no cosmos.

But for the Common Source, the One, to be expressed fully in the Many, there must be diversity in each unit of the Many. For if the One expresses itself in the Two, the Two cannot together manifest the One if they are the same, and what is true of two is true of millions. Just as each sector of a circle must be different from the others if the circle is to be complete, so for the One to be expressed in its entirety in the millions, each of the millions must have its own unique function and must be faithful to that function. This is Order and Cosmos, present even now among men and things but not present in the sense that it is not realized and made conscious. Thus the task of bringing the New Order into being is creation by realization.

For the creation of the New Order it is therefore necessary that there should be:

Personal Change

Change of attitude: individual

1 *From within* Beginning with himself, the individual must awake an inner realization of his twofold nature – of his identity with the Common Source, and of his uniqueness as a manifestation of that Source. Without this change in the individual there can be no corresponding change in the order of society, for any change which is less than this is an attempt to cure the symptoms of a disease instead of the cause. For at the root of the disease of man lie the desire to dominate and the desire to exclude, and these arise from the absence of this realization.

2 *A whole change* This change from within is no mere improvement but a change of the individual centre of gravity, his centre of consciousness. It is not a purification and strengthening of his present qualities but the creation of new qualities arising from a new attitude to life. Before this change, the individual is as one on the circumference of a circle imagining that his point on the circumference is the centre, while after the change he looks from the centre of the circle to the circumference and sees his own point on that circumference in its true relation to all other points. For this total change is the attainment of a true sense of proportion wherein the individual has regard neither for the universal alone, nor for the particular alone, but for both, for identity at the same time as diversity. And in the realization of his uniqueness he must express that uniqueness to its fullest extent so that its function may be fulfilled, while that uniqueness cannot be truly unique unless he has also the realization of his identity with the Centre; otherwise it would be domination and exclusiveness.

3 *World mutual* The change of one individual alone is not the New Order in its universal sense, for the New Order means universal realisation of the principles of identity and diversity. Thus the New Order is not to be achieved through the hermit

ideal of departing from society, but by men changing together in mutual assistance. For the hermit society is disintegration and a denial of identity; the fascist society is regimentation and a denial of diversity; but the organic society of the New Order is truly integration and co-ordination since it affirms both diversity and identity.

4 *A new world* Universal realization of the New Order must involve the creation of a new world with new institutions and new relationships in order to achieve a more faithful expression of the Order which already exists unrealized and in potentiality.

Change of attitude: social

1 *Personal Alliance as an Alliance of Persons*[44] To be truly a person each man must give the fullest expression to his uniqueness, must expand, assert and fulfil the function of his diversity. Yet in order to know what his uniqueness is, the individual must have an objective view of himself, and seeing himself thus he is not hurt by criticism or by hearing from others the truth about himself.

2 *Personal Alliance as a Human House*[45] But the social change is not effected by the expansion, assertion and expression of one person alone; it requires that every man should give to others the same opportunity for fulfilling their uniqueness as he would wish to be given to himself, and that he is prepared to accept and recognise their uniqueness as essential parts in the order of life.

3 *Personal Alliance as Senate First* The principle of Senate[46] is the seed in which the New Order exists in its totality though still in potentiality. Within that seed is the whole conception of the functional society, and for that reason no part of the conception can be rejected without abandoning the whole. For what is true of persons is here true of principles. The New Order must arise from this seed, from this Senate, and we say Senate First not only chronologically speaking but in terms of importance, for the unconditional acceptance of the whole conception of the functional society is the guarantee that the New Order will be The New Order and not A New Order.

THE PROCESS therefore is:

From INDIVIDUAL INITIATIVE
Through PERSONAL ALLIANCE
To THE ABSOLUTE COLLECTIVE.[47]

THE NEW ORDER
METHODS OF CHANGE: PERSONAL

CHANGE OF ATTITUDE: INDIVIDUAL

1 From within

2 A whole change

3 World mutual

4 A new world

CHANGE OF ATTITUDE: SOCIAL

1 Personal Alliance as an Alliance of Persons

2 Personal Alliance as a Human House

3 Personal Alliance as Senate First

THE PROCESS therefore is

From INDIVIDUAL INITIATIVE
Through PERSONAL ALLIANCE
To THE ABSOLUTE COLLECTIVE

SHAFTESBURY HOUSE
WIDMORE ROAD
BROMLEY, KENT [48]

12th June 1934

Dear Moeran [49]

Further to our telephone conversation of June 11th, I'm writing
to give you a suggestion for the amendment of the Constitution,
and I shall be grateful if you can manage to bring it up at the
meeting on the 13th.

It starts off by saying that the present system of society is
disastrous among other things to the spiritual well-being of the
people. I think it would be more apt to say that the present
spiritual condition of the people would be disastrous to any form of
society; that is to say, if we change the outward mechanism of
the state, that change must be balanced by an inward change of the
spirit, or Man will ruin the new order even though it may be a
better one. To take an illustration: a monkey in a top hat may
look more civilised than a monkey without one, but nevertheless he
is still a monkey. In the same way, I think it is true to say that if
you add to the material prosperity of society, you do not
necessarily improve society in the fundamental spiritual sense. It
may be that I have a very cynical view of human nature, but I do
feel that the New Britain Movement should lay especial emphasis
on the fact that the soul of improvement is the improvement of the
soul, if that is not too trite a phrase. It may be true that better
material conditions give people opportunities for spiritual
improvement which at present they are without, but at the same
time it is true that every man should try to rise superior in the
spirit to the circumstances under which he lives, however bad
they may be. Mere grousing at circumstance is not enough; for
even a small knowledge of history shows that the greatest
personalities have concentrated on changing the inner attitude to
life, rather than the outward ordering of society. Not that the
latter is unimportant, but the state of civilisation is so much a
reflection of the condition of our minds that no external reform
can be lasting and funda-mental without internal reform. If I may
quote an oriental saying, 'All that we are is the result of what we
have thought; it is founded on our thoughts; it is made up of our
thoughts'; or to use our own parallel, "We are not what we think
we are, but what we think, we are.'

Therefore I think the Constitution should lay more emphasis on
the mental change which is necessary for building the New Britain;
it should introduce some of the ideas expressed in a recent article
in NEW BRITAIN called 'A Testament to the Kingly' by Van Eeden.

If it were to include this it would be a Constitution almost unique in the history of politics, since every other political programme leaves out of consideration those ideas of personal alliance, spiritual endeavour and individual perfection which make the New Britain Movement a beacon of sanity in the political madhouse, and which add so much 'sweetness and light' to its proposals for constitutional and economic reform.

Hoping this will not be be regarded as 'carping criticism',

I am yours sincerely,

Secretary, Bromley Group

NEW BRITAIN GROUP
SHAFTESBURY HOUSE
69 WIDMORE ROAD
BROMLEY, KENT

20th June 1934

Watson Thomas Esq
New Britain Offices
53 Gower Street, WC1

Dear Sir

At a meeting of the S.E. London Area Council on Tuesday June 19th it was resolved that the following paragraph (or words to the same effect) should be suggested in addition to the first portion of the New Britain Constitution:-

The Movement believes that the organisation of the Community exists in order that every individual may be given the fullest opportunity for self-development, in alliance with other individuals. Moreover it believes that a fundamental change in society must be brought about as much by individual regeneration as by economic and political improvements.

It was felt that insufficient emphasis had been given to the spiritual aims and methods of the Movement, and that the Constitution was an inadequate expression of the New Britain philosophy and plan of action without some definite statement (as opposed to mere implication) of those aims and methods.

Yours faithfully

For & on behalf of S.E. London
Area Council

PART THREE:

Miscellaneous

MISCELLANEOUS
WRITINGS

•

THE WHOLE AND ITS PARTS (1937)

From psycho-analysis to psycho-synthesis is the trend of psychology today. This is in line with the teaching of the Ancient Wisdom of the East; and it would be difficult to find a more significant example of this tendency than that to be noted in the recent work by Dr Graham Howe, *I and Me*, which inspires the present remarks of our Contributor.

In the past, there has been much justification for saying that Western psychology is based on materialism, for most of its exponents regarded the mind as a by-product or 'epiphenomenon' of the body, and saw in all mental disorders the result of some physical disorder. Indeed, their materialism went farther than this, for they studied both mind and body as dead rather than as living things. That is to say, their technique was to separate things into their component parts and to try to undertand them by examination and classification of the pieces; their belief was that the best way of knowing a thing scientifically was to 'pull it to bits'. The natural result of this technique was that in pulling the mind and body to pieces they failed to discover any organism answering to the name of 'soul' and 'spirit', for to disintegrate is to kill, and the moment life disappears 'soul' and 'spirit' go with it. Many of these materialistic scientists admitted that they had never discovered what life is, hoping that one day, as their dissection of the human being progressed, they would at last detect some particle which could be labelled 'life' and regarded as the cause of movement and intelligence in the human body. That hope was, and is, absurd, since life consists not in any part of the living organism, but in the correlation of parts which make up the whole. For the same reason these scientists could find no 'meaning' or 'purpose' in the universe — all was 'a fortuitous congress of atoms' — because 'meaning', like 'life', is in wholeness rather than in disintegration.[54]

If we wish to discover the life and meaning of the human being, we shall not find it in the brain, the heart, the stomach, the entrails, the glands, the lungs, or the nerves. In the same way, the meaning of a word does not consist in any one of the letters composing it, and the wheel-ness of a wheel is neither in the hub, the spokes, nor the rim. If we take the wheel to pieces, arrange the spokes in a row with the hub at one end and the rim at the other, its wheel-ness no longer exists; we shall not understand the nature of the wheel by studying these different parts, for the whole, wherein is life and meaning, is greater than the sum of its parts.

Unfortunately, Western science did not confine its materialism to textbooks; it applied it, and in the field of medicine the result was the belief that a patient could be cured of a disease by treating some part of his organism. This belief is still prevalent, and its manifestation is the large number of 'specialists' who study one particular organ or groups of organs, professing to 'cure' diseases whose symptoms result in derangement of these organs. This, however, is medicine for the corpse – not for the living mind-body, for all diseases arise fundamentally from the wrong living of human beings as such, and not from the wrong functioning of particular parts of their bodies. But a new element has come into Western science in the form of psychotherapy, which was at first based on materialism, though subsequently many of its practitioners found that certain forms of mental disease or neuroses could not be removed by physical treatment. Whereupon they tried to apply this same technique of 'picking to pieces' to the mind; they attempted to analyse the mind in the hope of discovering some mental content which might be called the *cause* of the neurosis, and thus psycho-analysis was at first a method of disintegrating the mind so that its component parts might be examined as 'things-in-themselves'. But recently a tendency has arisen to change this technique; it is being realised that analysis, to be successful, must not be the separation of the mind into its various parts in order to find out which part is diseased, but separation in order that they may be properly related. Neurosis results, not from any 'bad' or 'unhealthy' mental content, but from a wrong relationship between all the contents which make up the whole mind, for the disease is a disorder of the whole and not of any one part. Therefore analysis must be merely the preliminary to arranging these parts in order instead of disorder, and to know what 'order' is it is necessary to study the mind as a living whole as distinct from a dead, disintegrated chaos. It is necessary to understand the entire behaviour of the mind, its attitude to life, its habits; in short – its soul.

This is one of the many fascinating themes of a remarkable book by a physician at the Institute of Medical Psychology – Dr E. Graham Howe.[55] Its title is *I and Me – A Study of the Self* (Faber & Faber, 7s 6d); it is an examination of the two aspects of man, the inner 'I' and the outer 'Me', and of the synthesis between the two which is essential to a balanced spiritual development.

> Whether we are thinking [writes Dr Howe] of yourself, myself, or himself, there are always *at least* two of them. Since these two selves are related as subject and object, observer and instrument, they may be conveniently referred to as inner 'I' and outer 'me'. . . . We may then ask ourselves the question: Which of these two selves is Reality? But then let us be warned not to take sides, and join the ranks of those who would exalt one of those aspects of self at the expense of the other.

For:

> in this relationship of the one and the two we can understand the genesis of all creation. Out of one nothing can ever happen; there is no making or movement until it has been divided into its two-ness. Only out of two can there be born a child.

The people who exalt the outer 'me' are those occupied almost entirely with external form, with 'good form' and 'bad form'; they like to have everything labelled and classified; their ideas and habits are rigid; they are the materialists who like to have everything dissected, who can never grasp anything whole, preferring instead to divide it up into good and bad so that the former may be kept and the latter thrown away. The 'I' people, on the other hand, are occupied exclusively with the subjective world; they are vague, unconventional, introvert, and undiscriminating. One might say that the difference between the two is that while the former cannot see the wood for the trees, the latter cannot see the trees for the wood. The balanced and integrated mind, however, is that which sees both the wood and the trees in their true relation to one another. This is the essence of Dr Howe's approach to psychology and psychotherapy, and the way in which he applies it to everyday life is unusually sound and valuable.

He shows that friction and unhappiness (or what the Buddhist would call *dukkha*) are produced by the alternation of the 'yes' and 'no' attitudes of life, by the affirmation of some things and the denial of others, the division of wholes into good parts and evil parts. This causes a deep conflict with life because it is a denial of that wholeness without which there is no life, only the death of a carcass whose flesh has been put in the cooking-pot and whose bones and entrails have been consigned to the dust-bin. While this attitude is more noticeably a characteristic of 'me' people, the 'I' people suffer from it in a more subtle form. They say 'yes' to the whole and 'no' to the parts, which again produces conflict because the one cannot exist without the other. Therefore this conflict is only to be brought to an end by the affirmation and acceptance of life as the synthesis of the whole and all its parts. In this way the individual does not isolate himself from life by retreating into the castle of egotism, for this retreat means, 'No, I will not play with you; I will run away and wage war on you from a safe place because I am afraid.' But Dr Howe shows that happiness can only result from abandoning this serious, strained state of war and joining wholeheartedly in the game of life with the relaxed and friendly attitude of one who plays.

> Life [he writes] is far too important to be taken seriously. This is not said cynically or in paradox, but because the play technique does in fact work better for hard-headed practical working people. . . . If we find that things are becoming a bit tight, then we must not trust to our instincts, but learn to be loose and relaxed, for fuss and worry can never help efficiency. If matters are really very difficult, then it is all the more important that we

should learn to take things easily ourselves. . . . Look at the fisherman: can we imagine anything more serious? But remember that he always *plays* his fish.

———————— • ————————

THE RUSTY SWORDS OF JAPAN (1939)

If it be true that Japan has well-nigh won her war against China[56] it is a political victory but a military tragedy; for it marks the final defeat of what was probably the greatest philosophy and system of warfare in the world. Much has been said about the ethical and political rights and wrongs of this conflict, but here we are not concerned with these, nor even with the rights and wrongs of wars in general. But, however inevitable wars may be, there are right and wrong ways of fighting, ways that ennoble and ways that degrade. There was a time when the Japanese were masters of the ways that ennoble, when their technique of fighting had the dignity of an art and a philosophy. That things have changed is by no means the entire fault of the Japanese, for the same change has occurred in some degree all over the world.

With the steely, cold impersonality of modern warfare, military chivalry in the old sense has gone, and its passing from Japan is especially tragic because in her old military arts there was a profound, almost divine, element of which few Western people have heard. But the West invented high explosives, bombs and airplanes, and taught the Japanese how to use them, and in a world armed with such weapons a great nation can hardly be expected to rest content with swords. And the impersonal machines of modern war seem to have a way of bursting into action of their own accord, as if they were too diabolical, too vast and impressive, for the human will to control.

Courage is still required of the men at the front, and even Prussians cannot surpass the Japanese for almost inhuman calm in the face of death, a calm which is generally attributed to 'oriental fatalism' and a peculiar brand of blind, unshakeable patriotism. But, though the Japanese have not lost a fraction of their old courage, the wildly extravagant manner in which that courage is exploited by modern methods must make the old samurai[57] turn in their graves. And the courage of which

193

no more is asked than to charge against a battery of machine guns in the certain knowledge that one will be slain is so easily degraded into a blind, dumb, mechanical fatalism; the soldier becomes as obedient as an egg flung at a stone wall – and about as useful. For degradation begins whenever the individual man with all his diverse faculties ceases to be of value as such, and courage loses all meaning when divorced from art and skill, becoming only the ability to go forward without turning back or stopping, like a stone dropped over a precipice.

No such waste of human faculties was ever contemplated by the old samurai, and the masters of swordsmanship would have regarded such haphazard methods of warfare as dropping bombs from airplanes with utter horror. It is hard to say how much they would have been moved by humanitarian considerations, but they would certainly have held it a military error of the worst order. For nothing is more liable than wanton slaughter to arouse bitter and permanent hatred in the foe and thus increase the power of resistance; furthermore, the greater the destructive power of his weapons, the more does the attacker lay waste and impoverish the very land which he sets out to conquer.

But, in the days of the samurai, mastery in swordsmanship involved much more than mere physical skill, more even than rigid aherence to a code of honour (bushido[58]). Strange as it may seem, the great masters of the sword had also to learn mastery in a certain form of religion which affected not only their state of mind in the face of death but also their actual technique of swordplay. From the earliest times the sword was always regarded as a semi-religious object; the swordsmith was no mere manufacturer – he was an artist, almost a magician. His work was done in ceremonial dress and performed before a shrine of the presiding deity, while the blows of his hammer were accompanied by incantations. But with the coming of certain forms of Buddhism from China the sword acquired an even deeper significance; it became a symbol of life as well as of death, a weapon to slay not only one's physical enemies but also the enemies of the soul – fear, hesitance and worldly attachments.

The form of Buddhism which had most influence on the art of the sword is known in Japan as Zen and in China as Ch'an or Ch'an-na, which is a corruption of the Sanskrit word *dhyana*, usually translated as 'meditation.' But what we, and even the people of India, understand by the word 'meditation' does not give any real idea of the meaning of Zen. For, although Zen came originally from India to China in the sixth century AD, the Chinese gave it a peculiarly lively and practical significance, and by the T'ang dynasty it had altogether lost its Indian characteristics and had become, as it were, the Chinese synthesis of Buddhism, Taoism and Confucianism. It is not at all easy to understand exactly what Zen is. A learned Japanese scholar, Dr D. T. Suzuki, has written eight considerable volumes in English to try to explain the subject, and he would probably be the first to admit that he has not succeeded. For Zen is something that can never be learned from books; it is a personal experience, and seeking its meaning from books is like trying to learn the art of love from a textbook on marriage. Perhaps we can arrive at some clue to its meaning by a study of its influence on the art of swordsmanship.

Originally the warrior class of Japan came to Zen to learn the secret of facing death with unruffled courage and calm. For, in common with other forms of Buddhism, Zen taught that life and death are alike aspects of the same existence, and that within the soul of man there is something greater than himself, something eternal and indestructible which is the only true reality in the universe[59]. Of this a Zen poem says:

> You cannot describe it, you cannot picture it,
> You cannot admire it, you cannot sense it.
> It is your true self, it has nowhere to hide.
> When the world is destroyed, it will not be destroyed.[60]

To the samurai, Zen seemed more effective than any other form of Buddhism in teaching the knowledge of this eternal being, and in the almost militaristic discipline of Zen monasteries there was something which appealed specially to the soldier-mind.

According to Zen, such knowledge cannot be attained by thinking about it; to chase it with thoughts is like turning round in circles in the attempt to see one's own eyes or trying to catch hold of the wind by shutting it in a box. Another poem says:

It is too clear and so it is hard to see.
A dunce once searched for fire with a lighted lantern.
Had he known what fire was
He could have cooked his rice much sooner.

To know this reality man must summon up all his courage and perceive it directly and immediately; thoughts, doctrines and ideas cannot be allowed to stand in the way, and even the effort to find it may itself be an obstruction. If you wish to concentrate on reading a book the only method is to go straight ahead and read the book; the moment you think about your own effort to concentrate, your attention is turned from the book to yourself. The samurai applied the same teaching to fighting with the sword. Action must be immediate and unpremeditated; for, if there is a moment's hesitation between your opponent's attack and your defence, you give him an opening for a deadly blow. Therefore the masters of the sword said that there must be no two movements, attack and defence; the two must be blended into one, and your own sword must move in perfect rhythm with your opponent's. Thus skilled combat with swords became a swift, even flow of movement which neither paused nor hurried, since it was most important not to confuse immediacy of action with mere speed. Speed there certainly was, but superbly controlled and without any of that feverish mental activity which turns speed into rush; the idea of rushing was considered yet another form of mental obstruction, something that held the mind's attention away from the actual task in hand.

Hence the mental condition of the swordsman was described as a 'not-stopping' attitude of mind, or as 'going-straight-ahead-ness.' The great fencing master Takuan[61] explained that, in fighting, the mind should never be allowed to 'stop' in any particular place; for anything that stops or holds your mind conquers it. If your thoughts become fixed on the enemy's sword you may fail to notice his other movements; if you think about the position of your own feet, your grip of the sword, what kinds of cuts or parries you will use, your mind is 'stopped' by your own body. Again, if the enemy does something unexpected, making you hesitate even for the fraction of a second, once more you give him a chance to strike home. Therefore when the mind is never stopped by any circumstance, when it flows evenly and the body follows it, then the swordsman becomes as elusive to his opponent as a bird, unceasingly twisting in the air, allowing not a moment's pause for an arrow to be aimed.

This was derived directly from the Zen teaching concerning one's attitude to the circumstances of life. For, when the mind is not 'stopped' by an occurrence, it becomes free, manifesting its true nature which is one with the ultimate reality of the universe. The Chinese observed this 'not-stopping' condition in all the operations of the natural world, concluding that these operations were outward signs of the activity of the Tao, or Way of Life. When the hands are clapped the sound does not stop to think before it comes out; there is no halting in the motions of the sun, moon and stars, in the flowing of streams, in the roar of a waterfall, in the procession of the seasons or in the movement of all life from birth to death. Hence, if the mind follows the same principle, it falls naturally into harmony with the Tao. 'The perfect man,' said the Chinese sage Chuang-tzu,[62] 'employs his mind as a mirror. It grasps nothing; it refuses nothing. It receives, but does not keep.' But, according to Zen, you cannot get into this harmony by thinking about it, as one who sits on the edge of a stream, wondering whether the water will be warm or cold, while every minute reluctance to take the plunge grows stronger in his mind. On the contrary, you must go right ahead and jump in without a second thought. Thus when a Zen master was asked, 'What is the Tao?' he replied simply, 'Walk on!'[63] Or to put it in the language of swordsmanship:

> Under the sword lifted high
> There is hell, making you tremble;
> But go ahead,
> And you have the land of bliss.[64]

A story is told of two generals, Kenshin and Shingen,[65] which illustrates this principle. Their two armies lay encamped opposite each other, and Kenshin, impatient of the slow progress of the battle, walked boldly into the enemy's camp, coming by surprise upon Shingen talking to his guards. Stealing up behind him, Kenshin whipped out his sword and held it poised just above Shingen's head, crying, 'What would you say at this moment?'

This was a typical Zen question, intended to test immediacy of response under trying and surprising circumstances. But, where most people would have been struck dumb with amazement, Shingen replied instantly, 'A snow-flake on the blazing stove,' at the same time striking the sword away with his iron fan. To a free and 'unstopped' mind such difficulties are indeed as snowflakes over a furnace, dissolving the moment they enter its heat. Thus another Zen poem says:

> Upon a soul absolutely free from thoughts and emotions,
> Even the tiger finds no room to insert its fierce claws.[66]

It should be noted, however, that 'free from thoughts and emotions' does not mean 'without thoughts and emotions'; the wise man may have both thoughts and emotions, but he is not carried away by them.

Economy of force was the second great principle of swordsmanship which came from China with Zen. There is no wild slashing, no aimless cutting and thrusting. The combatants face each other with hardly a movement, yet there is no stiffness or tension, only a relaxed poise. For when there is tension you may be just a second too late off the mark if the attack comes from an unexpected direction. So the swordsmen watch each other with the easy alertness of a cat watching a bird; suddenly there is a flash and an ear-rending shout of 'Ho!' and a point is won or lost.

But the principle of economy of force went further than mere technique. The sword, too, was a force, and the expert masters were those who employed most economy in its use. The master Bokuden[67] had three sons, whose attainments in swordsmanship he wished to test. Placing a pillow on top of the curtain at the entrance to his room so that any one who touched the curtain would upset it, he called to his sons one by one. The eldest came first, saw the pillow, took it down and replaced it again after entering. The second son followed, and as he touched the curtain the pillow fell, but, catching it before it reached the ground, he entered and replaced it in the same way as his elder brother. As the third son hurried in, the pillow fell and touched his shoulder, but before it could touch the floor his sword was out and the pillow slashed in twain.

Then Bokuden presented his eldest son with a sword, pronouncing him well qualified for swordsmanship. The second he advised to train himself still more carefully. But the third was reprimanded as a disgrace to the family.

On another occasion Bokuden was in a boat with a number of other passengers crossing Lake Biwa, near Kyoto. Among them was a huge, proud soldier who began to boast of his skill with the sword. Seeing that Bokuden was also carrying swords, the soldier approached and asked him to what school he belonged.

'My school,' answered Bokuden, 'is different from yours; it consists not in defeating others, but in not being defeated. It is known as the "without sword" school.'

'Why, then,' asked the soldier, 'do you carry a sword yourself?'

'This,' said Bokuden, 'is meant to do away with selfish motives, and not to kill others.'

This reply so incensed the soldier that he challenged Bokuden to fight him without using his sword, and the challenge was willingly accepted. The soldier ordered the boatman to make for the nearest land, but Bokuden suggested that they had better make for an island where a crowd would not collect and there would be no danger of hurting any one. To this the soldier agreed, and when they reached the island Bokuden handed his swords to the boatman while the solider stepped ashore. But just as Bokuden seemed about to follow he snatched the oar from the boatman and with a quick stroke pulled the boat away from the island into deep water, leaving the soldier stranded. 'Now,' he laughed out, 'you see my "without sword" school!'

Ultimately, success in swordsmanship depends on one's attitude to death. It often happens in duels in France and Italy that the expert with the foil retreats before the naked blade, leaving victory to a mere amateur. The supremacy of the old school of Japanese swordsmen was precisely due to the fact that their minds did not 'stop' at the fact of death; for death, as much as life, belonged to the Tao. Combat with swords was, therefore, a test of spiritual strength, and in battle each individual was alone responsible for his success or failure. When he slew it was with precision and economy, winning because he was a better man, not because he owned (or was owned by) a better machine whose projectiles had little precision and no economy. When he had to slay, he slew with almost surgical skill. Indeed, a Japanese sword is much like an enlarged scalpel, seeing that with one blow it should make a clean cut from shoulder to thigh. But now the tendency is to direct machines in accordance with fixed mathematical laws which most fools and all cowards can learn, touch the spring and release a hell-fire of wanton destruction that blasts and mangles combatants and non-combatants alike. In this new madness Japan was quick to follow the rest of the world. It might have been hoped that with her traditions she would have exercised somewhat more restraint in the use of these wild forces. Unfortunately, however, the past fifty years have seen the swift disappearance of the bulk of the pure *samurai* class through intermarriage with the peasantry. And over this mixture of *samurai* and peasantry rules 'Big Business,' having seldom birth or character but only money, and its handmaidens – figures, mathematics, machines, the new gods of the soul, which shall be made into their own image.

———————————— • ————————————

HOW BUDDHISM CAME TO LIFE (1939)

Of all the countries of the East none have been more profoundly influenced by Buddhism than China and Japan. That they are now engaged in war does not, perhaps, speak well for this influence, but so far as war is concerned the influence of Christianity in the West has been equally ineffective. In spite of the conflict we must not be blinded to the fact that there was an old China and an old Japan upon which our modern age has wrought many changes. Thus in speaking of the influence of Buddhism upon these two countries, we must think at first of olden times.

The West began its study of the teaching of the Buddha from India sources, and it is not always recognised that between Indian, Chinese and Japanese Buddhism there are vast differences. Although Buddhism was originally an Indian religion, emerging from the traditions of Hindu philosophy, it did not attain its full vitality until the times of the T'ang dynasty in China – about the eight century AD.

From times immemorial the aim of Indian religion has been to show man that, in spite of his feeling of isolation from and conflict with the universe, his self and the Self of the universe (*Brahman*) are in fact one. Separate things — men, animals, trees, rivers, mountains — appear and vanish, and by becoming attached to them, by looking to them for his happiness, man finds them unsatisfactory and productive of suffering. His own individuality is also subject to change and death, and he also suffers because he identifies himself with it. But, according to Hindu philosophy, the real Self of man and all other separate things is eternal, and this can be realised by giving up attachment to the transient selves which are simply fleeting aspects or manifestations of the Self. Thus, while the universal Self is real, other selves are only real insofar as they are rooted in the universal Self; but as separate things they are illusions (*maya*).

The early Buddhism of India was also a religion of non-attachment to individual things, but it divided into two schools, one of which was nihilistic in that it placed little or no emphasis on the eternal Self that would be found when the transient selves had been surrendered. This school, called Hinayana Buddhism[68], is the one chiefly studied by Western scholars, to many of whom it has seemed a morbid and pessimistic faith. But out of the Buddha's original teaching (no one knows quite what it was) there came also in course of time the Mahayana school[69], which, in theory rather than practice, carried the tradition of Hindu thought to its logical conclusion. Although the doctrine of Hindu philosophy was that the only reality in life was the universal Self, in practice there had always been a tendency to split the universe in twain, into the real and the false, the One and the Many, the life of the sage absorbed in solitary contemplation of the One and the life of the ignorant man absorbed in attachment to the Many. Thus Hindu sages became somewhat aloof, neglected the world altogether, so much devoted to the principle of unity that they denied themselves all diverse feelings and emotions until they almost ceased to be human.

But Mahayana considered this a one-sided view, and put forward the conception that, as all things are in fact the Self (they gave it another name), there can be no real division between the One and the Many. Therefore a man could realise his union with the Self and yet continue to be human. In India, however, this idea was less the occasion for practice than for an abundance of subtle philosophising to show in what sense the One was the same as the Many, and in what sense different. It was this Mahayana aspect of Buddhism that came to China about the first century AD, and by that time it had become the most complex metaphysical system in the world. It took the practical Chinese mind to apply it directly to life, to grasp its central principle and eliminate non-essentials. By the eighth century the Chinese had given it a dynamic quality that it had never had in India.

For the whole point of Mahayana is that every single thing, whether a Buddha, a fool, or a lump of stone, is actually at one with and in perfect harmony with the universe; man's only trouble is that he does not realise this, though even his lack of realisation is itself an aspect of that harmony because, as we have seen, there is no real difference between a Buddha and a fool. Thus, whereas ordinary men think there is a difference between themselves and the Buddhas, the Buddhas see no difference and hence have no spiritual pride. But the understanding of their identity with the ultimate reality of the universe gives them the use of a creative freedom and power of spirit which the ordinary man has but does not appreciate. One of the principal reasons that the Chinese were able to make practical use of this philosophy was the mental background given by their own religion of Taoism. The central concept of Taoism (said to have been founded by Lao-tzu about 600 BC[70]) is that all forms of life are aspects of the Tao – a term meaning much the same as *Brahman*, save that it has a rather more dynamic significance; it is the universal creative power rather than abstract Being. In common with Buddhism, the object of Taoism was to bring man into harmony with the Tao by teaching him to surrender his personal will and let the Tao work through him. But from the Mahayana point of view there is no real personal will to be opposed to the Tao; hence man's task is to appreciate that the Tao is already working through him – in spite of himself.

Thus Chinese Buddhism did not follow Indian in losing interest in the things of the world through regarding them as illusory aspects of the Infinite; on the contrary, the things of the world became a thousandfold more interesting just

202

because they expressed the Infinite Self. It was therefore natural that those who had this understanding brought a new feeling to the life of man and nature – a feeling which is best expressed in the Chinese painting of the period, especially in those Sung pictures[71] which appear to be far more works of nature than of man. For the highest expression of Buddhism, both in life and art, is concerned with ordinary, everyday things, with birds, tree branches and wisps of grass, with gathering rice and drawing water. Philosophy, Buddhas, bodhisattvas and religious rites are far less significant, and for this reason the greatest religious art of China does not appear to be religious.

The Chinese have a saying: 'To him who knows nothing of Buddhism, mountains are mountains and waters are waters. But when he has read the scriptures and knows a little of Buddhism, mountains are no longer mountains and waters no longer waters (that is, they are *maya*, illusion, and no longer worth considering). But when he has thoroughly understood Buddhism, mountains are again mountains and waters again waters.'

Generally speaking, the second stage is Indian Buddhism and the third Chinese.

Chinese Buddhism thus ceased to be a matter of otherworldly mysticism disregarding the ordinary objects and activities of the world. For these objects and activities became sanctified; it was just as much a religious act to chop wood as to sit absorbed in meditation, the essential point of Mahayana Buddhism being that every imaginable thing and activity is an expression of that ultimate reality which the Hindus call *Brahman* or the Self and the Chinese call *Tao*. Realising this in the heart of his being, man feels a powerful and liberating lift to his spirit, knowing that the whole might of the universe is at work in everything he does.

Look at the brush strokes of a master of Chinese painting or calligraphy who has been influenced by this knowledge. The Chinese artist does not work from his wrist, resting his arm on the table; he works from his stomach and all the power of his body goes into that stroke, which is made with a single, unhesitating and irrevocable sweep. If he pauses or falters, the silk or paper instantly absorbs the ink and leaves a blot; if he goes back to touch up a fault, it is plainly visible; if he makes a mistake, it can never be erased. Hence to do good work he uses the Buddhist principle of 'going-straight-aheadness' (*mo chih ch'u*), which is another name for keeping pace with life or the Tao. For life is always going ahead; it does not hurry; it does not lag; it never stops and never goes back to correct or wipe out what is past. Therefore the Chinese Buddhists said that he who performs his own activities in this way is in harmony with life. In doing things spontaneously and without faltering, keeping always 'on the move,' he becomes a free and unobstructed channel for the Tao. His mind moves like flowing water; nothing can catch hold of it; nothing can stop it.

Chuang-tzu, the Taoist sage, expresses it in another way: 'The perfect man employs his mind as a mirror. It grasps nothing; it refuses nothing. It receives but does not keep. And thus he can triumph over matter without injury to himself.' This was the Chinese view of Buddhist 'non-attachment.' It was not the complete abandonment of the things of the world; it was using them without getting caught by them, making one's spirit as elusive as water.

In *Ch'an* Buddhism, which was the principal and most representative school of China but which is perhaps better known in the West under its Japanese name of *Zen*, the Chinese evolved a new way of enabling people to understand Buddhism; a way that accorded strikingly with the underlying philosophy that religion was something intimately connected with the ordinary affairs of the world. When Buddhism first came to China the method used for attaining spiritual illumination followed the lines of Indian yoga; it was concerned with the practice of *dhyana* – a profound state of consciousness obtained by sitting for hours, days, months or even years in solitary meditation. But this did not really appeal to the practical spirit of the Chinese, who wanted a *dhyana* that could be applied to everyday life and that did not involve retirement from the world to become a hermit. Thus they developed a new technique, a method of bringing men to realise their identity with the Tao while engaged in ordinary activities having no necessary connection with religion. This method might be described as a form of 'shock tactics,' a way of presenting the truth so forcefully and unexpectedly that the mind would be jolted out of its usual ruts and see the whole thing in a flash.

The object of this method was to assist people to feel the truth 'in their bones' as distinct from having it just as an intellectual concept that does not necessarily express itself in actual life. The human mind is apt to remain content with such concepts, and is often unable to distinguish them from truly deep feelings and understandings. Therefore this method avoided intellectual concepts, striving to demonstrate the Tao itself instead of ideas *about* the Tao. Earnest disciples were deeply puzzled by the lack of any ordinary explanation or instruction from their teachers, and these surprising methods of demonstration created in their minds the necessary state of tantalisation and bewilderment which needs only a well-timed jolt to be turned into full understanding.

Thus on one occasion a group of disciples were gathered to listen to a sermon from their master. The master took his chair and was about to begin when a bird burst into song just outside the window. He waited respectfully in silence while the bird continued its song, and when it ended he announced that his sermon had been preached and went away.

In his *Essays in Zen Buddhism*, Dr D. T. Suzuki relates a story of the master Hui-t'ang being asked about the inner doctrines of Buddhism by a learned Confucian. He replied that there was a saying of Confucius which gave the answer: 'Do you think I am holding something back from you, my disciples? Indeed, I have held nothing back from you.'

The Confucian did not understand this laconic answer at all but some time afterward they were walking together in the mountains when they passed a bush of sweetly scented wild laurel.

'Do you smell it?' asked Hui-t'ang.

When the Confucian answered that he did, Hui-t'ang exclaimed, 'There, I have kept nothing back from you!'

At that moment, it is said, the Confucian understood the secret of Buddhism.

Dr Suzuki also tells how the master Tao-wu once had a disciple complain to him that, though he had been trying to learn from him for years, he had never had any instruction.

'Ever since you came to me,' replied Tao-wu, 'I have always been showing you how to study.'

'In what way, sir?'

'When you brought me a cup of tea, did I not accept it? When you served me with food, did I not partake of it? When you made bows to me, did I not return them? When did I ever neglect in giving you instruction?'

The disciple was more mystified than ever, so Tao-wu said again, 'If you want to see, see directly into it; but when you try to think about it, it is altogether missed.'

The unusual methods of Ch'an were not always quite as plain sailing as this. Surprise answers were often physically violent, for, having deep insight into his disciple's state of mind, the teacher would know just the right moment to administer a shock which would produce a phenomenon rather similar to the Christian 'sudden conversion.'

It will be seen that in Ch'an Buddhism there is a curious avoidance of religious discussion; its teachers considered that the highest truth of religion was completely and plainly manifested in the ordinary affairs of life, and one had only to look at it in the right way to see it. To them, thinking on specifically religious lines was like looking into the remotest parts of the sky for something that lay right at one's feet. To put it in another way, the truth was not so much in things looked at or thought about as in the looker and thinker himself. Thus the advice of Ch'an Buddhism is to take care that in seeking for truth you do not forget the seeker, for the Tao must be found in oneself and nowhere else. Pai-chang said that studying religion in the ordinary way is very much like looking for an ox when you are already riding on one.

The influence of Ch'an Buddhism is not always easy to estimate because of its avoidance of ordinary religious form. We know, however, that it had the widest popularity in southern China from the end of the T'ang to about the beginning of the Ming dynasty (850–1340), and its influence was certainly strong in the latter part of the T'ang. There is no doubt at all that many of the greatest Sung artists were deeply imbued with its teachings, and the great bulk of Ch'an literature (which is enormous) was compiled in this epoch, being composed mainly of anecdotes, typical examples of which have been given above. Generally speaking, however, we may say that in China its cultural influence was mainly in the realm of the arts, and from its literature we can judge that it also had far-reaching effects on personal life and character. Owing to the strong influence of Taoism, Chinese Buddhism was pervaded by an easy-going, mature, humorous and *laissez-faire* element which distinguishes it strongly from the Buddhism of Japan, and in early times the Ch'an monk was probably more akin to the Taoist 'old rogue' than to the disciplined soldier. But as its adherents grew it became gradually more formalised; the old yoga practices came more to the front and a definite system of meditation was evolved, together with a rigid monastic discipline. This systematisation was apparently necessary to prevent the teaching from disintegration, for the spontaneity and originality of the old masters were beginning to wane, and so informal a method of teaching might easily degenerate into nonsense and its inner meaning be forgotten.

At the same time Ch'an was beginning to fight its losing battle with another form of Buddhism – a form which shows no particularly Chinese characteristics, although at the present time it is by far the most popular Buddhist school in the Far East. This was the Pure Land school, the cult of Amitabha (in China, O-mi-to-fo; in Japan, Amida), the great Buddha of the Western Paradise (*Sukhavati*), who was said to have vowed that all who had faith in his name would be reborn after death in his Pure Land. This school holds that the highest enlightenment is impossible on this earth and unobtainable by human effort alone; only in the Pure Land can one work for enlightenment, and birth in this Land is had only through the saving grace of Amitabha. It is not surprising that this Buddhism of salvation by faith became far the most popular school among the masses. Apart from Ch'an and Pure Land there were yet other forms, such as T'ien-tai (in Japan, *Tendai*) and Hua-yen (in Japan, *Kegon*)[72] but essentially these were more Indian than Chinese or Japanese, being of a decidedly metaphysical and ritualistic trend. Thus it is mainly the Ch'an or Zen school that shows national characteristics to best advantage, and there is no doubt at all that of all schools it had the most profound influence on the educated classes.

Though Buddhism was first introduced into Japan in the sixth century AD, the Ch'an school did not arrive until the twelfth, and by this time it was beginning to enter upon its formalistic phase. It was not long before its theory and practice began to appeal strongly to the Japanese military caste, the samurai. In their hands its monastic discipline became more rigid than ever, and, being men who went constantly in fear of death, they found tremendous help in its philosophy of 'going-straight-ahead' and in the idea that life and death were alike aspects of the one, unchanging Tao. Never before had any form of Buddhism been so essentially a warrior's creed.

Westerners are often puzzled by the apparent inconsistency of warlike men embracing the Buddha's distinctly peaceable faith. Generally speaking, however, it may be said that in this respect the Japanese took over the philosophy of Buddha without his ethics, because, even in China, the Ch'an school took a somewhat amoral view of life. In the Mahayana system, good and evil are relative terms, Absolute Reality being neither one nor the other. Thus enlightenment, or union with that reality is not necessarily consistent with great morality, even though its attainment may require much self-discipline. This discipline is moral insofar as it forbids any activities which may distract the disciple from his task. But military duties are not considered a distraction, for their fulfilment involves hardships which strengthen the will.

The new form of Buddhism soon began to find favour among members of the aristocracy, for its priests had become the chief bearers of Chinese culture, travelling as merchants between Japan and China and returning not only with books but with all manner of artistic works which are now revered as Japan's most valued national treasures. Before long it found a firm footing in the predominating classes of this young, warlike and highly practical island people, and for the first time Buddhism began to be applied seriously to the smaller details of life. For the samurai, having secular duties to perform, did not often become regular monks. They would go to the monasteries for short periods, and, when they returned their home life would assume some of the qualities of the Zen monastery – absolute cleanliness, with a maximum of empty space and a freedom from overdecoration.

Westerners are always struck by the comparative emptiness of a Japanese home: the plain walls, the single picture and the dull yellow mats unobstructed with furniture – surroundings in which the mind is not distracted by fidgety knick-knacks. This is what the Japanese call 'Zen taste' – for, to the Buddhist mind, emptiness is full of potential power, suggesting freedom, room to move about, stimulating creative energy, just as a large white wall tempts a small boy to express himself with a piece of coal. The use of a single picture follows the all-important Buddhist principle of 'one-pointedness' of mind, which is controlled and concentrated thought, going straight ahead without wavering from one thing to another.

One of the chief reasons for the cleanliness of the old-fashioned Japanese home is that the Zen monastery was no place either for dirt or laziness, for in Zen one could never claim that one was too absorbed in religion to be clean or to do ordinary, menial work. On the contrary, Zen monks have always been given to art and industry because in their view these things are just as religious as meditation and ritual. And so far as art was concerned, the influence of Zen was, if anything, more profound even than in China. Painting, gardening, poetry, drama, tea-ceremony, pottery, architecture and even the military arts of *ju-jutsu* and swordsmanship (*kendo*) were transformed by the Zen view of life. In modern times the connections of these varied aspects of life with Buddhism may not always be remembered, but they are immediately obvious to the student of Zen and of Japanese history alike. There is hardly a department of Japanese culture where 'Zen taste' has not crept in.

Yet it may be regretted that, though the Japanese applied Buddhism far more efficiently and thoroughly to their life than the Chinese, it lost much of its spiritual *largesse*, which was perhaps only to be expected in an island community. Chinese Buddhism had a markedly Taoist atmosphere – along with an absence of triviality, it was easy-going, wise, old and mature, and savoured throughout with a profound sense of humour which was something much deeper than mere fun. But with the Japanese it became somewhat Prussianised, and with the passing of years seems to have been given rather more form and system than is good for its life and originality. Thus today Japanese Buddhism is almost as highly organized as any of the world's great religions, and in the case of Zen it is difficult to know whether its life has survived because of or in spite of organisation. Yet the evolution of an organised church from a loosely knit spiritual movement is a usual phenomenon in religious history, and it is highly probably that, had Ch'an continued to flourish in China, it would have been quite as much systematised as in Japan but lacking Japanese drive and efficiency.

There can be no doubt that this central stream of Buddhism, though crystallised into a church, still retains great vitality. Certainly its monks are often sent to the monasteries involuntarily as to a school, and certainly the fixed exercises and formulæ for meditation are apt to make it technique without inspiration: but where there is spiritual genius, rare as it may be, Zen flourishes magnificently, and those who have lived in modern Zen monasteries know well that, if their arduous schooling does not always produce great saints, it does produce great gentlemen.[73]

Yet those who would study Buddhism in its most vigorous, original and spontaneous form cannot do better than return to the early Chinese records of the T'ang and Sung dynasties, a time when the crutches of institutionalism were not needed, when the vitality came by inspiration from within the soul and not by technique from without. For this was the middle age of Buddhism, the prime of life when youth and maturity were joined.[74]

———————— • ————————

THE PROBLEM OF FAITH AND WORKS IN BUDDHISM
(1941)

It is generally assumed that philosophic Buddhism, and especially that form of it expressed in the Pali Canon,[75] is *par excellence* the way to salvation or illumination by self-help. For in the philosophy attributed to Gautama by the earliest records no place is given to a God or gods who can assist man in the development of spiritual life; the existence of such divine beings is not denied – it is ignored on the ground that no power on earth or in heaven can interfere with another's *karma*. And *karma* (Pali, *kamma*)[76] is a very inclusive term, for primarily it means 'action' or 'doing,' though in a secondary sense it has come to mean the law of cause and effect – a sense which has been much over-emphasised by Western theosophical interpretations. But it would seem that original

Buddhism does not only set aside the possibility of interference with *karma* for the reason that it is impossible to separate a cause from its effect (in the Christian sense of absolution). It also rejects the possibility of divine intervention at the causal end of the process, having no parallel to the Christian concept of Grace. In Christianity there is no human power which can, of its own resources, make for righteousness and salvation, for by reason of original sin it is impossible for man to move upwards without the gift of divine Grace. Buddhism, however, would appear to be a method of lifting oneself up by one's own belt, for according to a famous passage in the *Mahā-parinibbāna Sutta* (v. ii, 27–35), we are advised, 'Be ye lamps unto yourselves. Be ye a refuge unto yourselves. Take to yourselves no other refuge.'*

Both Hīnayāna and Mahāyāna Buddhism[77] in the historical development of their philosophy and practice have, for the most part, kept to this principle of absolute self-reliance. If any faith was involved, it was faith in one's own capacity to *work* out one's own salvation, and faith in the ability of Buddhism to supply the necessary method. In the Hīnayāna system the method was to exhaust the process of *karma* by perceiving the fundamental unreality of the individual (*atta*) who sets *karma* in motion. The Mahāyāna followed a variation of the same method, but, under the influence of Brahmanic thought, supplemented the idea of individual unreality with the concept of a universal, non-dual Reality similar to the Vedantist idea of Brahman. In one sense this Reality, called by such names as *Tathatā, Śunyatā,* and *Dharmakāya*,[78] was beyond *karma* (*akarma*), and thus the realisation that it alone existed involved deliverance from the toils of *karma*, even though one might continue to live in the 'world of birth-and-death.' But the radical non-dualism of, say, the *Laṅkāvatāra Sūtra*[79] refused even to make any absolute distinction between *karma* and *akarma*, the world of illusion and the principle of Reality, the transient, separate individual and the eternal, undifferentiated 'Suchness' (*Tathatā*):

---

* An interestingly different train of thought is suggested by this passage if we follow Mrs C. A. F. Rhys Davids' translation of 'yourselves' as 'the Self,' in the Upanishadic sense of *ātman*.

There is no Nirvana except where is Samsara; there is no Samsara
except where is Nirvana; for the condition of existence is not of a
mutually-exclusive character. Therefore, it is said that all things
are non-dual as are Nirvana and Samsara.[*]

The problem of faith and works in Buddhism, as we shall
discuss it, will be entirely in terms of the Mahāyāna school. To
understand its doctrinal and psychological background we
must pay particular attention to the Mahayanist doctrine of
non-duality, bearing also in mind that only in Mahāyāna has a
way of salvation by faith arisen.[80] Our attention will be
directed, however, to doctrinal and psychological aspects of
the problem rather than historical, for we cannot say precisely
whether the historical development of the way of faith came
as a logical result of certain philosophic trends or as an answer
to a natural human need. Furthermore, the historical aspect of
the problem is complicated by our uncertainty as to the exact
age of many of the important sutras involved. But we do
know that the way of faith developed quite early in Mahāyāna
history, playing an important role in the works of such early
patriarchs of the school as Nāgārjuna, Aśvaghoṣa and
Vasubandhu.[81].

Mahāyāna philosophy is centred upon two closely related
ideas. The first, descended from Vedānta, is that
Enlightenment (the Buddhist life-goal) consists in an inner
realisation of non-duality. All those things upon which
unenlightened man depends for his happiness are dual, and
thus conditioned by their opposites. Life cannot be had
without death, pleasure without evil. We cannot, therefore,
depend for our ultimate salvation and security upon any one
aspect of a given pair of opposites (*dvandva*),[82] for the two are
as essential to each other as back and front are essential to the
totality of any object. Thus, while we look to such limited
states for our salvation, we are involved in a world of ups and
downs which goes under the general name of Saṁsāra, the
wheel of birth and death.

From the beginning, the purpose of Buddhism was to find
deliverance from this wheel, to discover the state of Nirvāna,
differing from these limited states by being eternal,

[*] *The Laṅkāvatāra Sūtra,* translated by D. T. Suzuki (London, 1932), pp.
67 ff.

unchanging, and subject to no ups and downs. In the Pali
Canon there is no special emphasis upon the non-duality of
Nirvāna. It is here something quite outside and different from
Saṁsāra – an escape. But the Mahayanist Nirvāna is described
in much the same language as the Upanishads describe
Brahman, the 'One-with-out-a-second.' Here Nirvāna is the
experience which differs from all these limited experiences by
having no opposite. The Mahāyāna sutras are at such pains to
stress the non-duality of Nirvāna and Enlightenment (*bodhi*)
that they do not even allow Nirvāna to be opposed to Saṁsāra, or Enlightenment to be opposed to Ignorance (*avidya*). To
the fully enlightened man, Saṁsāra *is* Nirvāna; ordinary,
everyday experience of the world of opposites is for him
transformed into the supreme spiritual experience of
deliverance or freedom.

The second important principle of Mahāyāna is the
Bodhisattva-ideal. In one sense the Bodhisattva[83] is a lesser
Buddha. In another, he is one who, by patient striving
throughout countless incarnations, has attained the right to
Nirvāna, but who postpones final entry into its eternal rest in
order to come back into the world and work for the liberation
of 'all sentient beings.' But this rather picturesque view of the
Bodhisattva is actually taken from the Hīnayāna standpoint.
Nirvāna is still an *escape* from Saṁsāra, even though the
Bodhisattva has temporarily renounced it. But from the
thoroughgoing Mahāyāna standpoint, the Bodhisattva-ideal
is the necessary consequence of a philosophy denying the
duality of Nirvāna and Saṁsāra. The Bodhisattva has no need
to escape from Saṁ sāra because he realises that it is Nirvāna.
Thus, to quote the *Laṅkāvatāra Sūtra* again,

> those who, afraid of sufferings rising from the discrimination of
> birth-and-death, seek for Nirvāna, do not know that birth-and-
> death and Nirvāna are not to be separated the one from the other;
> and, seeing that all things subject to discimination have no
> reality, imagine that Nirvāna consists in the future annihilation of
> the senses and their fields. They are not aware ... of the fact
> Nirvana is the Ālayavijñāna (universal) mind)[84]. . .
>
> (Trans. *Suzuki*, p. 55)

But whatever the view of Nirvāna, the Bodhisattva is the
saviour, the one who makes vows (*pranidhāna*) to postpone
any final withdrawal from the world until he has seen all

living things liberated and raised to the level of his own understanding. Thus, in a number of Buddhist sects, the monk repeats daily the following vows to identify himself with the Bodhisattva-ideal:*

> How innumerable sentient beings are, I vow to save them all;
> How inexhaustible our evil passions are, I vow to exterminate them;
> How immeasurable the holy doctrines are, I vow to study them;
> How inaccessible the path of Buddhas is, I vow to attain it.

But it will be noted that, although the monk vows to save all sentient beings, he does not seem to expect anyone to save him. The remainder of his vows are firm affirmations of self-help, and this is in line with the main trend of Mahāyāna philosophy and practice in all but the popular sects, which have put the Bodhisattvas in the position of saviours to be worshipped and relied upon almost exactly as the Christian relies upon the saving power of the Christ. Thus there would seem here to be a huge inconsistency between popular and philosophic Buddhism in the Mahāyāna school. The purpose of this study, however, is to show that this inconsistency is more apparent than real.

In modern China and Japan, by far the most popular form of Buddhism is a way of salvation by faith. It has attained its most radical and interesting development in Japan, but, as we have seen, its origins are in India, far back in the early days of Mahāyāna history. Most students of Buddhism are at a loss to find any true similarity of purpose between these popular cults and the highly self-reliant Buddhism of Gautama and philosophic Mahāyāna. They are generally regarded as a mere degeneration of the creed, a pure concession to unregenerate human nature, which demands supernatural beings to achieve what men are too lazy and too frightened to achieve for themselves. There is no doubt whatever that there are plenty of lazy and frightened human beings, and that an easy method of salvation by faith would naturally appeal to them, especially in the more extreme forms which altogether discount the efficacy of works. But there are other

---

* Suzuki, *Essays in Zen Buddhism*, Vol. 1, p. 323.

considerations, and from a certain point of view these very extreme forms become full of the deepest interest. Here let it be said that I owe this point of view to Dr D. T. Suzuki, who has recently made a particularly suggestive study of the philosophy and psychology underlying the Buddhism of faith.* But as yet he has made no thorough study of the psychological relations of the way of faith and the way of works.† This seems to me a very necessary line of inquiry, because I believe that Western students of Christian background can never really understand the Buddhism of works unless they approach it through the Buddhism of faith, itself so close to Christian belief.

Generally speaking, the Buddhism of faith is founded upon the *Sukhāvatīvyūha Sūtra*[85] which, so far as we know, was compiled some three hundred years after Gautama's death. The *Sukhāvatīvyūha* tells of one Dharmākara, who, in some immeasurably distant age, made forty-eight vows concerning the liberation of sentient beings. Before making these vows he had devoted himself, for an equally incomprehensible span of time, to innumerable good works, thus acquiring for himself a store of merit sufficient to give abundant aid to the whole world. But he renounced the reward of Highest Attainment due to him for these works, in order that he might preside over the Buddha-land (*buddha-kshetra*) of Sukhāvatī, the Western Paradise, and there watch over the world until all living beings had been born into his Pure Land and thus assured of final illumination. From then on he was known as the Budda Amitābha (Boundless Light) or Amitāyus (Eternal Life). The Chinese form of the name is O-mi-to-fo, and the Japanese is Amida, by which he is most generally known. In the second part of the *sūtra* it is declared that those who, in complete faith, turn towards Amida and repeat his name will be born after death into the Pure Land.

But it is hard to find in the sutra itself sufficient ground for some of the later interpretations put upon it, and it was not

---

* See his essay, 'The Shin Sect of Buddhism,' in the *Eastern Buddhist*, Vol. VII, nos. 3–4 (July, 1939).

† With the one exception of an essay on the Koan exercise and Nembutsu in *Essays in Zen Buddhism*, Vol. II, p. 115. This, however, does not relate to our present theme.

until the time of the Japanese Amidist, Shinran *Shōnin*,[86] that there evolved a real philosophy of salvation by pure faith. In the *sūtra*, Amida is able to transfer his merit to others because, according to the philosophy represented by the *Avataṁsaka Sūtra*,[87] each single atom contains in itself the whole universe. Therefore, what is done by one individual affects all others; if one man raises himself, he raises at the same time the whole universe. But here Amida is not the sole source of merit as the Christian God is the sole source of goodness. In early Mahāyāna the transference of merit (*parinā mana*) is a process that may operate mutually between all beings, and, though the individual is helped by sharing Amida's merit, he is yet able to acquire merit by his own unaided efforts, thus adding his own contribution to a universal store. Thus, in the *Sukhāvatīvyūha* the possibility of self-help is by no means excluded, and Amida remains one among many Buddhas; he is not yet raised to the position of sole source of light and life and made the personification *par excellence* of the final, supreme Reality. His distinction is just that he has made a particularly large contribution to the store of merit in which all may share, and has put his *buddha-kshetra* at the disposal of all who seek it in faith. There is still the difference between *in* faith and *by* faith.

The growth of a cult around Amida was supported by a prevalent view that in this dark cycle (*kali yuga*[88]) of history it is impossible for anyone to attain Enlightenment here on earth, although some progress might be made towards it. Hence the advantage of being born after death into a realm unencumbered by the snares and impurities of earthly life in its dark cycle. And here we are able to note either a rationalisation of pure laziness or else the growth of what Christianity calls the conviction of sin, the realisation of man's impotence apart from God. There is, moreover, a remarkable parallel to this gradual break from the legalistic, ethical self-reliance of Buddhism in St Paul's revolt against the Jewish law – and for similar psychological reasons. Thus, in the seventh chapter of his *Epistle to the Romans* St Paul writes, 'Nay, I had not known sin, but by the law: for I had not known lust, except the law had said, Thou shalt not covet. But sin, taking occasion by the commandment, wrought in me all manner of concupiscence.'

In just the same way there were Buddhists who found that the rigid morality of monkhood, with its insistence on the negative precept, served only to aggravate the inner desire for vice. They found themselves in a spiritual impasse, unable to change themselves because the self that had to be changed was also the self that had to do the changing – a feat as impossible as kissing one's own lips. Certainly a deep insight into the psychology of the *Laṅkāvatāra* and the *Avataṁsaka* would have shown a way out of the impasse, a way which many of the self-help school discovered (as will be shown) but which many more missed. The trouble was not in the peculiar difficulties of that psychology, but in the obstacles to be overcome before one could get a glimpse of it. It lay hidden under a vast metaphysical structure which those unendowed with considerable powers of intellect could not penetrate, sifting the grain from the chaff. And even then they might be left with a grain that mere intellect could not appreciate.

It was, therefore, not surprising that Far Eastern Buddhism revolted in two quite distinct ways from a combination of metaphysics and self-discipline that might have been endurable separately, but hardly together. The first revolution was against the metaphysics, and this gave birth to the Chinese school of Ch'an (Japanese, Zen) whose profound intuitive grasp of the essentials of Mahāyāna made its ponderous intellectualism unnecessary. Zen discovered a way of communicating the meaning without words, and for once the Mahāyāna became, in practice, a psychology and a religion as distinct from a philosophy. But in doctrine and discipline Zen remained essentially a way of self-help. The real revolution against absolute reliance on works and self-discipline came last of all, in Japan. Its leader was Shinran Shōnin (1173–1262), a disciple of the great Pure Land (Jōdo) teacher, Hōnen Shōnin.[89]

Prior to Shinran, the Pure Land school had been only partially a way of salvation by faith, and even today there are two distinct forms of Pure Land Buddhism in Japan – Jodo-shu and Shin-shu, the former still placing a considerable emphasis on the efficacy of works. Thus Japanese Buddhism is divided into the two great divisions of *jiriki* (self-power) and *tariki* (other-power), the way to Enlightenment by self-reliance and the way by reliance on the Original Vow (*pūrvapranidhā-*

na) of Amida. Under *jiriki* we include the Zen, Shingon, Tendai, Kegon, and Nichiren schools,[90] under *tariki* the Shin,* while Jōdo comes more or less in between, though with a list to *tariki*.

Shinran began his Buddhist studies at the famous [Tendai] community of Mount Hiei, near Kyoto, where he attained a rank of some importance. But, in spite of such attainments, he was overwhelmed by the moral problem, recognising that in his heart he was no better than the merest novice. He was deeply conscious of his humanity and keenly aware that mere self-discipline was wholly inadequate to deliver him from the bondage of *karma*. Trying to work out *karma* with self-discipline was like trying to pick up soap with wet fingers; the harder you grasp, the faster the soap slips away. (The analogy is mine, not Shinran's.) More than any of his predecessors, he felt conscious of the overwhelming bondage of earthly life in its present cycle, and, as a man of feeling rather than intellect, he was finally attracted to the *bhakti-mārga*[91] of Pure Land in the person of Hōnen Shōnin (1133–1212). To Hōnen he unburdened his mind, and was advised to put his trust in Amida and to abandon the monkish life by marrying. Subsequently, Shin priests have never vowed celibacy[92]. Shinran did not remain in the Pure Land school to which Hōnen belonged; he founded his own school to preserve the purity of a faith which he felt that ordinary Jōdo priests did not fully understand.

There are two principal features of Shinran's religion. The first is his conception of *pariṇāmana*, or merit transference. For him, Amida was the sole and original source of merit. Birth in the Pure Land was no longer a question of directing ones' own store of merit towards Amida – as a strictly accurate reading of the *Sukhāvatīvyūha* would indicate. Shinran turned the sense of the words, making birth in the Pure Land dependent on Amida's turning his store of merit towards the individual. The second feature arises from the first, and is the doctrine of pure faith. According to Shinran, no possible human merit could ever earn the tremendous right of birth in the Pure Land, and to imagine that so great a blessing could

---

* Actually the full name of the Shin sect is Jōdo-Shinshū, but I use Shin alone to avoid confusion with Jōdo.

ever be claimed as the just reward for human effort was to him the height of spiritual pride. In the light of Amida's infinite compassion (*karunā*), all beings, whether worms, demons, saints or sinners, were equally deserving of love, as if Amida would say, 'I have the same feeling for the high as for the low, for the just as for the unjust, for the virtuous as for the depraved, for those holding sectarian views and false opinions as for those whose beliefs are good and true.' Those who would put faith in Amida must therefore offer themselves to him just as they are, not imagining that the Pure Land can ever be a reward for human virtue. Amida's love is not to be earned; it is as much universal property as the sun, moon, and stars – something to be accepted with humility and gratitude, but never measured against human merit. Thus Shinran said:

> You are not to imagine that you would not be greeted by Amida in his Land because of your sinfulness. As ordinary beings you are endowed with all kinds of evil passions and destined to be sinful. Nor are you to imagine that you are assured of birth in the Pure Land because of your goodness. As long as your *jiriki* sense is holding you, you would never be welcomed to Amida's true Land of Recompense.[*]

All that is necessary is to give up forever any idea of attaining merit by one's own power, and then to have faith that one is accepted by the compassion of Amida from the very beginning, no matter what one's moral condition. One must even give up the idea that faith itself is achieved by self-power, for faith, too, is Amida's gift. Thus man as man becomes spiritually passive and, by Amida's grace, lets the eternal love flow into him and save him just as he is, symbolising his faith by repeating the *Nembutsu*, the formula *Namu Amida Butsu* (Hail, Amida the Buddha!). According to the *Anjin-ketsujo-sho*:

> To understand the Vow means to understand the Name, and to understand the Name is to understand that when Amida, by bringing to maturity his Vow and Virtue (or Deed) in the stead of all beings, effected their rebirth *even prior to their actual attainment*.[†] [italics mine]

[*]Suzuki, *Eastern Buddhist*, VII, p. 253.

[†]*Ibid.*, pp. 249 f. The *Anjin* is a work by an unknown author, see p. 248 n.

The fact that Amida himself is the sole source of grace is further stressed in this passage quoted from Shinran in the *Tannisho* (ch. VIII):

> The Nembutsu is non-practice and non-goodness for its devotee. It is non-practice because he does not practise it at his own discretion, and it is non-goodness because he does not create it at his own discretion. All is through Amida's power alone, not through our own power, which is in vain.[†]

At first sight it would seem that the efficacy of Shin depends upon certain supernatural sanctions of a kind that ordinary *jiriki* Buddhists would have great difficulty in believing. Such difficulties will always be experienced while Shin is studied in terms of its theology, for to anyone but a Christian it would seem the merest wishful thinking. For it amounts to this: that it is possible to become virtually a Buddha by pure faith. According to Suzuki:

> Being born in Amida's Land means no more than attaining enlightenment – the two terms are entirely synonymous. The ultimate end of the Shin life is enlightenment and not salvation.[‡]

Thus Shin devotees refer to their dead as *Mi hotoke*, or 'Honourable Buddhas.' But as soon as we examine the *psychology* of Shin as distinct from its *theology*, it becomes possible to relate it to the deepest experiences of Mahāyāna as expressed, for instance, in the *Lankāvatāra* and in some of the writings of Zen teachers, notably the *Lin-chi-lu* (Japanese, *Rinzai-roku*[93]). For we have to ask not what Shin believes, but what are the causes and results of that belief in terms of inner feeling, of those inner spiritual experiences which words alone can never fully communicate.

For example, let us take the case of any person acutely aware of his shortcomings, his fears, desires and passions, his lack of insight, and of any sense of union or harmony with the life of the universe – in fact, just such a man as Shinran. Then someone tells him that, if only he will open his eyes and see

[†]*The Tannisho*, translated by Ryukyo Fujimoto (Kyoto, 1932), p. 10.

[‡]Suzuki, *Eastern Buddhist*, VII, p. 264. By 'salvation' Suzuki means simply birth into Amida's Paradise after death, using the word in its eschatological rather than mystical sense. In the latter sense, salvation would be almost synonymous with Enlightenment.

it, he is a Buddha (is saved by Amida) just as he is, and that any attempt to make himself into a Buddha by his own ingenuity is rank spiritual pride. By adopting *jiriki* he is ignoring what is offered to him from the very beginning by the laws of the universe, and is trying to manufacture it for himself, so that he can take the credit for having earned it. When we say that a man is a Buddha just as he is, what does this mean in terms of psychology? It means that he is divine or *fundamentally acceptable* just as he is, whether saint or sinner, sage or fool. In Amidist language we would say that he is accepted for birth in the Pure Land by Amida's compassion, which is 'no respecter of persons' – in other words, that man is given the sense of freedom to be what he is at this and any moment, free to be both the highest and the lowest that is in him. This results at once in a great relaxation of psychic tension. All self-powered striving and contriving (*hakarai*) is set aside in the realisation that Buddhahood can neither be attained nor got rid of because it alone *is*. For, in Mahāyānist non-dualism, the Buddha principle, *Tathatā*, has no opposite and is the only Reality. And while the *Anjin* says that Amida effected our rebirth into the Pure Land 'even prior to actual attainment,' the *Laṅkāvatāra* says that, if they only realised it, all beings are in Nirvāna from the very beginning. Here are two doctrines, but one psychological experience.

In practical terms this experience is one of exhilarating spiritual freedom, amounting almost to the sanctification of ordinary, everyday life. For, when man feels free to be all of himself, there is a magic in every littlest act and thought. Thus the Zen poet, Hokoji,[94] says:

> How wondrous strange and how miraculous, this –
> I draw water and I carry fuel.

One cannot resist quoting Herbert[95] from the Christian standpoint:

> All things of Three partake;
> Nothing can be so mean
> But with this tincture 'For Thy Sake'
> Shall not grow bright and clean.

> A servant with this clause
> Makes drudgery divine;
> Who sweeps a room as for Thy laws
> Makes that and the action fine. . . .

221

This is the famous stone
That turneth all to gold,
For that which God doth touch and own
Can not for less be told.

This experience may be clarified and related more closely to the *jiriki* way by further consideration of the *Laṅkāvatāra* and the writings of certain Zen teachers. It will now be clear that Shinran's faith has a right to be considered as philosophic Mahāyāna expressed in rather colourful, symbolic imagery, even though it appears to be quite dualistic in conception. Philosophic Mahāyāna would not allow the dualism of self and other, man and Amida; but, if it is followed far enough, Shin arrives in experience at what Mahāyāna states in philosophy – although complete non-duality is actually beyond philosophic description. Furthermore, the *Laṅkāvatāra* insists that Saṃsāra, the world of life and death, *is* Nirvāna, and Saṃsāra just as it is, with all its pain and suffering. So, too, Shinran insists that we are saved by Amida just as we are, with all our imperfections. In other words, ordinary men are Buddhas just as they are, and, according to Hui-neng, of the Zen school, those whom we call Buddhas are simply those who understand this truth. Thus it is often remarked in Zen literature that one's 'ordinary thoughts' or 'everyday mind' is Enlightenment (*satori*). I quote a peculiarly suggestive passage from the *Rinzai-roku*:

> You must not be artful. Be your ordinary self . . . *You yourself as you are – that is Buddha Dharma.* I stand or I sit; I array myself or I eat; I sleep when I am fatigued. The ignoramus will deride me but the wise man will understand.[*]

And further on the text states:

> Wherefore it is said that the everyday mind is the true law.

Suzuki translates another passage from this text to the same effect; here Rinzai says:

> The truly religious man has nothing to do but go on with his life as he finds it in the various circumstances of this worldly

---

[*] I am much indebted to the Rev. Sokei-an Sasaki[97], Vice-Abbot of Mamman-ji, for allowing me to consult his unfinished translation of the *Rinzai-roku*, which is otherwise unavailable in English.

existence. He rises quietly in the morning, puts on his dress and goes out to his work. When he wants to walk, he walks; when he wants to sit, he sits. He has no hankering after Buddhahood, not the remotest thought of it. How is this possible? A wise man of old days says, If you strive after Buddhahood by any conscious contrivances, your Buddha is indeed the source of eternal transmigration.[†]

This kind of writing is very easily misunderstood, for one would naturally ask, 'If ordinary life is Nirvāna and ordinary thoughts are Enlightenment, whatever is Buddhism about, and what can it possibly teach us, other than to go on living exactly as we have lived before?' Before trying to answer this, we must quote two *mondo*, or Zen dialogues. The first is from the *Mu-mon-kan* (XIX)[96]:

> Joshu asked Nansen, 'What is the Tao?' 'Usual life,' answered Nansen, 'is the very Tao.' 'How can we accord with it?' 'If you *try* to accord with it, you will get away from it.'[‡]

The looks very much like pure *tariki* psychology. Then Suzuki gives the following from Bokuju (Mu-chou):

> A monk asked him, 'We have to dress and eat every day, and how can we escape from all that?' Bokuju replied, 'We dress, we eat.' 'I do not understand.' 'If you don't understand, put on your dress and eat your food.'[*]

Clearly the monk's question involves much more than mere dressing and eating, which stands for life in Samsāra as a whole – 'the trivial round, the common task.'

Applying philosophy to this more direct language, we find that the Zen teachers are demonstrating that Samsāra, just as it is, is Nirvāna, and that man, just as he is, is Buddha. Zen does not say so as a rule, because the terms, *Nirvāna* and *Buddha*, are concepts which do not move the soul deeply and lead easily to mere intellectualism. Zen wants us to *feel* non-duality, not just to think it, and therefore when we say, 'Nirvāna is Samsāra,' we are joining two things together that were never in need of being joined. For both Zen and Shin aim, in different ways, to effect a psychological or spiritual

[†] *Essays in Zen Buddhism*, II, p. 260.
[‡] I follow Sohaku Ogata's translation.
[*] *Essays in Zen Buddhism*, I, p. 12.

state that moves the whole being, not the head alone. They are trying to set us free within ourselves, and to make us at home with ourselves and with the universe in which we live. This freedom is known when we give up 'contriving' and accept ourselves as we are, but it does not seem to me that the experience can be effective unless there has first been a state of contriving and struggle. In Zen this is self-discipline; in Shin it is coming to an acute awareness of one's insufficiency through a previous attempt at self-discipline. It is difficult to see how the Shin experience could be fully appreciated unless, like Shinran, one had first tried the *jiriki* way. The danger of continuing in the *jiriki* way is that one may so easily become a victim of spiritual pride, expecting to *make* oneself into a Buddha; the danger of the *tariki* way is that the experience may come so easily that its true meaning is unseen and its force unfelt.[98]

Spiritual freedom, however, involves much more than 'going on living exactly as you have lived before.' It involves a particular kind of joyousness, or what the Buddhists term bliss (*ānanda*). It is the discovery that to accord with the universe, to express the Tao, one has but to live, and when this is fully understood it becomes possible to live one's life with a peculiar zest and abandon. There are no longer any obstacles to thinking and feeling; you may let your mind go in whatever direction it pleases, for all possible directions are acceptable, and you can feel free to abandon yourself to any of them. Nowhere is there any possibility of escape from the principle of non-duality, for 'you yourself as you are – that is Buddha Dharma.' In this state there can be no spiritual pride, for union or identity with the Buddha principle is not something achieved by man; it is achieved for him from the beginning of time, just as the sun has been set on high to give him light and life.

Yet, in the life of the spirit, it is much harder to receive than to give; it is often such a blow to human pride to have to accept from Amida, God, or life what it would be so much more distinctive to achieve for oneself. In Shin terms, we should say that the meaning of freedom is that you can think any kind of thought, be any kind of person, and do any kind of thing without ever being able to depart from Amida's all-embracing love and generosity. You are free to do as you like, and also as you don't like, to be free and to be bound, to be a sage and to be a fool. Nowhere are there any obstructions to spiritual activity. At the same time, there is an intense awareness of the joy of that activity; one feels impelled to exercise it and feel the ecstasy of its abandon, much as we imagine a bird must feel high up in space, free to soar up, to swoop down, to fly north, south, east, or west, to circle, climb, tumble, or hover. For 'the wind blowest where it listeth, and thou hearest the sound thereof, but canst not tell whence it cometh nor whither it goeth. Even so is everyone that is born of the spirit.' Or, in the more matter-of-fact language of a Zen teacher,

> There are no by-roads, no cross-roads here. All the year round the hills are fresh and green; east or west, in whichever direction, you may have a fine walk.[*]

There remains the moral problem. To a superficial understanding the freedom of non-duality seems to be an invitation to libertinism of the most flagrant kind. In terms of philosophy, the Mahāyāna sūtras state very frankly that the principle of non-duality is beyond good and evil, and that its attainment has no essential connection with morality. And morality here includes all kinds of works, both social and spiritual. Certainly the sūtras speak of *sila*, or morality, as one of the necessary stages, but sometimes it seems as if *sila* were advocated simply as a safeguard against misuse of the enormous, amoral power of supreme knowledge. Thus the *Laṅkāvatāra* says:

> In ultimate reality there is neither gradation nor continuous succession; [only] the truth of absolute solitude (*viviktadharma*) is taught here in which the discrimination of all the images is quieted . . . But [from the absolute point of view] the tenth stage is the first, and the first is the eighth; and the ninth is the seventh, and the seventh is the eighth . . . what gradation is there where imagelessness prevails?
>
> (Suzuki's translation, p. 186)

In yet another passage we read:

> Some day each and every one will be influenced by the wisdom

---

[*] Yeh-hsien, Suzuki, *The Training of the Zen Buddhist Monk* (Kyoto, 1934), p. 83.

and love of the Tathāgatas of Transformation to lay up a stock of merit and ascend the stages. But, if they only realised it, they are already in the Tathāgata's Nirvāna for, in Noble Wisdom, all things are in Nirvāna from the beginning.

An even stronger statement of the philosophy will be found in the *Saptasatikaprajñāpāramitā Sūtra*:

> O Sāriputra, to commit the offences is to achieve the inconceivables, to achieve the inconceivables is to produce Reality. And Reality is non-dual. Those beings endowed with the inconceivables can go neither to the heavens, nor to the evil paths, nor to Nirvāna. Those who commit the offences are not bound for the hells. Both the offences and the inconceivables are of Reality, and Reality is by nature non-dual . . . In the real Dharmadhātu (Realm of the Law) there is nothing good or bad, nothing high or low, nothing prior or posterior . . . Bodhi (Enlightenment) is the five offences and the five offences are Bodhi . . . If there is one who regards Bodhi as something attainable, something in which discipline is possible, that one commits self-arrogance.[*]

Here, besides an unequivocal statement of non-duality, there is again an example of *tariki* psychology, speaking of the arrogance of striving to attain Bodhi by discipline.

Mahāyāna does not disguise the fact that its wisdom is dangerous and we know that monks of the *jiriki* schools are subjected to rigid disciplines just to pre-condition them against abuse of knowledge, which is unfortunately a fairly frequent occurrence. But it would seem that such abuse is only possible when the experience of freedom is feebly appreciated or improperly understood. Oddly enough, although the experience itself and the thing experienced (*Tathatā*) is non-dual and beyond good and evil, the result of a truly deep experience is morality. Shinran speaks very strongly against those who make use of Amida's vow and then go on behaving as immorally as ever. He likens them to those who, because they have found an antidote to a poison, just go on taking it. But this is rather a negative way of looking at the problem. From the positive standpoint, Shin would say that Amida's compassion for us and all other beings, when realised, calls out a corresponding compassion in ourselves.

[*] *Saptasatika*, pp. 232–34. Suzuki, *Essays in Zen Buddhism*, Vol. II, pp. 251–252 n.

In terms of philosophic Mahāyāna, we should say that, having understood that we and all creatures are Buddhas, we therefore treat them with the reverence due to the Buddha principle.

A second factor which makes for morality is the gratitude felt for the freedom to be all of oneself, a gratitude so deep that men will often renounce some of that freedom as a thank-offering. Obviously there is more opportunity for this feeling of gratitude to grow when the Ultimate Reality is personalised in the form of Amida. From the philosophic standpoint there is no real ground for gratitude, because in non-duality there is neither giver nor receiver. Hence the danger of a merely philosophic understanding. But from the emotional standpoint there appears to be every reason for gratitude. In discovering freedom to be all of oneself one has a similar experience to the Christian forgiveness of sins; however black your soul, it is not outside the love of God, which is as omnipresent as God Himself, and in this connection it is worth citing a remarkable passage from the work of a Catholic theologian:[*]

> For we are never really outside of God nor He outside of us. He is more with us than we are with ourselves. The soul is less intimately with the body, than He is both in our bodies and souls. He as it were flows into us, or we are in Him as the fish in the sea. We use God, if we may dare to say so, whenever we make an act of our will, and when we proceed to execute a purpose. He has not merely given us clearness of head, tenderness of heart, and strength of limb, as gifts which we may use independently of Him when once He has conferred them upon us. *But He distinctly permits and actually concurs with every use of them* in thinking, loving or acting. This influx and concourse of God as theologians style it, ought to give us all our lives long the sensation of being in an awful sanctuary, where every sight and sound is one of worship. *It gives a peculiar and terrific character to acts of sin . . .* Everything is penetrated with God, while His inexpressible purity is all untainted, and His adorable simplicity unmingled with that which he so intimately pervades, enlightens, animates and sustains. Our commonest actions, our lightest recreations, the freedoms in which we most unbend – all these things take place and are transacted, not so much on the earth and in the air, as in the bosom of the omnipresent God. [Italics mine]

[*] F. W. Faber, *The Creator and the Creature* (Baltimore, 1853), p. 65.

There are important points in which Faber's words diverge from Mahāyāna philosophy, for, in Christianity, God is essentially Other. But, insofar as doctrine is a symbol of inner experience, I can see no important difference between the inner feeling suggested by Faber's words and the inner feeling of Mahāyāna Buddhism, especially in the Amidist cults. Thus the experience of freedom or Enlightenment is like discovering an immeasurably precious jewel in one's littlest acts and lowest thoughts. One discovers it where all jewels are first found – in the depths of the earth, or lying in the mud. Those who appreciate jewels do not leave them there; they lift them up from the depths, polish them, place them on velvet or set them in gold. This polishing and adornment is our symbol of morality, the expression of our joy and gratitude in realising that:

> This very earth is the Lotus Land of Purity,
> And this very body is the body of Buddha.*

It is here interesting to note that considerable importance is given to worship in the Zen school which, philosophically, is the most inconoclastic form of Buddhism. Perhaps there is a clue to the apparent inconsistency of worship and non-duality in the following incident from the *Hekigan-shu*:

> Huang-po (Japanese, Obaku)[99] stated, 'I simply worship Buddha. I ask Buddha for nothing. I ask Dharma for nothing. I ask Saṅgha for nothing.' Someone then said, 'You ask Buddha for nothing. You ask Dharma for nothing. You ask Saṅgha for nothing. What, then, is the use of your worship?' At which remark, Huang-po gave him a slap on the face!†

The Buddhist feeling of worship and gratitude is most notably expressed, however, in the Bodhisattva-ideal, based on a profound intuition of the basic unity of all creatures and things. Those who, having attained Enlightenment, do not become Bodhisattvas, helpers of the world, are termed *pratyeka-*

---

* From the *Song of Meditation* by Hakuin (1683–1768), one of the most famous Japanese Zen teachers.

† I follow the version of Kaiten Nukariya. Cf. his *Religion of the Samurai*, p. 96. Buddha, Dharma and Saṅgha (the Buddha, the Law and the Order of monks) are the Three Refuges (*tri-sarana*) taken by all Buddhists.

buddhas[100], which, in Mahāyāna philosophy, is almost a term of abuse. They are not willing to share their experience of freedom with their other selves, and, strictly speaking, Enlightenment is no Enlightenment unless it is shared and circulated. It is no one's property, and those who try to possess it for themselves do not understand it. Service, morality, and gratitude are our response *as men* for a gift to which we cannot respond *as Buddhas*. The Buddha-principle is beyond morality, but not so the human principle. From the standpoint of non-duality, these two principles are one; yet what is so often overlooked in the study of Mahāyāna is that from the *same* standpoint they are two. For non-duality excludes nothing; it contains both unity and diversity, one and many, identity and separation. Japanese Buddhism expresses this in the formula *byodo soku shabetsu, shabetsu soku byodo* – unity in diversity and diversity in unity. For this reason, philosophically, morally and spiritually, Buddhism is called the Middle Way.

PART FOUR:

Writings for

Buddhism in England
and
The Middle Way

FURTHER WRITINGS

———————————— • ————————————

THE PARABLE OF THE COW'S TAIL (1939)

A famous Zen *koan* asks: 'When a cow goes out of its enclosure to the edge of the abyss, its horns and head and its hoofs all pass through, but why can't the tail also pass?' Commenting on this, an old master says:

> If the cow runs it will fall into the trench;
> If it returns it will be butchered.
> That little tail
> Is a very strange thing.

In the quest for understanding of life there comes a time when everyone is confronted with 'that little tail' – the one tiny obstacle that stands in the way of complete fulfilment. We know that it is only a fraction of a hair's breadth in thickness, and yet we feel it as a million miles wide.

There is in mathematics an equation which, when drawn as a graph, appears as a curve that always nears but never touches a given line. At first the curve sweeps boldly towards that line, and the head, horns and hoofs go clean through the gate, but, just as the tail is about to pass, the curve straightens, leaving just a fraction of an inch between itself and the line. As it moves on, that fraction grows less and less, but still curve and line do not touch, and even though it be continued for a thousand miles or a thousand million miles the gap remains, though at each successive point it becomes smaller.

This curve represents the progress of human intellect towards Enlightenment, grasping more and more subtle nuances of meaning at each stage of its journey. It is as if we stood bound to illusion by a hair; to weaken it we split it with the knife of intellect, and split it again until its divisions become so fine that to make its cuts the mind must be sharpened indefinitely. Yet however much we split this hair, the sum total of its divisions is not a whit thinner than the original hair, for the more fragile we make our bonds, the more is their number.

Philosophically this condition is known as infinite regression, and psychologically it is that mad, exasperating state that must always precede the final experience of awakening. We can demonstrate this by the famous triangle puzzle of Mahayana philosophy. The two base points of this triangle represent the pairs of opposites which confront us at every moment of our experience – subject and object, I and you, positive and negative, something and nothing. The apex represents the relation, the meaning between them, the principle that gives them reality, the One as distinct from the Many. But the moment we set this One apart from the Many we create yet another pair of opposites, thus initiating a process which will continue indefinitely with ever-increasing complications.

In the *Bhagavad-Gita* we are told to stand aside from our thoughts and feelings, to realise that they are not the Self and learn that the Self is not the actor in actions but the Spectator of actions. But why not stand aside yet again from this first standing aside and perceive that it is not the Self that stands aside, for the Self performs no action? This, too, may continue for ever.

The first step in Buddhism is Right Motive, and to attain Enlightenment it is said that we must do away with selfish desire. But if we have selfish desire in the beginning, surely the desire to get rid of it is also selfish. We desire to be rid of our selfishness for a selfish reason, and again we may easily have a selfish reason for getting rid of the selfish reason for wanting to be selfless.

An even more fundamental illustration of the problem may be found in the simplest statement of Eastern philosophy, namely, that there is only one Reality and that all diversity is illusion. This is a statement which almost all students of Eastern wisdom take very much for granted: it is the first thing they learn but in fact it is about almost all there is to learn, for the rest is mere embroidery. It is the central principle of Vedanta, Mahayana and Taoism alike: there are no two principles in the universe; there is only Brahman, Tathata or Tao, and Enlightenment is just the realisation of one's identity with it. But here the complications begin and the cow's tail gets stuck in the gate, for the moment we think, 'This is Tao' or 'That is Tao' we immediately make a distinction between Tao and this and that. Furthermore, as soon as we think that the object of religion is to identify ourselves with the Tao, we create the dualism of the Tao and ourselves that are to be identified with it. Dualism appears the moment we make an assertion or a denial about anything; as soon as we think that This is That or This is not That we have the distinction between This and That. And even when we say that in Reality there are no distinctions, we have the opposition of Reality and distinctions.

Moreover, let us consider this problem: if there is only Tao, how can there be any divergence from it? If there is only one Reality, our thoughts, enlightened or unenlightened, must be it. There can be no distinction between Reality and illusion if there is only Reality. Whether you can concentrate your thoughts or not, whether they are of compassion or hatred, whether you are thinking about Buddhism or chewing your nails, you cannot by any means diverge from the Tao. You may love life or you may loathe it, yet your loving and loathing are themselves manifestations of life. If you seek union with Reality your very seeking is Reality, and how can you say that you have ever lost union?

To put it in another way: it is said that to be enlightened we must live in the eternal. Now, that infinitely small and therefore infinitely great point of time which is called the present moment. The universe exists only in that moment, and it is said that the wise man moves with it, clinging neither to the past nor to the future, making his mind like the mirror that reflects everything instantly as it comes before it, yet making no effort to retain the reflection when the object is removed.

'The perfect man,' says Chuang-tzu, 'employs his mind as a mirror. It grasps nothing; it refuses nothing. It receives, but does not keep.'

Yet, when the matter is carefully considered, we find that this is a description, not of what we should do, but of what we cannot help doing in any case. For whether we think of the past or the future, and whatever we think about either of them, our thoughts exist in and partake of the eternal Now;

otherwise they would not exist at all. We cannot separate ourselves from this present moment, and if we imagine that Enlightenment consists simply in living in the present, in thinking only about what is going on now, we find ourselves in the dualism of now and then. The point is that we can only think of what is going on now, even if we are thinking of the past or the future. For our thoughts about past and future are going on now, and we are thinking them. There is only one Reality![101]

Therefore it will be asked: 'Is Enlightenment simply to live and think like any ignorant fool, not bothering about philosophy, mysticism or morality, knowing that whatever you do you cannot get out of harmony with the Tao?'

If we answer, 'Yes,' we assert; if we say, 'No,' we deny. The tail is still caught in the gate. But if you think that you will attain Enlightenment by living like an ignorant fool, you are still caught in the dualism of the *you* that must attain *Enlightenment*. Indeed, there is no prescription for Enlightenment, for as soon as we start saying that it is this or it is not this, we try to make two realities in the universe instead of one. In fact, you can think about philosophy, or about eating and drinking, you can love mankind, you can hate it, you can do as you like, you can do as you don't like, you can discipline yourself, you can run wild, you can seek wisdom, you can ignore it, but you can't diverge from the Tao, for everything, anything and nothing is Tao.

Is it? Beware of that 'is.' The sting is in the tail.

———————————— • ————————————

THE SECOND IMMORTAL (1940)

Once upon a time there was a man who lived much as other men live. He had a wife and three children and a shop in the Street of Happy Sparrows where he sold cakes, vegetables and sweet pickles. He rose at dawn and went to bed at sunset; he ate rice three times a day; he smoked two pipes of tobacco in the hour; he talked of buying and selling with his neighbours; he picked his teeth after eating and had his wife scratch his back in the noonday heat. In spring he watched the young grass peeping out from behind the stones; in summer he lifted an eye at the lazy clouds; in autumn he followed the leaves that danced in the wind; and in winter he woke to see the tracks of birds in the snow. And in all seasons, between talking and smoking and selling cakes, he chewed water-melon seeds and amused himself by plaiting straw ropes round his toes.

One day, when he went to burn incense at the Temple of Amiable Dragons, his friend the priest approached him, saying: 'You are getting on in years and your eldest son is of an age to take care of your shop. It would not be proper for a man such as you to spend the rest of your days in empty activities, for you will go to the grave as insignificantly as old refuse is flung into the river.'

'Such being the lot of man,' answered the cakeseller, 'how can I complain?'

'So many are mere vegetables.' said the priest. 'But if you are willing to take the trouble you can find yourself a place among the Immortals.'

'And who,' asked the cakeseller, 'are the Immortals?'

'They are those who do not depend on their own power to keep themselves alive. Man is a small creature whose life is like a snowflake. But the wind blows on for ever; the sun and moon eternally maintain their courses and the rivers have flowed since time began. The Immortals are they who learn the secrets of these things; instead of relying on their own resources, they allow themselves to be maintained and directed by that which maintains and directs the wind, the sun, the moon and the rivers.'

'But how can one become an Immortal?'

'You will have to find an Immortal to teach you,' said the priest. 'I am not wise enough.'

'Well,' said the cakeseller. 'I must find one. But there are so many people in the world, and how can one recognise an Immortal?'

'That should not be difficult,' answered the priest. 'It is said that their breath is operated by the wind; that the sun gives them the light of the right eye and the moon of the left; that their shouting is assisted by the thunder, their whispering by the murmuring waves and their laughter by the mountain streams. The earth, it is said, maintains their flesh, while their bones and vital juices are supplied by the rocks and the rains. Their thoughts and moods are directed by the coming and going of the seasons and the elements, and having such mighty ones as the movers of all their functions they are said to be free from all the ordinary limitations and more powerful even than the gods.'

'Such a strange being,' observed the cakeseller, 'should be easy to recognise,' and immediately he returned home, set his affairs in order, instructing his eldest son in the care of the shop, and the same evening left the city on his journey in search of an Immortal.

After many weeks upon the road he came to a hut inhabited by an ancient personage of severe aspect who seemed to him to be at least two hundred years old. His white beard caressed the upper part of his shoes and the top of his head glistened like the elbows of an old coat. Noticing his venerable appearance, and also the many volumes of the classics with which he was surrounded, the cakeseller at once approached him and begged for instruction, thinking that surely this must be an Immortal, for he was the most aged person he had ever seen.

'It is a long time,' said the venerable one, 'since my advice was asked upon anything, for this is a dissolute age, and the mastery of life is not understood by those who fail to observe the forty-eight precepts and fail to avoid the ninety-one indiscretions. Sit down, and I will instruct you in the words of the ancient sages.'

Whereupon he began to read from the classics, and the cakeseller sat and listened until the sun went down. And on the following day he read yet more, and again on the next day and the next and the next, and so on, until the cakeseller almost lost count of time. And he was instructed and made to discipline himself in the eight virtuous deeds, the twenty-nine laudable thoughts, the one hundred and eight ceremonial observances, the forty-two marks of superior character, the thirty-seven acts of filial piety and the four hundred and three propitiations of ill-disposed spirits. And all the while the cakeseller grew in righteousness and high-minded conduct, and was disposed to believing himself well on the way to immortality. But one day he remembered suddenly that he had now been with the venerable scholar for some twenty years; the days of his life were growing shorter and yet he knew nothing of the secrets of sun, moon, rivers, wind and the elements. At this he was filled with agitation, and in the night set out upon the road again.

After some weeks of wandering in the mountains he came upon a cave where a strange being sat at the entrance. His limbs were like the trunk of a gnarled pine, his hair like wisps of smoke drifting on the wind and his eyes staring and fiery like those of a snake. Duly impressed, the cakeseller again begged for instruction.

'Immortals,' said this person, 'have the wind as their breath, and to learn this you must cultivate the art of the Expansive Lungs. But this cannot be learnt by such as you who chew melon seeds and smoke two pipes an hour and eat three meals a day. If you would have the wind as your breath, you must eat but one grain of rice in a day and drink one cup of water. You must clear the smoke from your windpipe, and learn to breathe but twice in a day. Only then will your lungs be able to contain the wind.'

So the cakeseller sat down at the mouth of the cave, ate but one grain of rice and drank but one cup of water a day. And under the instructions of the sage he was made to lessen and lessen the speed of his breath till he thought his eyes would proceed from their sockets and the drums of his ears disturb all the birds of the forest with their bursting. But for many years he practised until he did indeed breathe but twice a day, at the end of which he saw that his body was as a skeleton hung with skin as spiders' webs cover the branches of a bush, and with a display of exceedingly ill-regulated conduct he fled from the cave.

For many more months he searched for an instructor, and finding none began to wonder whether he had perhaps not persevered enough with his teacher. So he began to make his way back to the mountains. On the way he caught up with an itinerant trader who carried a pole over his shoulder to which was attached a bundle containing an assortment of pots, beads, combs, dolls, kitchen utensils, writing materials, seeds, scissors, and sticks of incense. For a while they kept each other company, conversing on idle matters such as the state of the crops, the best ways of driving out fleas, the pleasures of soft rainfall and the various kinds of charcoal useful for making fires. At length the cakeseller told the trader of his desire to find an Immortal who could instruct him and asked whether he knew of any such person.

'Have a melon-seed,' said the trader, offering him a handful.

'Indeed, I regret I cannot eat melon-seed,' cried the cakeseller, 'for if I chew them it will take away my power of Expansive Lungs.'

The trader shrugged his shoulders, and for a while they walked on in silence, broken only by the cracking of melon-seeds between the trader's teeth – a sound which filled the cakeseller with a variety of emotions. On the one hand he began to feel an urge to break his discipline, and once more feel that eminently satisfying crack of seeds between the teeth; on the other he felt he should persist in his search and again ask the trader about the Immortals. Perhaps, he thought, the trader had never heard of Immortals, but it might be that he would recognise such beings if he knew what they were like.

'I was wondering,' said the cakeseller, 'whether in your journeyings you have happened to meet with anyone of strange and powerful aspect, whose breath is operated by the wind, whose right and left eyes are given light by the sun and moon respectively, whose shouting is assisted by the thunder, whispering by the murmuring waves and laughter by the mountain streams; whose flesh is maintained by the earth, whose bones and vital juices are supplied by the rocks and the rains, and whose thoughts and moods are directed by the coming and going of the seasons and the elements.'

'Oh yes,' answered the trader, 'I have seen many such beings. Why, I believe that two of them are making their way along this road.'

'What!' cried the cakeseller. 'On this very road? Let us hurry so that we can catch up with them!'

And so they increased their pace, and when night fell they did not pause to rest, for the cakeseller, persuaded the trader that it would be well to gain upon them by a night's journey. At sunrise they found themselves on the top of a hill from which they could see the road ahead for many miles, but as they looked down upon it there was no one anywhere to be seen.

'It may be,' said the cakeseller, 'that we overtook them during the night.'

Whereat they looked behind, and again a view of many miles showed them an empty road. At this the cakeseller was very sad.

'They must have taken a side-track into the mountains,' he said, 'for it seems that we are the only people on this road.'

'Oh,' said the trader, 'I forgot to tell you. When they go about in pairs one of them is always invisible. You are looking for two men travelling together. Let us look again.'

Once more the cakeseller gazed up the road and down the road, but saw no other man upon it than his companion, the trader.

'No,' sighed the cakeseller, 'we have missed them. I see neither two nor one.'

'Are you sure?' replied the trader. 'I really believe I can see one. Look again.'

'No,' said the cakeseller, 'I see no man on the road at all, excepting yourself.'

At this the trader began to laugh, and as he laughed it seemed to the cakeseller that his laughter was like the sound of a mountain stream.

'You!' he exclaimed. 'Are you an Immortal? But you look like an ordinary man!'

'Indeed,' laughed the trader, 'I must confess it. You see, I have to go about in disguise, for otherwise I should be followed all over the place, which would be most inconvenient.'

'But your invisible companion,' asked the cakeseller, 'is he also here? Does he look like an Immortal? Describe him to me.'

'Surely,' answered the trader. 'His breathing is operated by the wind but you do not notice it; the light of his right and left eyes is given by the sun and moon, but you do not see it; his shouting is of the thunder, his whispering of the waves and his laughter of the mountain streams, but you do not hear it; his flesh is maintained by the earth, and his bones and vital juices by the rocks and rains, but you do not understand it; his thoughts and moods are directed by the coming and going of the seasons and the elements, but you are not aware of it. He does not rely on his own resources; he allows himself to be maintained and directed by that which maintains and directs

241

the wind, the sun, the moon and the rivers, but you do not recognise it.'

'Marvellous indeed must he be to look upon!' exclaimed the cakeseller. 'Please ask him to become visible so that I can understand his secrets.'

'You had better ask yourself,' replied the trader. 'Only you have the power to make him visible. There is a magic by which you can make him appear.'

'Tell me about it.'

'The magic,' answered the trader, 'is this: in spring to watch the young grass peeping out between the stones; in summer to lift an eye at the lazy clouds; in autumn to follow the leaves that dance in the wind; in winter to wake and find the tracks of birds in the snow. To rise at dawn and go to sleep at sunset; to eat rice three times in a day; to talk of buying and selling with one's neighbours; to chew the seeds of water-melon and to plait straw ropes around the toes.'

And at this the cakeseller discovered the second Immortal.

———————————— • ————————————

THE MYSTERY OF SHIN (1940)

There is a certain form of Buddhism which has always been a puzzle to Western Buddhists or to those of us who value the teachings of Gautama. In Japan it is known as Shin, but Shin is actually a branch of a whole school of Buddhist thought known both in China and Japan as the Pure Land School.[102] In the Far East this school is, in numbers, far superior to any other – a superiority which many people ascribe simply to its undoubtedly accommodating and comfortable gospel, so nearly resembling what some consider the most ridiculous element of Christianity. For the Pure Land School is a way of salvation by faith in the saving power of the Buddha Amitabha (Ch., *O-mi-to-fo*; Jap., *Amida*), the personification of Boundless Light whose cult originates in the two *Sukhavativyuha* sutras. The Shin sect is purely Japanese, and is of particular interest because it presents the Pure Land faith in its most extreme form. Its immediate founder was Shinran Shonin (1173–1262)[103] and his special contribution to Pure Land doctrine was the laying of the entire emphasis on faith as distinct from works as the means of salvation.

This article is not intended, however, as an historical outline of the faith nor as an exhaustive study of its relations with other forms of Buddhism. Its purpose is to suggest a way of approach to Pure Land teaching, which reveals a profundity which few Western students have suspected. I would even go so far as to say that in the doctrine and practice of the Shin sect we have a key to the central secret of Buddhism. Actually, Buddhism has no secrets, just as there is no secret about great artistry, for the mysteries of life are quite open to those who have eyes to see them. And it is true, of course, that Shin presents that 'secret' in highly symbolical form. But this very symbolism blinds us to its tremendous value – a value which I doubt if I should have guessed if it had not been for a way of approach to Shin suggested by Dr D. T. Suzuki. (See Vol. 2 of his *Essays in Zen*, 'Passivity in the Buddhist Life,' also his article on Shin in Vol. 7, Nos. 3–4 of the *Eastern Buddhist*.)[104] As yet, however, Suzuki has not carried this way of approach very far in relating Shin to other forms of Buddhism; he has, in fact, done no more than describe the inner meaning of Shin quite objectively and without comment.

The principle of this way of approach to Shin is this: to regard religious doctrine just as the symbolical expression of a psychological or spiritual experience. In other words, we have to ask, not, 'What does Shin believe?' but 'What are the causes and results of this belief in terms of inner feeling, in terms of those experiences which cannot directly be described in words?' Then we have to enquire into the relation of that feeling to the feelings which underlie wholly different systems of doctrine. Doctrines are as different as languages. Thus we have the words *boy, garçon, ragazzo, puer* – all as different as they could be, but all describing the single experience or being of a male child. Possibly we have a similar situation in religious symbolism and experience. All religious experiences are not absolutely identical; after all, there are certain differences between English, French, Italian and Roman boys, but the words are much more unlike than the realities. This is no means of explaining away the differences between religions, because if any two religious experiences are utterly different our method will soon discover the divergence. But there is reason to believe that the Shin way of salvation by faith is not so far from Zen, for instance, as a mere comparison of doctrines might make us believe.

There are two main forms of Mahayana Buddhism, called in Japanese *jiriki* and *tariki*. *Jiriki* means 'self-power' or the way to Enlightenment by total reliance on one's own efforts. *Tariki* is 'other-power,' or the way to Enlightenment through the help or grace of some power which is symbolized by a great Buddha or Bodhisattva. Generally speaking, Zen is regarded as the extreme of *jiriki* and Shin as the extreme of *tariki*. But, proverbially, there is a point where extremes meet, not in the middle but at the ends. This point is 'infinity,' the Goal, Nirvana. It may be even closer than that. In general, Buddhism is supposed to be a *jiriki* way of life, for, according to Gautama, we are advised to be lamps to ourselves, a refuge unto ourselves and to take to ourselves no other refuge. Mrs Rhys Davids' translation of this passage, however, suggests a subtle difference, for she would render 'yourselves' as 'the Self,' and in Hindu terminology the Self, *Atman*, is Brahman, the ultimate and only Reality. Obviously there is not much difference between Brahman and Amitabha, whose other name, Amitayus, means 'Eternal Life'. It would be a mistake to be misled by popular anthropomorphism to dismiss the cult of Amitabha as superstition because, for mass consumption, the Eternal Principle is dressed up in personal imagery. Such imagery, however, is yet another of Mahayana's many devices (*upaya*) for conveying a deep experience, and so long as the experience is conveyed we need not grumble about the devices. If you are sick, the main thing is that you should be healed, and the good doctor is he that can cure you whether his method be surgery, osteopathy, psychotherapy, radiology, homoeopathy or herbalism. And if Amitabha is but another name for that Principle which the more philosophically-minded have called Brahman, Tathata and Tao, what is the real meaning of Shin Buddhism?

First, we must state the general, exoteric doctrine of Shin. In some immeasurably distant age the Buddha Amitabha vowed that he would never enter the final Enlightenment until all 'sentient beings' were ready to enter it with him. Now Amitabha presides over the Western Paradise of Sukhavati, the Pure Land, where the attainment of Enlightenment is not set about with the myriad obstacles which we find here on earth. Therefore, Amitabha promised that whoever put faith in his vow should be born after death into his Pure Land, wherein eventual Enlightenment would be a relatively simple matter. Thus Shin devotees refer to their dead as '*O hotoke,*' or 'Honourable Buddhas.'

On the face of it, putting faith in this vow involves very little. Shinran insists that faith, and faith alone, is involved; that Amitabha's salvation cannot possibly be earned by works because no human being can ever expect to be virtuous enough to claim this tremendous reward as a right. He therefore states explicitly that if you put faith in Amitabha you are saved *as you are*, whether you be criminal, lunatic, murderer, drunkard, philosopher or saint [105]. For Amitabha says, 'I have the same feeling for the high as for the low, for the just as for the unjust, for the virtuous as for the depraved, for those holding sectarian views and false opinions as for those whose beliefs are good and true.' To him (or It) all beings are Buddhas and, therefore, call forth *karuna*, the infinite compassion which knows no pride of rank or merit. Everyone can share in this compassion and its results; it is offered as freely to the fool as to the sage and, therefore, it is impossible to *earn* it. You already have it, if you will only stretch out your hand and take it.

But there are those who feel that they have no right to it and cannot share in it until they have done something to make themselves worthy of it. This, according to Shinran, is spiritual pride. It is one thing to feel unworthy of it, but quite another to imagine that by our own efforts we can claim it as our desert. Enlightenment cannot be earned because it cannot belong to anyone; it is universal property, like the sun, moon and stars, which shine alike for saint and sinner. We may not feel worthy to behold their brilliance and their ordered rhythm, but we have them in spite of ourselves. You may be moved to virtue out of gratitude for having them, but only a lunatic would refuse to look at the skies until he has mastered all the precepts of Buddhism. How much merit could ever deserve the stars? Are they to be valued in terms of morality? Only a morbid interest in self-righteousness could ever measure human merit against the eternal, and in pride imagine that the gift of stars depended on personal sanctity.

Of course, it sounds very easy. It would be delightful indeed to have Enlightenment or even birth in the Pure Land as readily available as the heavenly bodies. But is this true in reality? Furthermore, grubs and worms cannot see the stars; we see them only because we have grown to be men, and it may be that we must grow to be Buddhas before we can see Enlightenment. But what is the process of growing? Must it be performed by our own, unaided efforts, or is there another way?

The best answer is to study the psychological process which the practice of Shin involves. Let us take the case of an ordinary human being, painfully aware of a hundred shortcomings, of his vices, actual and potential, of his ignorance, his lack of wisdom and his absence of the sense of harmony with life. Suddenly he is informed that, if only he will open his eyes and see, if only he will have faith, he is virtually a Buddha. And this 'he' does not mean some remote, mysterious 'Higher Self'; it means himself as he is, with all his ignorance and all his faults. For Amitabha has accepted that self as a Buddha, worthy to enter the Pure Land. Shorn of all doctrinal symbolism, this means that the man is invited to accept himself as he is, for in terms of psychological experience such words as 'Buddha', 'God', 'Brahman' and 'Tao' mean that which is ultimately and fundamentally acceptable. Thus, when the Zen teacher says that your 'everyday mind' is Buddha (cf. *Rinzai-roku*[106]) or that ordinary thoughts are *satori*[107], the psychologist would interpret this as indicating that your ordinary state of mind, whatever its nature, is wholly acceptable. In other words, you are absolutely free to think your usual thoughts, absolutely free to be what you are at any moment, absolutely free to be all of yourself, your depths as well as your heights. To use the actual words of Zen master Rinzai, 'You must not be artful. Be your ordinary self. . . . You yourself as you are – that is the Buddha Dharma. I stand or I sit; I array myself or I eat; I sleep when I am fatigued. The ignoramus will deride me but the wise man will understand.'*

Almost every psychologist knows the enormous sense of

---

* From a tentative translation by the Ven. Sokei-an Sasaki, Abbot of Jofuku-in.[108]

release and inner freedom brought about by this kind of acceptance. Two factors are involved: first, a relaxation and loosening of all the tension's of one's being so that there is a sense of being utterly at ease with oneself and with the world; and, second, a new feeling of zest for life, an urge to use and exercise this new-found freedom for the pure joy of feeling its movement.

But is this sense of freedom the same as Enlightenment in the Buddhist meaning of the word? Shin makes a distinction between birth into the Pure Land and final Enlightenment, and I believe that the former represents this inner freedom. Yet we can find the same psychological process at work in many other forms of Buddhism and Oriental philosophy. After all, most forms of Oriental philosophy are little more than embroidery upon one central fact – *Tat Tvam asi*, THAT art thou.' There is but one Reality; all else is *maya*; Brahman, Buddha-nature, Tao alone exists. Strangely enough, this means exactly what it says. Your own self-nature is Buddha-nature; you cannot *make* yourself into a Buddha, nor can you ever be anything else; open your eyes and see it! The challenge of this tremendous gospel is so often refused by removing Buddha-nature to the safe and nebulous distance of a 'Higher Self' and by constant harping on the appalling dangers of identifying the 'higher' self with the 'lower.' Naturally, there is danger is every spiritual enterprise, and there is no power in the universe which cannot be used either for good or evil. This is especially true of spiritual freedom, for a merely intellectual, *unfeeling* comprehension of *Tat tvam asi* is easily made the sanction for unbridled licentiousness. For if we are indeed THAT whether we are saints or sinners, why worry with morality?

But as soon as that freedom is felt, as soon as it becomes more than head-understanding, morality becomes a necessary consequence, even though THAT itself is beyond good and evil. The experience of this freedom arouses a sense of deep gratitude, which expresses itself in morality and love. It is as if you had discovered a priceless gem lying buried in the deepest slime of your own being. If you appreciate that gem, you lift it out of the slime and set it in gold. But all too often the constant harping on the dangers of this understanding is simply the rationalization of a pride which

247

will not *accept*. In the spiritual realm it is much harder to receive than to give. Pride makes it difficult for us to accept what has been achieved for us since the beginning of time; we would much rather manufacture it for ourselves and take the credit, and so we remain blind to that which stands right before our eyes. In the words of the *Lankavatara Sutra*[109], 'But, if they only realised it, they are already in the Tathagata's Nirvana, for, in Noble Wisdom, all things are in Nirvana from the very beginning.' And this, too, means just what it says.

What, then, is the difference between *jiriki* and *tariki*, between Enlightenment by one's own efforts and Enlightenment by faith? Make no mistake – Shin does *not* state that by faith in Amitabha we can be absolved from the consequence of foolish acts; it is no escape from *karma*. We continue to live in the midst of our *karma*, yet in our hearts rise above it, learning that 'Nirvana and Samsara's world of life and death are aspects of the same thing.' For faith in Amitabha is the faith that, from the beginning, self-nature is Buddha-nature – a fact achieved by universal law, not by personal effort. In the end, the *jiriki* way comes to this same experience.

Thus in the Zen text *Mu-mon-kan*[110] Joshu asks Nansen, 'What is Tao?'

'Ordinary life,' answers Nansen, 'is the very Tao.'

'How does one get into accord with it?'

'If you try to accord with it, you get away from it,' is Nansen's reply, which is the purest *tariki* psychology.

The particular advantage of the *jiriki* way is that, after so much effort, the final *tariki* experience comes with a feeling of sudden, overwhelming and intense relief. Its disadvantage is the pitfall of pride. On the other hand, with *tariki* alone the experience may come too easily and thus be insufficiently appreciated. Hence the wisdom of the middle way. Furthermore, if one gets lost in the symbolism of *tariki*, the experience may be superficial; as Jung would say, the experience is provisional rather than actual.

Morality, of course, is the 'hub' of the problem, but it should be understood that morality can no more create wisdom than the tail can wag the dog. Morality without wisdom (or spiritual freedom) is imitation of the sage's external behaviour; it is not really genuine; it is an act of duty, not of love. True morality is the expression of love and is thus the consequence rather than the cause of wisdom. It is the logical expression of that creative energy which is released within us when we realise with joy and gratitude that:

> This very earth is the Lotus Land of Purity,
> And this very body is the body of Buddha.

———————————— • ————————————

THE BUDDHIST WAY OF LIFE (1941)

For a Western man, Buddhism is a wonderful eye-opener – in many senses. Firstly, it reveals the meaning of his own religion, Christianity,[111] because it enables him to find the true psychology of spiritual experience which Christianity has concealed in historical and theological doctrines. Buddhism is the only psychological religion in the world, because it sets out the conditions of this experience free from symbolism. Secondly, in the form of Zen, it reveals the meaning of ordinary life and ordinary experience. For who would think that walking down the street, watching the kettle boil, or feeling angry was anything but a series of limitations imposed by physical existence? And yet Zen Buddhism points to such common experiences as these in answer to the most profound questions about the universe. This is because most religions have split the universe in two – God and the world, spiritual and material, higher and lower, Reality and Illusion. Even when they try to unite these opposites in consciousness, they still presuppose their separateness. But to unite things which are already joined is like trying to kiss your own lips.

Buddhism breaks up this vicious circle of lip kissing, or looking for sight with wide-open eyes, and shows us the unity of Nirvana and Samsara, eternity and time, simply by demonstrating the living fact. Comments are unnecessary and often misleading, for they are like painting the reflection on a mirror or putting legs on a snake. As the great religion of non-duality, Buddhism kicks us out of the vicious circle of trying to lift ourselves up by our own belts, and shows us that our present experience is already united with Buddha-experience, that all things demonstrate their one-ness by being multiple and diverse.

Thus a flower or an old tin can demonstrates eternal truth

neither by symbolism, nor by illusory aspect of the Infinite – but by being a flower or an old tin can. Buddha taught the great doctrine of *anatta*,[112] which means that things are as they are, unique, individual and impermanent, having no mysterious essential and in-dwelling immortal self. This is what is so excellent about them. You clap your hands, and where does the sound go? If it stayed, it would not be a clap; if things did not end, they would not have a beginning, and thus would never exist. When we try to perpetuate them, we kill them; when we try to unite the temporal with the eternal, we destroy it. What is the need? Eternity is in the moment, not in everlastingness. He knows eternity who lets the moment go, who lets it be momentary, who lets himself be mortal and limited in time and space.

Try as we may, we cannot prevent ourselves from doing this, and therefore Buddhism teaches that we are already in Nirvana in spite of ourselves.

Surely this is excellent news.

———————— • ————————

TOMORROW NEVER COMES (1941)

When we say that all things in the universe are the creative activity of God, this is really like putting legs on a snake or painting the reflection on a mirror. It is not to be compared to seeing that activity as it is, although we say that it is God's activity to draw attention to it in a particular way. But the trouble is that people spend so much energy looking for the God that they fail to see the activity, which is surely a sad state of affairs. What is this activity? The rivers flow; the flowers bloom; you walk down the street. Really we should need to say no more than this, but it is sometimes called the activity of God to point out a certain understanding to the sort of person who might retort, 'The rivers flow; the flowers bloom; you walk down the street – so what?'

So what? Well, what else are you looking for? Here is someone who eats out the grocer's store and still complains that he is starving. But the word and concept *God*, *Brahman*, *Tao* or what you will, was really introduced for such unappreciative stomachs. It is a way of emphasizing actual life to draw attention to it in much the same way as we underline words or put them in italics. Thus we call the universe the activity of God to induce the so-whatter to pay some attention and reverence to it, because he always bolts his life instead of rolling it appreciatively round his tongue. He always thinks of the second and third pieces of cake while he is eating the first, and thus is never satisfied with any of them, and ends up with a thoroughly disordered digestion. This is called the vicious circle of having lunch for breakfast, or living for your future. But tomorrow never comes.

The snow is falling on the window-sill. Is this the activity of God? Maybe. But if anyone watches it *in order* to see God he will surely be disappointed. 'No man hath seen God.' No, and in looking for God he may fail to see the snow. 'Thou art Brahman!' But if you look in yourself *in order* to find Brahman, you will be very disappointed indeed. Yet all this trouble has started because people have taken a simple device much too far. The idea of God is a finger pointing the way to Reality, but when people try to join God and Reality, to identify the one with the other, to find the former in the latter, they are trying to join together two things that were never in need of being joined. This is like trying to make the eyes see themselves.

Yet how do we arrive at the state where to watch the snow falling is so much one with God that we need no more introduce God than put red paint on the roses? Whence all this hurry to arrive at a state? Are you not already watching the snow? Are you not already face-to-face with the eternal mystery? Take it easy for a while; just watch the snow falling or the kettle boiling, and not so much hurry. What's wrong with watching the snow or the kettle that anyone should want to arrive at a state? It is possibly that any ordinary moron can do this just as well, and why not go him one better? How splendid is his ignorance! Like the stones, the grass and the wind, he has Enlightenment without knowing it, and cannot appreciate his good fortune. Yet he, too, is a so-whatter, for he asks 'So what?' when others go questing for God. He is not free to watch the snow because he can do nothing else, and especially because he does not appreciate his freedom.

But you are free to abandon yourself to actual life and to know that living in God is another name for this abandonment, for watching the snow and walking down the street. And you are free not only because you have once been a so-whatter, but also because you have been living in this abandonment all the time, though without knowing it. If you had actually to get into it, to arrive at a state of abandonment where you had not previously been, you would not be free, for this would involve *going somehwere*, arriving tomorrow at a place where you were not yesterday. And tomorrow never comes.

You say you do not feel this abandonment right now. What do you expect to feel? It is not *a* feeling; it is feeling. It is not *a* thought; it is thinking. If it were a particular thought or feeling there could be coming into it and going out of it; but God is One and all-inclusive, and here there can be neither coming nor going, inside or outside. More than this, the great abandonment of Enlightenment does not depend even on feeling and thinking, consciousness or unconsciousness, living or dying. As the verse says:

> This you can not describe, nor paint,
> Nor yet admire, nor feel.
> It is your real self, that has no hiding-place.
> Destroy the universe, and it remains.[113]

No, you can't feel IT – but then how can you know anything about it at all? Because you can *use* it and feel its use, just as 'the wind bloweth where it listeth, and thou hearest the sound thereof but canst not tell whence it cometh nor whither it goeth.' What is it like to feel its use? This is told in another verse:

> Sudden the cold airs swing.
> Alone, aloud,
> A verse of bells takes wing.
> And flies with the cloud.

•

WHAT IS REALITY? (1941)

People often say that they are looking for Reality and that they are trying to live. I wonder what that means?

Some time ago a group of people were sitting in a restaurant, and one of them asked the others to say what they meant by Reality. There was much vague discussion, much talk of metaphysics and psychology, but one of those present, when asked his opinion, simply shrugged his shoulders and pointed at the salt-shaker. He was amazed to find that no one understood him, yet he had intended to be neither clever nor obscure. His idea was just to give a commonsense answer to the question, on the ordinary assumption that Reality is whatever exists. He was not understood because his friends, in common with many others, regarded Reality as a special kind of existence and Life (with a capital L) as a particular way of living. Thus we often meet those who talk about the difference between being a mere clod, a mere 'animated stomach,' and a *real* person; between those who simply exist and those who really live.

In Chinese philosophy *Life* is called *Tao*, and the Chinese speak of the wise man as one who realises (makes real to himself) his accord and harmony with Tao. Therefore, it is asked whether Tao means Life in the sense of simple existence, or whether Tao is Life lived in a special way, lived faithfully, thoroughly, vitally and with a certain zest born of the joy of being alive.

The answer to this question depends solely on why it is asked. Let's see what the Chinese themselves say about it.

A pupil asked his teacher, 'What is the Tao?'

He answered, 'Everyday life is the Tao.'

'How,' went on the pupil, 'does one get into accord with it?'

'If you *try* to accord with it,' said the teacher, 'you will get away from it.'

Indeed, we have all met those who are trying very hard to be real persons, to give their lives Reality (or meaning) and to live as distinct from existing. These seekers are of many kinds, highbrow and lowbrow, ranging from students of arcane wisdom to the audiences of popular speakers on pep and personality, selling yourself and making *your* life a success. I have never yet met anyone who *tried* to become a real person with success. The result of such attempts is invariably loss of personality, for there is an ancient paradox of the spiritual life whereby those who try to make themselves great become small. The paradox is even a bit more complicated than this; it also means that if you try, indirectly, to make yourself great by making yourself small, you succeed only in remaining small. It is all a question of motive, of what you want. Motives may be subtly concealed, and we may not call the desire to be a real person the desire to be great; but that is just a matter of words.

So many modern religions and psychologies make this fundamental mistake of trying to make the tail wag the dog, which is what the quest for personality amounts to. Old-fashioned Christianity was never so stupid, for its aim was never to achieve greatness (or great personality) for man. Its aim was simply to serve God and ascribe *all* greatness to Him. But in these days so many people find themselves unable to believe in the Christian God, and His more abstract substitutes fail to inspire any genuine devotion and reverence.

So we return to the original question, 'What, then, is Life; what is Reality, that it may inspire us with devotion?' If we regard it as a particular way of living or as a particular kind of existence and accord our devotion to *that*, what are we doing? We are reverencing its expression in great personality, in the behaviour of those whom we consider 'real persons.' But here is the snag. When we revere real personality in others, we are liable to become mere imitators; when we revere it as an ideal for ourselves, here is the old trouble of wasnting to make yourself great. It is all a question of pride, for if you reverence Life and Reality only in particular types of personal living, you deny Life and Reality to such humble things as, for instance, salt-shakers, specks of dust, worms, flowers and the great 'unregenerate masses' of the human race. We are reminded of the Pharisee's prayer, thanking God that He had not made him sinful like other men. But a Life, a Reality, a Tao that can be at once a Christ, a Buddha, a Lao-tzu and an ignorant fool or a worm, this is something really mysterious and wonderful and really worth devotion if you consider it for a while.

The Buddhist scriptures say: 'When every phase of our mind is in accord with the Buddha-mind, there shall not be one atom of dust that does not enter into Buddha-hood.' For Life and Reality are not things you can have for yourself unless you accord them to all others. They do not belong to particular persons any more than the sun, moon and stars.

———————— • ————————

METAPHYSIC AND RELIGION[114]

A Note on the Study of Oriental Doctrines in the West
(1950/1)

It is always difficult to adopt a new point of view. Faced with an unfamiliar idea, we are apt to interpret it in accordance with old patterns of thought, which are usually so habitual as to be almost unconscious. The result is that the essence of the new idea is lost. It becomes merely a novel and exotic dress for the old. For this reason, much of the study and practice of Oriental doctrines now current in the West has the character of a mummery.

During the last hundred years Western civilization has been exposed, as never before, to the spiritual traditions of Asia. In this relatively short time, works on Buddhism, Taoism, and Vedanta have appeared like the proverbial night growth of mushrooms, and there is no sign that the process is anything more than a simple beginning. The decline of Western spirituality has created a hunger for Oriental wisdom which is not likely to decrease, and its growing popularity will surely have the deepest effect on the life and thought of the Western world.

It can hardly be doubted that the present culture of the West is beset by a grave spiritual confusion manifested in the apparent collapse of our own religious traditions. There is thus the danger that the study of Eastern wisdom may result in a mere dressing-up of these confusions in Sanskrit and Chinese terminology, borrowed and misapplied. For there are already many signs that in adopting spiritual treasures from Asia, we are adopting only words and missing the basic principles which underlie them. Too often Western 'Buddhism' is nothing more than 'scientific rationalism' poorly expressed in Pali. And, since Western religion has so largely degenerated into mere moralism, it is often said that such 'milk-and-water' Christianity is after all 'one in essence' with what are supposed to be the 'moral principles' of Confucius and the Buddha. Assimilated in ways of this kind, Oriental wisdom will not enrich us at all; it will become simply a new form of the vicious circle in which we are already revolving. Such is the inevitable consequence of failing to see how much the Oriental doctrines differ in principle from many of our own basic, and largely unconscious, assumptions.

One of the most significant misunderstandings now current underlies the custom of referring to Buddhism or to Vedanta as *religions*, as if they were something of the same order as Christianity or Judaism. It is perhaps natural that in a civilization where there is nothing truly resembling Buddhism, it will be compared with its nearest equivalent. But this 'equivalent' is so unlike it that to put Christianity and Buddhism in the one class of 'religion' is to make the word so inclusive as to be almost meaningless. There may be dispute as to the exact definition of religion, but the lumping together of such different things in a single class shows a serious incomprehension of their natures. It leads, furthermore, to absurd comparisons and utterly unnecessary conflicts. It is like trying to argue the respective virtues of a symphony and a ballet without realizing that they are two distinct art-forms.

A very obvious difference between Christianity on the one hand, and Buddhism, Taoism, and Vedanta on the other, is in the language used to denote the Absolute or Ultimate Reality. Christianity, a religion, generally employs positive language. God is the Father; he is Being; he is Love and Goodness. But the major Oriental doctrines use negative language. The Buddha referred to the Absolute as 'the unborn, unoriginated, uncreated, unformed' and refused to give any positive doctrine about it at all. Likewise Vedanta speaks of Brahman as *'neti ... neti ...'* – 'Not this, not this,' and Mahayana texts abound with passages insisting that Enlightenment requires that the mind be freed from all concepts (i.e. finite notions) of Reality.

Now if both Buddhism and Christianity are religions, it will seem that Christianity has something which Buddhism lacks – a God. To Christians it will thus seem that Buddhism is an inferior religion, and to atheists a superior religion. Missionaries will try to obliterate Buddhism, while rationalists will espouse it – both completely missing the point.

The point may be understood by a simple analogy. There is some resemblance between trying to describe Reality to one who has not realized it and trying to describe colour to a blind man. You may tell him that colour is not round or square, hard or soft, warm or cold, liquid or solid, though if you go on in this way he will think that you are talking about pure nothingness. Or you may say that colour is like musical sounds or variations in temperature, as for example that red is like warmth and blue like cold. This will let him know that colour is a definite reality, but it will mislead him if he forgets that you are using analogy and comes to believe that red is warmth. In short, you can tell him either what colour is not, or what it is like; you cannot tell him what it *is*. It is the same with the Ultimate Reality. Because it must be infinite, it cannot be described positively since all positive things are finite. It is therefore more accurate to say what it is not than to try to say what it is. But if you confine yourself to saying what it is not, you are not saying that it is pure nothingness.

How, for instance, can you describe consciousness? What colour, size, shape, or weight is pure awareness? Of course, all such terms are of no use in describing awareness, but we have no other terms of description at our disposal. Awareness is colourless, sizeless, and shapeless, and yet it is most certainly not nothing; it is the entire basis of knowing anything at all. It is that without which there would indeed be nothing in our experience.

Thus the difference between Christianity and Buddhism is not between two differing sets of religious doctrine, one including something which the other lacks. It is a difference between kinds of doctrine, between two types of language. Christianity is saying what the Absolute *is like*, and it becomes absurd as soon as we think it is saying what the Absolute *is*. Its doctrines are analogical, and this is the chief characteristic of a religion, in the sense of the word here used. The best term for doctrines in the negative form, stating what the Absolute is not, is probably *metaphysic*. This should not be confused with academic 'metaphysics,' with logical speculations about the Absolute divisible into differing and conflicting systems. Metaphysic, as found in Buddhism and Vedanta, is an immediate knowledge, or realisation, of that which is beyond (*meta*) the whole finite order of nature (*physis*).

Metaphysic is, then, twofold. Its inner and essential part is immediate knowledge – not speculation. It is an effective realization of the Absolute in which there is no distinction between the knower and the known. Its outer and contingent part is doctrine, and the form of the doctrine is negative. The reason for the negative form is that realization comes about when the mind is freed from ideas. This is not empty-mindedness, a state of no ideas in the mind. It is a state of mind which entertains ideas but does not cling to them. We cling to ideas — ideas of God, of immortality, of soul, of mine and thine — to make our ego feel secure. To let go of such ideas is to let go of the ego; to let go of the ego is to realize the Absolute. In reality, mind (or pure awareness) is not an ego, an individual. It is *anatta*,[115] that is, supra-individual and infinite. Ego is an idea in the mind with which it seems to be identified, as a mirror reflecting red seems to be red.

Religion, on the other hand, is not and does not even claim to be an immediate knowledge of the Absolute. Christianity, for example, insists that it comprises a knowledge of the Absolute in the likeness of Jesus Christ, and this is analogy. Religion is threefold, consisting of creed, code, and cult. The creed is a system of positive doctrines describing God in terms of finite ideas and events: he is like a Father, or like the human nature of Jesus. The code or moral system embodying the will of God is a representation of the divine nature in terms of human relations and conduct - again analogy. The cult is a system of symbolic actions or sacraments which express, by analogy, the relation between God and man in concrete and physical terms.

It follows that a metaphysic, such as Buddhism, does not comprise a morality in the same sense as a religion. The Five Precepts of Buddhism are not understood as analogies of the nature of God, and thus should never be mistaken for an indication that, in Buddhism, there is some notion of an *absolute* moral law. Morality has to do with relations, and is thus quite obviously relative as distinct from absolute, and the common Western notion that Buddhism replaces God with a moral Law-Principle administered by *karma* is purely fantastic. The point of the Five Precepts is simply that they are conducive to realization, not because they mirror the Absolute but because they are temporary devices for letting go of the ego. All precepts in the metaphysical doctrines are simply convenient supports or crutches to prepare the mind for Enlightenment, to remove the hindrances to realization.

Unlike religion, metaphysic is not concerned with offering

the individual any consolations as to his future state. On the contrary, it is concerned with transcending the individual point of view. It is thus quite beside the point to go in for Buddhism because it is more consoling that Christianity, because it has no doctrine of eternal damnation, because it explains inequalities and injustices by rebirth, because it has no God of jealousy and wrath. Nay more, while religion consoles the individual with promises of future glory, it terrifies him with the prospect of certain doom if he should let the spiritual pride of egoism become his master. Thus to make of Buddhism a consoling religion with all 'nasty threats' removed is the very height of sentimentality, besides being a total misunderstanding of its supra-individual (*anatta*) nature.

There was a time when Christianity and Western culture comprised a metaphysic. This was the 'mystical theology' of Dionysius the Areopagite[116], followed by such spiritual giants of the Western tradition as Erigena, Albertus Magnus, Eckhart, Denis the Carthusian, and even Thomas Aquinas. This is the one real point of contact between the Oriental and Western viewpoints, whereas 'modernist' Christianity, which is almost pure moralism, and all the myriad varieties of naturalism with which modern thought abounds have nothing whatsoever in common with metaphysic – the super-natural and in-finite.

There is no doubt that this foisting of our own ideas upon the Oriental doctrines is the greatest obstacle to their proper study, and that in approaching them we need to be fully aware and keenly critical of both our motives and our assumptions. This is the more true in that misinterpretation has already gone so far that Ananda Coomaraswamy[117] could say, 'Although the ancient and modern scriptures and practices of Hinduism have been examined by European scholars for more than a century, it would hardly be an exaggeration to say that a faithful account of Hinduism might well be given in the form of a categorical denial of most of the statements that have been made about it, alike by European scholars and by Indians trained in our modern sceptical and evolutionary modes of thought'.

PICTURE WITHOUT A FRAME (1956)

The mind of man makes sense out of life by looking at it through frames. Within frames, within limits, something can be achieved; right and wrong can be laid down; success and failure can be determined; important and unimportant can be distinguished. By constructing a frame whose boundaries are birth and death, we can, within those limits, live out a life which appears to be meaningful and to accomplish something in terms of time. But a strange disquiet arises when we look outside the frame, for before birth we are not, and after death we leave only brief memorials. Frames are the very substance of rational knowledge, for we handle our experience of the world by putting it into classes. What *is*, is defined by the frame which distinguishes it from what *is not*, and *vice versa*. Motion is defined by the frame which separates it from stillness, so that if the frame be removed and we find ourselves in a world where all is in motion, the idea of motion ceases to mean anything. This is why the logicians say that there cannot be a class of all classes, a frame including all frames – for a frame with nothing at all outside its edges would not be a frame. It would be as inconceivable as the colour of the eyeball's lens.

Within human society we bring order into being and make communication possible by means of frames. We identify ourselves in terms of narrowing frames of reference – as that I am human, male, Caucasian, adult, American, professor, and so forth. When the frames are larger than human – mammal, organic, existent — they begin to lose meaning. The same is true when they become smaller than the frame designated by my proper name – tissue, cells, molecules, atoms, electrons, etc. Yet, large or small, every one of these identifying terms is the name of a frame, and there seems to be no way of saying or thinking what I am except in terms of frames. This gives me a peculiarly empty feeling, so that I begin to feel like the Irishman's definition of a net – 'a lot of holes tied together with string.'

The curious human mind has always wanted to know *what* is inside the frames, and for an answer it gets only the names of still smaller frames. In modern philosophy it is no longer considered proper to ask *what* anything is, unless you are simply speaking about its class or frame, or unless you are asking what it does – unless, that is, you are asking for an 'operational definition.' But even operational definitions — running, jumping, hopping, wobbling — are the names of frames, of classes of movement and behaviour. The problem is that thought and language have no terms except frame-terms, and there is really no way of even phrasing one's question so as to speak of what is not a frame. To ask 'What?' is to ask 'What frame?', for there are no means of saying what anything is save by denoting its class, by describing its *difference* from other things — which is simply to designate its boundaries, its frame.

In many schools of philosophy, stray thoughts which quarrel with this conclusion are simply outlawed as meaningless nonsense. The philosophers must at all costs convince themselves that life is composed of frames and frames alone – overlooking the fact that frames are 'airy nothings' in their enthusiasm for the fact that, hollow as they may be, they are at least definite. The philosophers will also contend that such knowledge amounts to far more than a vain effort to catch the wind in nets. After all it is the very nature of scientific knowledge, and look what science has achieved in the realm of concrete experience – at the innumerable ways in which it has made it easier and more pleasant to survive in this world as human beings.

One may wonder how close Western philosophy is coming to a realisation that the 'real material world' composed entirely of these frames is a vast net of abstractions. This will, perhaps, be difficult to see so long as we pretend to be really satisfied with the technological miracles of science – so long as the prospects of longer and more pleasant lives can distract our attention and keep it well within the limits of the frame called birth-and-death. But men have never been willing to remain closed in boxes for very long, and the wiser orthodoxies have used them as wise parents provide play-pens for their babies. On the one hand, the pen is a safe place where baby can stay out of trouble. On the other, there is a proper parental pride in seeing the baby grow strong enough to climb over the fence. The trouble with so many Western orthodoxies is that they have been living inside the pen with the baby. They have never allowed those who went outside to return unless they promised never to go out again. It is for this reason that the great Western orthodoxies, religious and scientific, have been strictly exoteric and profane. They have never had the secret smile of the parent who lays down rules in the hope that they will eventually be disobeyed. But that is the smile on the face of the Sphinx – and on the faces of meditating Buddhas.

To know the universe in terms of nothing but frames is almost exactly what Indian philosophy means by *maya*, and by the idea that all such knowledge is in some sense an illusion. The very word is related to our terms 'metre,' 'matrix,' and material', since it comes from the Sanskrit root *matr*, to measure. And measurement is framing – describing, as circles are described with dividers, defining, as limits are set with rulers, and dividing with hairlines, as minutes are marked out on a clock. These make up the frail mesh of abstractions with which the human mind tries to grasp the world, always, ultimately, in vain. For the sense of achievement, whether in knowledge or in action, is maintained only so long as one keeps one's gaze within a limited frame. But if the angle of vision is widened in both space and time, we begin to feel a frightening sense of futility. It begins to dawn upon us that our knowledge of the world and of ourselves is entirely hollow, and that all our efforts of muscle and brain have gone for nothing.

A despair of this kind is the starting-point of Buddhism. But those who close their minds to it never discover that despair has two faces – that the sigh of 'giving up the ghost' transforms itself into the sigh of relief, of liberation. This is, I think, the proper meaning of Nirvana, to 'blow out', to 'de-spirate'. It is here, too, that we discover the meaning of Buddhist and Taoist passivity: of the peculiar wisdom of a certain almost indescribable kind of inaction.

If there is any one psychological problem which really baffles the student of Buddhism, it is that desire (*trishna*) or grasping cannot put an end to desire – or, in other words, that to seek Awakening (*bodhi*) is to thrust it away; that to try to become a Buddha is to perpetuate ignorance. To imagine that the self can deliver itself is to foster the very illusion of self which constitutes bondage. For when Awakening, the actual vision of reality, is conceived as something to be grasped, something to be reached in the course of future time as if it were an object of success, then it is at once degraded to the level of frame-knowledge. Hence the strange insistence of such Zen masters as Rinzai[118] and Bankei[119] on the life of 'not seeking.'

In the words of Rinzai, 'Don't have a single thought in your mind about seeking for Buddhahood. How can this be? The ancients say, "If you desire deliberately to seek the Buddha, your Buddha is just *Samsara* (birth-and-death). "... There is no place in Buddhism for using effort. Just be ordinary, without anything special. Relieve your bowels, pass water, put on your clothes, and eat your food. When you're tired, go and lie down. Ignorant people may laugh at me, but the wise will understand ... if a man seeks the Tao, that man loses the Tao.'*

Or as Suzuki translates the words of Bankei, 'If you have the least desire to be something better than you actually are, if you hurry up to the slightest degree in your search of something, you are already going against the Unborn [i.e., the un-framed].'†

It is at this point that the *jiriki* (or self-powered) and *tariki* (other-powered) forms of Buddhism meet, for Rinzai and Bankei are here saying what the followers of the Jodo Shin-shu or [True] Pure Land School express in other terms. According to their view, the notion that a man can attain Buddhahood by his own effort or contriving is sheer pride. He must recognize that his own resources can lead nowhere but to the *naraka*, the so-called hells, the places of perpetual self-frustration. Deliverance from this bondage must come through a complete disillusionment with his own efforts, in which he has no recourse but to trust himself completely to the 'other-power' of the Buddha of Boundless Light, Amitabha, which will raise him just as he is to the Land of Purity. But this trust in the 'other-power' requires the total abandonment of all forms of 'self-powered' thinking, including the concern as to whether one's faith is sufficient or sincere.‡

---

* *Ku-tsun-hsu Yu-lu*, fasc. 1, *chuan* 4, pp. 6, 7, and 24.

† *Living by Zen*, p. 178.

‡ It should be understood that Amitabha considered as 'other' than

The difficulty of realising this total abandonment of seeking or 'self-power' is that the notion, 'I must do something to get it,' is so deeply ingrained that even giving up or 'not doing' is approached in the spirit of something to be done. This is why the Pure Land School insists that even concern as to whether one has faith or the power of self-surrender is to be abandoned, and why Zen says:

> This cannot be attained through thinking;
> This cannot be sought by not thinking.

Which is to say the same thing as Suzuki quotes from the Pure Land mystic Kichibei[120], 'When all the ideas of self-power based upon moral values and disciplinary measures are purged, there is nothing left in you that will declare itself to be the hearer (i.e. the one who gives up and accepts the other-power), and just because of this you do not miss anything you hear.'*

Self-surrender is not, then, a voluntary act, but something which happens when man finds himself in an ultimate quandary – at a crossroads where every road offered is the wrong road, every choice — and even making no choice — a mistake. The function of such Buddhist disciplines as meditation and the koan[121] is to precipitate this quandary, to exhibit the futility of 'self-power' by exercising it to the limit. Yet such meditations become somewhat farcical when done *in order* to realize what cannot be done; when, as it were, you try to make a hand catch hold of itself in order to realise that it can't. Of such artificial efforts to get oneself into this quandary, which Zen calls the state of 'Great Doubt,' Bankei said: 'It is like a Buddhist priest misplacing his only ceremonial robe, which he fails to locate in spite of his most anxious hunting. He cannot even for a moment give up the thought of the lost article. This is a doubt genuinely aroused. People of these days try to cherish doubt merely because the

oneself is not essentially different from what *jiriki* types of Buddhism call the innate Buddha-nature or 'original mind' (*honshin*). This is easily understood from the analogy of the heart-beat. From one point of view, I (the conscious ego) am not making it happen, but from another point of view I (as something more or other than the ego) am doing it.

* *Living by Zen*, p. 130.

old masters had it. This is no more than a make-believe; it is like searching after a thing which one has never lost.'*

Our difficulty in understanding such men as Rinzai, Bankei and Kichibei is that their Buddhism sounds too easy. To judge from their words, the great Buddhas and sages realized a state of mind so close to our ordinary everyday mind that we seem forced to one of two conclusions: that there is nothing specially important in Buddhism after all, or that we have completely misunderstood what they were saying. It seems inconceivable that these spiritual giants of the past should have gone through all their disciplines and labours for nothing, so that in the end all that they have to say is, as Nansen said to Joshu, 'Your ordinary mind is the Tao,' and 'By intending to accord with it, you immediately deviate.'

But the problem here is, again, one of framework. Buddhism was originally no more than the Buddha's experience of Awakening. After 2500 years of explanation and discussion it has been so conformed to the frames of human thought that our view of what a Buddha is has undergone a radical distortion. Our very natural reverence for these spiritual giants, coupled with the intensity of our aspiration to the same state, has inevitably made Awakening a coveted prize. It has, in other words, raised it to the very highest degree of a scale of values in which it has no part at all – the scale of success. Yet it would be nearer to the point, though still short of it, to say that Awakening is ultimate failure.

In the symbolism of the Buddhist Wheel of Becoming[122], the state of Buddhahood lies nowhere in the six divisions of the Wheel. At the highest point are the *devas*, the angels at the very crown of spiritual success. But, on the circular path, high leads to low, and in the depths are the *naraka* realms which represent the extreme of sentient misery. Ascent, in other words, does not lead to Nirvana, to Buddhahood – only to the temporary *deva*-world. In other words, there can be no association of Awakening with ideas of attainment, of spiritual superiority, of success, of mastery, or of claims to any prerogative. It is only quite figuratively — that is, within the misleading frames of human thought — that the Buddhas are termed higher than Ishvara[123], higher than the highest

* *Living by Zen*, p. 179.

gods. 'Higher' must here be translated as meaning altogether outside the scale of values in which high and low have any significance.

Yet, on the other hand, the state of Awakening is just as remote from that envious hostility to greatness, that insensitive disregard for the relative values of superiority which expresses itself in shallow egalitarianism. This is a kind of profane mimicry of the classlessness of the Buddhas which is by no means freedom from class but mere antagonism to it. And antagonism is another form of bondage.

The status of a Buddha is immeasurable, not because of its height or depth, but because Buddhas do not measure, do not *maya*, and so, in a way, do not matter. It is all the same word. They are, in Zen language, *muji* — nothing special — without affecting to be ordinary.

Above all, to a Buddha it is meaningless to think that he is a Buddha. For there is no 'he,' no frame.

Appendices

•

1 A READER'S REPLY TO THE 'MYSTICS OF TODAY' ARTICLE ON THE OXFORD GROUPS, AND ALAN WATTS' REPLY

Château Juan-les-Pins,
Juan-les-Pins (A.M.).
Feb. 24th [1938]
To the Editor of *Modern Mystic*

Sir,
As a constant reader of your magazine may I, also, be allowed to say a few words in answer to Mr Alan Watts' article on the Oxford Groups and to a letter published in your February issue. Before going on I wish to state I am not a member of the Oxford Groups, but have been interested to study the results they have obtained rather than their literature. My observations are addressed for reasons which I hope will be obvious.

After carefully reading Mr Watts' article, I think his viewpoint may be summed up in his following remark: 'All this may save civilisation from war and establish the brotherhood of man. But some of us would rather have civilisation perish in blood and fire than have to live on and endure such a brotherhood.'

When Master Jesus, overshadowed by the Christ, came to give His Teaching in Jerusalem, there were then, also, those who scornfully refused — perhaps through that most subtle form of egotism, spiritual pride — to listen to the 'still small

267

voice of Love' spoken in humble places. Should not students of the Secret Doctrine[124] be the first to know the Teachings are given in the language that is needed, where and when it is needed?

Has it been overlooked that many children of the West cannot fathom the veiled idiom of the East? For them, in their modern world of 'unadorned realism,' a new language had to be found. Perhaps just that platitudinous cheeriness, so scathingly criticised, is necessary for what Mr Watts terms their 'awkward age'. If indeed they be at this awkward age is that any less the reason — even if it offends the modestly declared sensitiveness of Mr Watts' fastidious ear — that they should be deprived of a much needed spiritual impetus? At this time of internal and external strife, when the forces of destruction are utilising chaos and class hatreds to further their ends, this Group is proving its value where others, with the greater responsibility of knowledge, sit idle. May it not be that their value lies in the fact that they speak in the scorned language of the masses? Perhaps it were better to close those too sensitive ears — unfortunately, it would seem, cut off by the intellect from the Voice of the Heart — from contact with what may well be inspired by One Who was not too proud to stoop to simple words, to simple people, to accomplish His Will for the Brotherhood of Man.

Admittedly this crude modern version 'works.'

And who is Mr Watts to deny that 'Wherever two or three are gathered in My Name, there am I in the midst of them'? Or is it for him to choose the place and limit the means?

For such as those who prefer to rely on 'dignified ritual' — as an occultist Mr Watts should be aware this same ritual is even now obsolete and being used by the forces of destruction — instead of active Service through the Heart, they may indeed, if that be their wish, awake some day to find they have perished in 'blood and fire' rather than 'live[d] on and endure[d] such a brotherhood' - truly a 'peculiar state of mind'!

'Judge not that ye be not judged.'

ALSO A READER

•

To the Editor, *The Modern Mystic*

Sir,

Your correspondent 'Also a Reader' has written a particularly beautiful letter, and, if it had any relation to the facts, I should be forced to withdraw my remarks and stand very thoroughly corrected. But I cannot see any clear connection between the Oxford Groups of his letter and the Oxford Groups of reality, as they are to be found in London and the various university centres of this country.

I think I ought, first of all, to clarify the passage from my article quoted in the second paragraph of his letter. Naturally I do not mean that I would rather civilisation should perish than have to live on and endure a real brotherhood of mankind wherein all 'loved their neighbours as themselves.' But the Groups do not seem to constitute this brotherhood, nor even to be working towards it. Of course, I, in my spiritual pride, may not be able to perceive any humble awakening of the brotherhood of man in these gatherings in country houses and expensive hotels for the mutual retching up of the less savoury contents of the human mind. I may be superior and fastidious, but surely it is a mistake to confuse the humble with the vulgar and dirty. But I still maintain that it is dirty for young people to group together for these pathological analyses of their souls, and that the whole tone of their propaganda is vulgar. And figs will not grow on thistles.

If these things had really come to pass in 'humble places,' I should have written a very different article. But I feel your correspondent is wholly mistaken in regarding the Groups as a movement for the great masses of the people, speaking to them in their own language. Compared with the language of the Groups the talk of peasants and working men is the sweetest music of a genuine simplicity, quite unlike this cheap, sophisticated jargon which is the sorry attempt of 'superior people' to be simple. For the Groups are not recruited from the masses to any great degree. When they tried to 'convert London' they worked in Mayfair rather than Hoxton,[125] and their members consist mainly of university students, young people of the middle classes and that sprinkling of rich people which is to be found in almost any curious cult. These people, I feel, ought to know better. If they want to influence the masses, they should work with Toc H[126], the Salvation Army, the Catholic Church or any other movement that is doing real hard work among the poor. But for the most part the Groups find favour among supposedly educated youths and so absorb them in 'drawing-room religion' that they neglect their proper work.

The 'still, small voice of Love' is certainly being spoken in humble places, but not by the Groups, whose voice is neither small nor still. To hear it one should go to such people as the Methodist minister who talks at lunch hours on Tower Hill – not to the 'hearties' at Brown's Hotel, Dover Street, WI.

Your correspondent asks who made *me* a judge over the Groups. The answer is, 'Nobody,' for I am simply the advocate (for the prosecution); the Judgement we leave to a Higher Law, and if that decides against me, well, I must be wrong.

I am, Sir, Yours faithfully,
Alan W. Watts.
Chislehurst, Kent

——————————— • ———————————

2 THE THRESHOLD OF A NEW AGE, A REPLY TO MR ALAN WATTS' ARTICLE 'IS RELIGION NECESSARY?', BY ELEANOR C. MERRY[127]

Mr Watts' article in last month's *Modern Mystic* did not seem to me to reach any conclusion though it came to an end with the following sentence: 'It is not a question of what *you* do, but of what God does, and you cannot save yourself by any means, either by doing or not doing. God is always saving you, but this is not easy to understand.' In discussing the question of what is God's purpose in creating the universe and man, together with all the accompanying problems of Sin and Grace, of the separative nature of sin and Ultimate Unity with God, he merely repeats all the familiar arguments and throws no fresh light upon them.

The question of 'doing' and 'not doing' anything to help ourselves perhaps comes rather strongly to Mr Watts' mind because of his oriental studies; but it needs to be understood by the Western mind by developing, in a new way, its innate historical sense: that is, by fertilising history with the teaching of re-incarnation.

The East has never really achieved the historical sense, and 'non-action' belongs to the whole renunciatory spirit of the ancient Orient – asceticism towards the fruits of action because action entangles the soul more and more in the 'wheel of births' – that is, in the necessity to re-incarnate. In the West, the 'fruits' of action are desired, because the historical sense urges men on to achievement; the problem for the Western man is how to desire results, *but not to desire them for himself.*

This is the 'morality' for our time which Mr Watts seems to find so teasing a conundrum. But I do not want in this article to deal separately with the various points raised by Mr Watts, but rather to approach the whole question from a different angle.

The morality which I believe we have to discover cannot be described as mere so-called 'rightness of conduct.' It has not so very much to do with that. But it has everything to do with *compassion.* In this, East and West could find common ground. It was the fundamental principle of Buddha's life; and so it was of Christ's. But Christ added something more. I will try to explain it.

Buddha pointed *away* from the earth. One was to be compassionate, but one was to do away with all those causes whose results called forth compassion — the miseries of life — by striving for liberation from the necessity of re-incarnation.

Christ pointed *to* the earth. Most clearly did He do so in the Sermon on the Mount, especially in the Beatitudes: and He announced His intention of always staying with humanity 'even unto the end of the world.' He made compassion into something positive. If men did charitable actions, they would be doing them 'unto Me.' His positive compassion was crowned by the death on the Cross. Steiner once said that Buddha taught the Wisdom of Love, and that Christ brought to men the Force of Love. Which is the same as the 'force of Ascension.' Both ideals are right. But Christ also said 'Be ye therefore perfect, as your Father in heaven is perfect.'

That is a distinct call to some kind of action other than simply external goodness in action; it is action directed towards self-development; we are to become perfect. The

Christian ideal is to establish the kingdom of heaven on the earth; the idea of the Eightfold Path is to be so moved by compassion that the liberation of all beings from the sorrows of the earth is attainèd. If we study the Gospels carefully we shall see how wonderfully balanced is the idea of inward perfection with the idea of outward moral actions, rooted in the inwardly created love.

Wherever we look in searching for the springs of religion we find these two aspects: the aspect of the inner life, and that of the outer life. Before the time of Christ the old Mystery Schools tended in one or the other direction; those in the more southern parts of the world had as their primary consideration the science of the soul, and in the more northern parts of the world, the science of Nature. There are ancient legends suggesting that all knowledge is inscribed upon *two* pillars or 'tables' of stone. The Christian ideal unites them.

As regards our present time, it is quite clear that our problems are rooted in the one supreme problem, which is: how to reconcile what we feel to be humanity's innate sense of 'goodness' — the innate sense that we have *in* us possibilities of a real and true 'inner life' and a capacity for spiritual experience — with the confusion that we have somehow, in spite of ourselves, created in the external world; and not only with that, but also with the apparent slow and inevitable destruction to which the physical world seems to be doomed.

So we are compelled to enquire – what is the purpose of it all? Why are we here? The very fact that we ask such a question is at any rate one hesitating step forward in our evolution.

Now it seems to be quite clear that when we have before us two opposite poles — let us say Light and Darkness, Spirit and Matter, the inner life and the outer life, and so on — a third factor must be discovered which in some way bridges the gap; much as the crossing of the vision of our eyes produces the single vision. What makes us able to *distinguish* the 'inner' from the 'outer' – so that we can appreciate the difference, for example, between the fact of a thunderstorm and our feeling or emotion about it? Nothing else than our ability to realise ourselves as 'I.' No one else can say 'I' about us; we can only say it ourselves. And this 'I' looks in two directions – inwardly and outwardly. It is itself the bridge.

So we are certainly something or somebody. How did man become able to recognise himself as an 'I'? Only by being placed between opposites; only by having the power of choice. The story of Paradise tells us pictorially how man, in the course of his evolution, becomes definitely aware that he is passing from the period when he lived in a kind of dreaming 'mystical' co-operation with supernatural powers, to the period when he meets the dawn of his own selfhood.

The Tree of Life and the Tree of the Knowledge of Good and Evil were said to be not separate trees, but intertwined with one another. Adam and Eve ate the fruit only of the Tree of the Knowledge of Good and Evil. They became, as the serpent foretold, not gods, but *as* gods. Formerly they *were* gods – children of the Divine; they fell into a state which was lower; so that they only resembled gods. Why? Because only in this lower state, standing between the opposites 'good' and 'evil,' could they develop, as humanity, more and more, through immense ages and many incarnations, what we call *individuality*.

Everything that happens today which crushes out the freedom of the *individual* in his path of evolution from primitive selfhood to higher selfhood is against this moral law, and a retrograde step in evolution.

Why is individuality — the strong sense of 'I am' — so necessary? Because unless you are first separated from 'mass-consciousness,' even from the natural call of the blood, you cannot know the secret of Love. Unless you can say 'I,' you cannot say 'thou.' So mankind had to develop, from the Fall, towards a *new* polarity: myself – and the other.

That is why the ego may be a 'two-edged sword' proceeding out of the mouth of man. With this sword we can kill or we can make alive, hate or love, have antipathy or sympathy. So what appears as the polarity of 'I' and 'thou' needs bridging over by a third element. And this is the *social life*. But the social life cannot be built up on mere 'moral rectitude'; because we are not yet sufficiently advanced to see our motives for moral rectitude clearly. It needs something else. And this is *Compassion*; which is the first step towards Christ's words 'Thou shalt love they neighbour as thyself.'

The Eightfold Path laid down by Buddha is in reality an outline of a much later stage of human development, when we shall return again, through self-sacrifice — which is positive action — to the *wisdom* of Love.'

In our time the mystic desires to escape from diversity to uniformity – to lose himself in divine union. The occultist desires to educate mankind to a right understanding of diversity, which will lead to a real co-operation of individuals towards a common purpose. This is true religion, and will be free from the bondage of creeds. For when it is understood that the development of conscious egohood is necessary for the developing of love, then the 'purpose' behind human life reveals itself as divine.

Religion means a 're-binding'.[128] Human beings, *free* in their souls because they grasp their spiritual origin, become *bound* together because they have each of them an interest that is higher than a personal one. When you become really an 'ego' in this sense, you can be the greatest possible egoist *because the interests of the whole world have become your own!** This, it seems to me, is the real Unity which is the goal of the earth. Then it doesn't matter if the material earth perishes or becomes like a moon, because men will have tasted the Tree of Life (Freedom), and a new earth — even a new planet for our habitation — can arise as the result of their positive creative selflessness.

All this seems very far away from our everyday life. But it is Mr Watts' fault, for venturing on — and inveigling us to follow him — arguments about the nature of 'God's purpose' for the world. And as a last word on this particular question, I would like to say that I do not see why one should not permit oneself to imagine that God desired to see those Spirits, whom we call 'human,' reach a higher degree of perfection than they had in heaven in the beginning, by bestowing on them the great Initiation of passing through material existence on a material planet. Life itself, in all its incarnations, is supreme initiation. Those whom we call the great Initiates have simply gone ahead of the rest of humanity and are their teachers. Man is the only hierarchy of spirits to whom has fallen the difficult task of assuming bodies of flesh. So it was said of him

---

* This is a saying of Rudolf Steiner's.

that he is made 'a little lower than the Angels, but crowned with mercy and honour.'

But now let us return to more immediate questions.

If it is true, as I am sure it is, that a real compassion will generate a new socal order, then we must look deeper and see how such compassion can arise in the first instance. I think the answer is that we have to develop the capacity to see, in all human beings, the evidence of the presence in them of their 'I,' which is their immortal spirit. That would be reading the riddle of the Sphinx: 'I am that which was, and is, and will be. No *mortal* can lift my veil.' No; only the immortal can recognise the immortal in another; one 'I' recognises another 'I.' The royal purple of the 'kingly robe' is around the shoulders of each one of us.

From this, we should recognise as self-evident that in the Spirit — but in the Spirit alone — there is *equality*. All 'I's' are equal. We should not try to create a Utopia in which we enforce this equality upon all spheres of life, because that would be a contradiction of the nature of the Spirit.

Secondly, the next step would follow of itself, because in recognising the spiritual nature of man, the spiritual nature of his surroundings — of the whole earth, which sustains him in physical existence — would also be recognised.

Compassion is not mere 'pity.' Compassion is 'an experiencing *with*,' really a kind of intuition. Behind the physical world, just as behind the physical bodies of men, the needs of the kingdoms of nature below man would become apparent. The whole creation, said Paul, 'groaneth and travaileth,' waiting for this recognition by the 'sons of God.' So through compassion a new outlook would be possible upon the fact that the earth is a living whole, and as a whole, desires to bestow its physical gifts upon all men equally. Then World-economy would arise! The products of the earth would be made accessible for all nations.

In the right economic distribution — right action indeed! — BROTHERHOOD would be a natural result. There would be no desire to fight over what is common to all.

Then this recognition would lead to the recognition of human FREEDOM.

'Is Religion Necessary?' was the title of Mr Watts' article. It is a question he did not succeed in answering. But I think it follows naturally from what I have said that the recognition of Equality and Brotherhood — *in their respective spheres* — would give a character to the whole of life which would itself be Religion. And all religions, or creeds, would find their own place, in freedom, in human hearts. With this Freedom, Justice and Mercy are united. One of the first necessities would prove to be an entire revision of the alien laws.

Equality – Freedom – Brotherhood!

Where is now the 'tension' between the dualities of life which Mr Watts says so much about? There is in reality no such thing. Because no opposites exist at all without a third thing, which is the consciousness that is aware of them. Thus we can have no actual conception of a duality or polarity without its immediate assumption into a trinity. This *ends* tension; a trinity is not static but dynamic. It moves freely within itself. It is equilibrium. Between good and evil man walks erect and balanced.

Such a conception of a trinity may mark only one stage in the long course of human evolution. But I believe it is something that is struggling to assert itself, as spiritual truth, within this modern age of self-consciousness. It need not any longer remain in the realm of metaphysics, but may be made actual.

Moreover the secret of the Triad may be discovered everywhere. It mysteriously rules the world. If in our civilisation we reject it when it wishes to appear, we are out of tune with the present stage of God's 'purpose.' The beginning of its discovery is compassion. I could also say it begins with veneration.

One might well despair that any such awakening could ever come to humanity when one sees every day in every newspaper the ghastly proofs of human bestiality. We have believed too well in the Darwinian theory that we have descended from the animals; we are in danger of becoming lower than they....

But I have no expectations that any propaganda could be made — let us say for the inauguration of world-economy, or the revision of alien laws — by any such arguments as I have put forward here in the *Modern Mystic*. Nature herself, and human reason making its practical observations, will secure the propaganda sooner or later. 'What must, will surely come to pass.' The facts which surround us urge us to begin with the physical world. The mystic may begin at the other end. The occultist may have the spiritual and the physical in view and will do what he can. But meanwhile Nature seems to be preparing her obvious lessons; and through world-pain, we may be roused to compassion, and strenuous effort.

Mr Watts seems to think we have only to 'admit that we are what we are,' and that in this humble admittance we are immediately 'transformed and transfigured.' I am sure that this is self-delusion, unless it is regarded as a preliminary step; if not, you might just as well say you have walked from Bloomsbury to Westminster when you have put one foot forward[129]. That we are *able* to walk from Bloomsbury to Westminster is due to 'Grace'; that we do it is our own affair We shall not be lifted up and wafted over the traffic.

And one other thing. Let us get clear about this fleeing from the past or running after the future. Mr Watts says: 'We are fulfilling the divine purpose at this moment, whether we know it or not, simply by being what we are.'

That is true in one sense. But only if we understand Past, Present and Future as another — and tremendous — triad. What is it that makes the Present? *Man!* In the consciousness of man alone lies the continual collision between Past and Future. The Future does not stretch away from us; it comes towards us. So does the Past. But, being 'man,' we can exercise memory, which is the prerogative of egohood, and in a certain sense separate ourselves from the Past and look back upon it – because the Past has made us what we are. But it makes us only through the miracle of its never-ending birth out of the on-coming Future. Man is the Magician, standing between these two pillars, whose heights and depths are eternity. Because he is there — *present* — they exist.

What then? In his self-consciousness, in his awakened awareness of himself, man commands the Present within the limits of his self-made personal destiny. If we believe in reincarnation, we believe that our *karma* is a very real thing. We created it ourselves – out of present moments that are past. So we can redeem it also. The *ability* to do so is bestowed. Whether we do it or not depends upon our power of 'self-recollection' – which means holding ourselves in a state of conscious equilibrium where Past and Future meet.

What applies in this way to the single human being applies to humanity as a whole. The world of men is being called upon to awake – to have self-recollection, balance, and compassion; and from these to find the way to Equality in the Spirit, Freedom in the soul, and Brotherhood in the body.*

* In connection with this subject see *The Threefold Commonwealth* by Rudolf Steiner.

Notes On The Text

———————————————— • ————————————————

1 The Metropolitan Line is a railway linking London with the commuter suburbs and home counties to the north-west of London. Now part of the London Underground system, it interfaces with the Circle Line at Baker Street station. Coming himself from the southern suburbs of London, Watts was familiar from an early age with the stultifying rhythms of commuter life – and no doubt resolved to escape.

2 'Back to nature movement'. Even back in what we should today regard as the relatively salubrious ambience of the 1930s, sensitive people were devising ways to escape the rat race and the artificialities of commercialized city life. Their dreams were of a more honest and authentic existence in the unspoiled countryside, pursuing traditional arts and crafts, perhaps, or running a market garden or small-holding, and generally living in accord with the seasons and the rhythms of nature.

3 *Avatar*. In classical Hindu mythology, the 'descent' or incarnation of a god, notably Vishnu, who comes into the world when a crisis has been reached. He has appeared many times — as Varaka, Narada, Dattatreya, Rama, as Krishna, as Buddha — and he will next appear as Kalki.

4 Etymologically 'Manu' is derived from *manas*, 'to think', and hence is associated with 'human'. Manu himself was, according to classical Hindu mythology, the first man and king, the lighter of the sacrificial fire and the originator of the social and moral order through his pronouncements on *Dharma* or Law (his so-called Laws). Dimitrije Mitrinović believed that the notion of a threefold order, which in the social context results in trivision into the economic, cultural and political spheres, originated in the Laws of Manu.

5 It is doubtful whether the composers of the Upanishadic verses

279

were, in any realistic sense, 'mere peasants' who 'could not even write', but rather great *yogis* and *rishis* who boldly rejected both conventional social life and Brahmanical orthodoxy to seek direct knowledge of Brahman or Ultimate Reality for themselves in the solitude of jungle and mountain retreat.

6 Shankara (also known as Shankara Acarya): the foremost of all Indian religious thinkers. The Advaita Vedanta philosophy that he expounded asserted the non-duality of Brahman and Atman (see note 8). According to his biographer, Madhava, he lived in the 8th century, was born in the south Indian region of Kerala and died at Kedarnath, a holy place in the Himalayan foothills.

7 *Dharma*: a Sanskrit word with a wide range of connotations. With a capital 'D' it signifies the Laws of the Universe – the way things are, the way they operate. The sensitive person will seek to live in accordance with *Dharma*. It can also signify Moral Law, or a specific set of religious teachings (e.g. the Buddha's). There is also a sense in which each person has his or her own *dharma* (with a small 'd') – his or her own particular destiny, function or social role.

8 Brahman, Atman: Brahman is the transcendental Ultimate of the Hindu Way. It is a great mystery, impossible to capture in words or concepts, hence the tendency of many sages to refer to it solely in negativistic terms: *Neti, neti* – 'Not this, not this...' Atman is technically its immanent aspect. In fact, however, the distinction between Brahman and Atman is spurious for in the last analysis they are One. So each of us somehow embodies the Ultimate in its entirety – a hard notion to swallow, perhaps, but ineluctably the infinite and eternal cannot be sliced up and portioned out. It is always the All.

9 All this is somewhat questionable. In the earliest texts *Tao* means quite simply 'road' or 'pathway'. It later began to widen to encompass connotations of showing the way, guiding, teaching, doctrine. *Te*, on the other hand, is primary power or virtue – the vital force that makes things work. Putting *tao* with *te* therefore sparks a notion like 'the way the Universe works', or the underlying numinous Law of the Universe.

10 *Karma yoga, bhakti yoga, gñana yoga*: *karma yoga* is certainly the yoga of action, e.g. of charitable or religious good works in the world. *Bhakti yoga*, on the other hand, is devotional; it is religious surrender through unqualified faith to a *guru* (teacher) or deity. Finally, *gñana yoga* is the yoga of transcendental wisdom or insight – which is not simply intellectual (i.e. verbal-conceptual), as Watts states. Here then are three primary ways of approaching the Divine: 1 through action, 2 through faith, and 3 through a higher form of knowledge.

11 Johannes Jacobus van der Leeuw, LlD. (1893–1934): prominent

NOTES ON THE TEXT

Dutch Theosophical writer. 1921: ordained a priest of the Liberal Catholic Church in Australia. 1930–1: General Secretary of Netherlands section of the Theosophical Society, founder of Practical Idealist Association for Youth and the King Arthur Society (Neutral Bay, 1922). 1931–2: lectured in the USA. Died in a crash during a solo flight in South Africa. Books include *The Fire of Creation* (Subba Row Medal, 1925), *Conquest of Illusion*, *The Dramatic History of the Christian Faith*, *Gods in Exile*, *Task & Education in World Crisis*, etc.

12 Jiddu Krishnamurti (1895–1986): a south Indian who was groomed from childhood by Mrs Annie Besant (*née* Wood, 1847–1933), C. W. Leadbeater (1847–1934) and other luminaries of the Theosophical Society to be the new world teacher. He rejected that mantle, however, and disbanded the organization set up to promote his mission (the Order of the Star), proclaiming 'Truth is a pathless land.' But although subsequently rejecting conventional religion and all submission to authorities and teachers, he went on to attract enormous followings himself, spawned many institutions (including schools) and a library of books, tapes and videos. Thus he willy-nilly became a teacher or authority for many. Paradoxically, then, the teaching that there are no teachers was reified into a teaching; the church of no-church was inaugurated. Watts perceptively touches on these problems in this essay, pointing out that those who were following Krishnamurti were clearly not getting the point. Biographies of Krishnamurti by Mary Lutyens (3 vols: *The Years of Awakening, The Years of Fulfilment* and *The Open Door*, London, 1975, 1983 and 1988), and by Pupul Jayakar (*Krishnamurti: A Biography*, San Francisco, 1986).

13 Carl Gustav Jung (1875–1961): the Swiss originator of Analytical Psychology and, with Sigmund Freud and Alfred Adler, one of the pioneers of modern psychology and psychotherapy. Jung took much interest in the religions of the East – see *Psychology and the West* (London, 1978). His collected works run to 20 volumes (tr. R.F.C. Hull, ed. G. Adler, M. Fordham and H. Read, Princeton, 1953–79). Biography by B. Hannah (*Jung – His Life & Work*, New York, 1967); also personal memoir (*Memories, Dreams and Reflections*, C. G. Jung, ed. A. Jaffé, New York, 1965).

14 Pavlov, Hollander. **Ivan Petrovitch Pavlov (1849–1936)**: The distinguished Russian physiologist most famous for his study of conditioned reflexes. His experiments with dogs have become part of popular mythology. Professor and later Director of the Institute of Experimental Medicine in St Petersburg: winner of the Nobel Prize (1904). Life by B. P. Batsin. **Bernard Hollander (1864–1934)**: naturalised British physician specializing in mental and nervous diseases. He made a special study of mind and character, and their deviations from normal; he also developed theories on the location of functions within the brain. Born Vienna, educated King's College, London, etc., Founder and President of the Ethological Society (1904–22), etc.. Numerous papers and books, including *The Insanity of Genius* (1913), *In Search of the Soul & the Mechanism of Human Thought, Emotion & Conduct* (1920) and *Psychology of Misconduct, Vice and Crime,* (1922).

15 Lindworsky, Dimnet and Leslie Weatherhead. **Johannes Lindworsky (1875–1939):** German psychologist, born Frankfurt am Main, educated at the University of Münich, etc., died Essen. He served on faculties of the University of Cologne (1920–8) and the Germany University, Prague (1928–39). His main concern was with the will, which he regarded as a 'switching mechanism' secondary to motivation. 'Will training occurs when an appreciation of values and motives is produced.' He interpreted the spiritual exercises of Ignatius Loyola in this light. Books include *Der Wille* (1919), *Experimentelle Psychologie* (1921), *Theoretische Psychologie* (1932) and *Psychologie der Aszese* (1935). **Abbé Ernest Dimnet (1866–1954):** priest, lecturer and writer in French, English and American periodicals; born Trélon; Hon. Canon Cambray Cathedral, Professor at Collège Stanislas, Paris, Lowell Lecturer at Harvard (1919), French Lecturer at Williamstown (Mass.) Institute of Politics (1923). Publications include *La Pensée Catholique dans L'Angleterre Contemporaine* (1905), *Figures des Moines* (1908), *The Art of Thinking* (1928), *What We Live By* (1932), etc. **Leslie Dixon Weatherhead (1893–1976):** a charismatic Methodist preacher and writer, born in London and educated at the Universities of Manchester, London and Edinburgh. Between 1936 and 1960 he eloquently occupied the pulpit at the City Temple in London. He was an examiner in psychology for Wesleyan Methodist ordination candidates and a lecturer in psychology for the Workers' Education Association. At a time when psychology was fashionable, Weatherhead combined it with religion for evangelical purposes and seemed to believe in both equally. Books include *Psychology in Service of the Soul* (1930), *Jesus & Ourselves* (1931), *How Can I Find God?* (1934), *Psychology, Religion & Healing* (1952), etc. Biography: *Dr Leslie Weatherhead of the City Temple*, by Christopher Maitland (1960).

16 This is a very crucial point.

17 Daisetz Teitaro Suzuki (1870–1966): a Japanese who trained in Zen Buddhism with Imagita Kosen Roshi and Soyen Shaku at Engaku-ji in Kamakura. After an enlightenment experience around 1897, he worked for many years in the USA for the Open Court Publishing Co. of LaSalle, Michigan, where he developed the necessary skills for his great life's work of introducing the riches of Zen Buddhism in particular and Mahayana Buddhism in general to Western audiences.

From 1909 his activities were mainly confined to Japan itself, but between 1949 and 1958 he travelled many times to the West (mainly the USA) to teach, holding official posts at Columbia University (New York) and elsewhere. Suzuki's visit to London in 1936 was a crucial experience for Watts, his mentor Christmas Humphreys and other leading British Buddhists. Suzuki was sent over by the Japanese Government as a kind of cultural ambassador to take part in the World Congress of Faiths, a great ecumenical gathering conjured out of the aether by Sir Francis Younghusband, an old imperialist war-horse who had, ironically, undergone a profound religious transformation after leading a victorious British army to the holy city of Lhasa, capital of Tibet, in 1904. Suzuki produced many influential books on Zen. Biography by A. Irwin Switzer 111 (*D. T. Suzuki, A Biography*), edited and enlarged by John Snelling (London, The Buddhist Society, 1984).

18 One of the sayings of Layman P'ang (lit. 'Lofty Interior', c. 740–808), a simple Chinese family man who, according to legend, was able to achieve the highest level of spiritual enlightenment by ardently following the Ch'an or Zen way. One of his great acts was to dispose of his house and then sink all his money and possessions in the river so as to be free of them once and for all. Surely the action of a deeply wise man!

19 From *Song of Meditation* by Hakuin Zenji (1685–1768), the revitaliser of Japanese Rinzai Zen and restorer of the *koan* system. Hakuin set the trend for developments in Zen to the present time. (See D. T. Suzuki, *Essays in Zen Buddhism* (First Series), London, 1949, p. 337).

20 The highlight of Suzuki's 1936 visit to London for the World Congress of Faiths was a great public meeting at the Queen's Hall on July 9th, where the topic those on the platform were asked to address was 'The Supreme Spiritual Ideal', a rather ponderous one by any token, as Suzuki, who began in a very low-key way but went on to utterly steal the show, was quick to point out. Accounts of the meeting are to be found in Switzer's biography of Suzuki, pp. 32–3, and in *Both Sides of the Circle*, by Christmas Humphreys (London, 1978), p. 91.

21 'Oxford Groups' is in fact a misnomer for a movement founded by Frank Buchman (1878–1961), an American evangelist. In 1921, believing that the demise of civilisation was imminent, Buchman instigated the Group Movement at Oxford, England. This did not aspire to be a new sect but rather to catalyse existing religious institutions. It emphasised divine guidance and adherence to four principles: honesty, purity, unselfishness and love. Members participated in compulsory 'sharings' of their shortcomings. After 1938 the movement rallied under its slogan

'Moral Rearmament', and after World War II it adopted a more political stance as an alternative to both communism and capitalism. See Buchman's *The Oxford Group and its Work of Moral Rearmament* (1954) and *America Needs an Ideology* (1957).

22 *Tantum religio potuit suadere malorum*: 'Such evil deeds could religion prompt' or, as a modern translator puts it, 'Such are the heights of wickedness to which men are driven by superstition', a quotation from Book 1, line 101 of *De Rerum Naturum* ('On the Nature of Things' or 'The Nature of the Universe') by the anti-religious Roman poet Lucretius (c 99–55 BC).

23 Archbishop Randall Davidson set up a number of Archbishops' Commissions and Committees in 1922. Besides the Commission on Church Doctrine dealt with by Alan Watts here, which he appointed in conjunction with the Archbishop of York, others in the same year concerned themselves with Church music, relationships with other churches, etc. Interestingly, in 1920 a Lambeth Conference Committee on Spiritualism, Christian Science and Theosophy deliberated between July 5th and August 7th. Biography of Randall Davidson by G. K. A. Bell (2nd ed., Oxford University Press, 1938).

24 Gilbert Keith Chesterton (1874–1936): English critic, writer (novels, short stories, journalism, etc.) and poet, noted for his robust humour and mastery of the device of paradox (which he often used as a weapon to deflate Victorian hypocrisy); also for his religious and theological concerns. Born London; educated St Paul's School, the Slade School of Art, and London University; converted to Roman Catholicism in 1922. Most famous novels include *The Napoleon of Notting Hill* (1904), *The Man Who Was Thursday* ((1908) and the 'Father Brown' detective books (1911, 1914, 1926, 1927 and 1935). Most famous poem: 'Before the Roman Came to Rye'.

25 Ernst Heinrich Haeckel (1834–1919): German naturalist who, anticipating Darwin, was the first to describe the genealogical tree of animals and the process of sexual selection. He maintained that the life history of an individual is a recapitulation of its species' historic evolution. He is generally thought to have rather moulded the facts to fit his own theory of materialistic monism. Books include *Natürliche Schöpfungeschichte* (1868), *Anthropogenie* (1878).

26 L. Cranmer-Byng: editor of John Murray's 'Wisdom of the East' series, in which Watts' first book, *The Spirit of Zen*, appeared. His son continued the series for a time after his death. Author of *The Vision of Asia* (London, 1932).

27 566 BC is a generally though not universally accepted date for the Buddha's birth.

28 Watts is here falling into one of the classic double-binds: talking about that which cannot be talked about. However, he is not alone; hence the libraries of books that have been written about that elusive entity 'beyond words and concepts', Zen.

29 Can one will oneself to forget oneself? Another classic double-bind, surely!

30 Second Congress of the World Congress of Faiths (1937): Watts shared quarters at Balliol College, Oxford, with Baron Hans Hatto von Veltheim, 'a former Zeppelin commander turned ardent disciple of Rudolph Steiner'. He also 'had long conversations in bad French... with Ernesto Buonaiuti, a courteous and inquiring young scholar who walked round and round the quadrangle with me...' See *In My Own Way*, by Alan Watts (paperback edition: New York, 1973; pp 143-4).

31 Eleanor C. Merry (1873/75?–1956): a prominent English Anthroposophist, daughter of Herbert Kynaston, a headmaster of Cheltenham College, who later became Canon of Durham Cathedral. Married a son of Dr Merry, Vice-Chancellor of Oxford University; her husband died in 1922. After an initial encounter with Theosophy, she was introduced to Rudolf Steiner's ideas in 1919 'and found in his teaching the unity she was seeking.' Worked closely with D. N. Dunlop, Chairman of the Anthroposophical Society in Britain, with whom she organised summer schools at Penmaenmawr, North Wales (1923) and Torquay (1924), which Steiner attended. After a visit to Steiner in Paris in 1925, developed her Anthroposophical style of painting; she later held exhibitions and gave classes. Also wrote poetry and many books, including *Pure Colour* (1950), *I Am: The Ascent of Man* (1944, 1963), *Art, Its Occult Basis and Healing Value* (1961), *Easter – The Legends & the Facts* (1933, 1967), etc. Spent a dark, lonely period in London towards the end of her life 'with no job, little money, going from lodging to lodging; separated from all my friends, my son and daughter dead, no pupils any more; and terribly lonely.' Died at a nursing home in Frinton, Essex in 1956.

32 Bloomsbury is the artistic and intellectual quarter of north London; the British Museum and London University are situated there. There was also the famous 'Bloomsbury Set', of which the best-remembered member is Virginia Woolf. Westminster, about two miles to the south on the Thames Embankment, is the site of the Houses of Parliament and many government offices.

33 *Nirvana, Moksha: Nirvana* is the spiritual ultimate of Buddhists, *Moksha* of Hindus. While both represent liberation from rebirth — or, more technically, from the painful round of cyclic existence (*samsara*) — it is debatable whether they are identical, at least from the Buddhist point of view. The Buddha experimented with various Indian spiritual disciplines and found that they did not lead to the absolute liberation from suffering that he was seeking. They certainly could induce rarefied bliss states (or heavenly states) above the turmoil of ordinary human existence, but such states, though of long duration, were still subject to the Law of Impermanence and the practitioner would sooner or later have to quit them – with much chagrin. The Buddha therefore set off to find a lasting liberation, and this he did through the application of spiritual disciplines that he himself evolved, notably Insight Meditation (*Vipassana*).

34 Intuition, sensation, feeling, intellect – Jung's fourfold typology.

35 *Vajra:* the powerful symbol of enlightenment in Tantric Buddhism; derived from the thunderbolt of the Indian god Indra.

36 See note 10.

37 'Life like a dome of many-coloured glass': P. B. Shelley, *Adonais*, verse L11.

38 Percy Wyndham Lewis (1884–1957): English modernist painter, novelist and critic; founder of BLAST!, the journal of the Vorticist school (with Ezra Pound). Born in Maine (USA); studied at the Slade School of Art. Books include *Tarr* (1928), *Childermass* (1928), *Men Without Art* (1934), *Blasting & Bombadeering* (1937) and *Rude Assignment* (1950). Studies by Porteous, Kenner, Tomlin and Read.

39a Randolph F. E. S. Churchill (1911–68): pugnacious English journalist and Tory pundit, educated at Eton and Oxford, the son of Sir Winston Churchill. 'Born to succeed, doomed to failure' summed up his life, though this was not quite fair either. Privilege, great gifts and other advantages, including a greater father, seemed to predestine him for the heights. But in many ways his advantages, augmented by certain defects of character (wilfulness, argumentativeness, etc.), worked against him and he never fulfilled his father's or the world's expectations of him. He was passionately interested in politics and fought and lost many elections; in 1940 he was returned unopposed but lost his seat in 1945. Before World War II he stressed the need to re-arm and build up a common front with the USSR against the growing menace of Nazi Germany. During the War he served with distinction on the Western Front and as an Intelligence Officer in Yugoslavia. Subsequently, working as a journalist, he was acute and fearless – even to the extent of on occasion biting the hand that fed him (i.e. criticising the British press). Alan Watts' remark here may have something to do with Winston Churchill's quarrel with Stanley Baldwin over India Policy, which made the Tory machine little interested in furthering Randolph's political career. Books include a biography of Lord Derby

(1960), *The Rise & Fall of Sir Anthony Eden* (1959), *The Fight for the Tory Leadership* (1964) and the first two volumes of an uncompleted biography of his famous father (whom he idolised).

39b Twofold Basis and Threefold Structure: two Mitrinović ideas, the one signifying unity amidst diversity, the latter the organic division of functions whereby, in terms of the state, there is a division into the cultural, economic and political spheres. This is examined in our Introduction. The notion of such a threefold order can, so Mitrinovic's colleagues believe, be traced back to Plato's *Republic* and to the Laws of Manu (see note 4). Note too how in this piece Watts talks of the British Empire being invested with a kind of manifest destiny for bringing about the New Order.

40 Georg Groddeck (1866–1934): psychoanalyst of Baden-Baden (Germany) famed for his somatic approach to psychological malaise. Brutally simply put, his theory was that any physical symptom was the result of a psychological problem, usually a frustration of the shadowy 'It' that is the real driving force and architect of our lives. Thus we go against the 'It' at our peril. Books include *The Book of the It*, *The Unknown Self* and *Exploring the Unconscious*.

41 Arthur Wragg: British illustrator, born 1906 near Manchester. After studying at Sheffield School of Art, Wragg began working on magazines in London in 1923. Later he worked on books: 'His book illustrations had a *succès d'estime* in the 1930s, being valued for their political and spiritual message as well as for their powerful designs' (*Dictionary of British Book Illustrations: the 20th Century*). He drew for *The Eleventh Hour*, but, so far as we have been able to find out, his connection with the New Britain Movement went no further than that. Besides *Jesus Wept* his own books include *The Psalms for Modern Life* (1933) and *Seven Words* (1939).

42 In the quirky context of English thinking, a so-called 'public school' is in fact a very expensive and highly exclusive private school. 'National schools', on the other hand, is the old name for state-sponsored schools. Watts himself attended one of England's most prestigious public schools — King's, Canterbury — on a scholarship.

43 This and subsequent pieces in the section, all previously unpublished, are from the archives of the New Atlantis Foundation, now based at Ditchling in Sussex. They were kindly contributed by Harry Rutherford, a trustee of the Foundation who worked with Dimitrije Mitrinović for 20 years until his death and who was also a friend of Alan Watts. They show the extent to which, when working in the context of the New Britain Movement at least, Watts was influenced by Mitrinović's ideas, notably the regeneration of the world and society by a new movement in which the interests of the individual and the collectivity would be organically and consciously reconciled. Watts himself was very strongly drawn to the notion of the primacy of each individual's right to fulfil his or her own potential, but in Mitrinović's view this individualism had to be balanced by genuine social integration. The basis for the reconciliation was spiritual, for both individual and collective participated equally in a Supreme Ultimate – a Source or Centre, no doubt cognate with the Hindu Brahman, the Buddhist Buddha-nature, the Christian Christ Spirit, etc.

44 Alliance of Persons: 'the alliance of persons who were prepared to be accepted simply as human beings apart from any special abilities or attainments' (Harry Rutherford). A key Mitrinović idea.

45 Human Household: another key Mitrinović idea; authentic world unity, based not on national, tribal or blood ties but rather on a sense of fundamental shared humanity – 'within which differences are acknowledged and respected, difficulties honestly faced, but underpinned in the final analysis by a fundamental commitment to each other as people, as individual members of the wider human family' (*Initiation & Initiative*, by Andrew Rigby, Boulder, 1984; p188). And Mitrinović himself:

> We are discovering that our world is our common human household and truly one species only. Our kingdom is becoming a commonwealth and a family; a republic and a common cause... (*World Affairs* by 'M. M. Cosmoi', reprinted from *New Britain*, May/July 1933, by the New Europe group, undated and unpaginated.)

46 Senate: another key Mitrinović idea. The New Britain Movement had thrown up the crucial but vexed question of leadership and authority. Thereafter, Mitrinović's thinking was that the new order that he envisaged would have to have some kind of integrating body that could balance the inevitable differences among free, autonomous individuals and groupings. This was not conceived as an authoritarian body. Rather it would be composed of persons from every grouping or function in society, acceptable to the community by virtue of possessing deep understanding of the totality and genuine concern transcending self-interest. Senate would offer guidance but have no special powers to enforce it:

> The function of senate would be to possess a clear vision of the necessary functions in the social state and their proper relationship to one another, and to steer the various groups in society towards a genuine functional relationship through devolution and federation (Andrew Rigby, op. cit., p145)

Senate would furthermore play a vital part in initiating the new order from its very inception, hence Mitrinović's work with close groups of individuals after the demise of the New Britain Movement (1935 onwards).

47 Absolute Collective: the title of Erich Gutkind's second book, in which he adumbrated his vision of socialism. As developed by Mitrinović, the term implies the fulfilment or consummation of collective potential organically initiated by individuals through alliance (Alliance of Persons – see Note 44 above):

> Men and women of Old Britain, of this dangerously decaying Britain and her Commonwealth, conceive a novelty! And give birth to a Society, a State, and a nation that are new because conceived in a mode that is new: the mode of Individual Initiative, through Personal Alliance, for the sake of the Absolute Collective of this nation and of mankind! (from the Editorial, *New Britain*, 25th October 1933 issue)

48 69 Widmore Road, Bromley: a house owned by Watts' uncle, Harry Buchan (father of his childhood playmate, Joy). Watts' parents moved there during a period of hard times when they were forced to rent out their own family home — Rowan Tree Cottage, Holbrook Lane, Chislehurst — and his mother, Emily Watts (*née* Buchan), took in extra embroidery work to make ends meet.

49 Edward Moeran: by profession a solicitor, he was a leading light in the London New Britain Groups and leader of the Stanmore Group. He continued to be in touch with Mitrinović and his colleagues after the demise of the New Britain movement in 1935.

50 Quotation from *The Dhammapada*, a pithy and poetic summary of the Buddha's teachings composed in the Pali langauge. See Penguin translation by Joán Mascaró (Harmondsworth, 1973); also others by Narada Mahathera (London, 1954), etc.

51 *Testament to the Kingly*, by Frederik van Eeden (b. 1860). With Erich Gutkind (1877–1965), Wassily Kandinsky, *et al.*, the Dutchman van Eeden was a vital formative influence on Mitrinović and the prime mover behind the Blutbund (lit. 'Blood-brotherhood'), a community of kindred spirits dedicated to initiating a moral regeneration. Wealthy by birth, he trained in medicine and psychology, wrote novels, plays and poems, and was a Utopian activist. In 1898 he established a Utopian Socialist commune at Bussum in Holland which lasted to 1907; later he tried to initiate similar schemes in the USA. He believed that true socialism could not be inaugurated by the alienated and oppressed working classes, but only by an enlightened élite or spearhead, hence his concept of the 'Kingly of Spirit', which he apocalyptically proclaimed in his *WORLD SENATE: Unite in Heroic Love! Testament to the Kingly of Spirit* (London, published by the Nova Atlantis Publishing Co. for private circulation to members of the New Europe Group, undated):

> The Kingly man — the Prophet, the Poet, the Sage — will only be understood by the few at first. His spirit is alive, and every day he finds something new. The multitude calls that 'inconsequent' and 'unreliable'. He alienates and does not convince. He offers no firm resting-place. He always needs mediators who make his truths acceptable to the multitude...
>
> The Kingly man, however, desires neither to obey nor to be obeyed; he demands permission to share with every man the best that he has, his divinity; he is not satisfied with subjection. He wishes to help the weak to liberty and self-dependence, since they cannot stand without the prop of authority...
>
> The conflicts between the Kingly of Spirit and the herd always have their root in money... *To the Kingly of Spirit, every saying contains a lie and all money is false...*
>
> The Kingly man does not long for peace, but for that which peace must bring – unity and understanding.

Mitrinović's introduction to Gutkind and van Eeden, around 1913, was through a small book given him by Kandinsky. It was called *World Conquest through Heroic Love* and contained two essays, one by Gutkind under the pseudonym Volker, called 'World Conquest', the other by van Eeden, called 'Heroic Love'. When Mitrinović had the two essays translated into English and published as separate pamphlets, he added further titles.

52 Watson Thomson (died 1969): a central personality of the New Britain movement. A graduate of Glasgow University who had worked in Jamaica and Nigeria, he returned to London in 1931, attended a series of lectures delivered by Mitrinović at 55 Gower Street to promote the New Europe Group and was deeply impressed: 'Here, I thought, is a very great man. Here is the kind of wisdom the world desperately needs...' With David Davies, he co-edited the first edition of the *New Britain Quarterly* (October 1932) and wrote the leading article. After working as a prominent activist in the New Britain movement, he remained a member of Mitrinović's inner circle until 1937. He was detailed by Mitrinović to check inner group members for failings like 'artificiality', and the so-called 'Thomson's Ticket' was handed to those who made the grade. Later he emigrated to Canada, where he became prominent in the educational world and a broadcaster, but kept in touch with the New Atlantis group until his death. Memoir: *Turning into Tomorrow* (New York, 1966).

53 S.E. London Area Council. Some of the members of the Adler Society wished to put their psychological understanding into practice socio-politically, so in the late 1920s the New Europe Group was formed, into which Mitrinović entered wholeheartedly. Later some group members wished to do something on the home front; the result was the New Britain Group, in which Mitrinović, not being a British citizen, did not feel he could play a direct part, though he was very much in the background. This initiative caught the public imagination, however, and gathered such great momentum that by 1933 'the people gathered around Mitrinović in their Gower Street headquarters had found themselves at the centre of something akin to a mass social political movement – the New Britain Movement (NBM)' (Andrew Rigby, loc. cit., p 112). This launched a vigorous publicity campaign and held conferences. Local groups also emerged in London — Alan Watts was the leading light in the Bromley Group — as well as in the provinces. These came under area councils, like the S.E. London Area Council, of which again Alan was also a leading light, and ultimately under a Provisional National Council with its London headquarters at 3 Gordon Square.

54 Of course Watts is here discoursing on what we should today label with the buzz words, 'holism' and 'reductionism'. He also touches explicitly on the currently fashionable topic of 'holistic medicine'. All of which only goes to show yet again how far ahead of his time he was in his thinking.

55 Dr Eric Graham Howe: a psychiatrist with consulting rooms in London's Harley Street and 'cosy living quarters' in the mews behind, where he and Watts lunched together one day around 1936. When he came to write his memoirs, what lodged most forcibly in Watts' mind from that meeting was that Howe had served scrumptious baked potatoes doused with runny butter. Watts did not become a patient, however; Howe just 'let me in on his mind' – and in this way he became an important formative influence. Howe was also linked to esoteric circles, including the Buddhist Lodge founded by Christmas Humphreys. Besides *I and Me*, his books include *War Dance, A Study of the Psychology of War* (1937), *Mysterious Marriage, A Study of the Morality of Personal Relationships and Individual Obsessions* (1949), and *The Triumphant Spirit* (1943).

56 Japanese War in China. The Japanese expansion into China, focused first on Manchuria, began in earnest at the end of the 1920s. In 1931, Japanese troops attacked Mukden and were deployed over the whole of the region. Subsequently the puppet state of Manchukuo was set up. Hostilities then escalated into war with China and in 1932 Shanghai was attacked. In 1937 full-scale, though undeclared, war broke out, and by the end of 1938 the Japanese controlled most of the great cities and ports as well as the major railways of China. The Chinese Nationalist government of Chiang Kai-shek (1887–1975) meanwhile retreated to Chungking. The brutality with which the Japanese prosecuted their offensives in China have become legend, notably at Nanking, which they reached in 1937 and where terrible slaughter took place.

57 Samurai: the warrior caste of ancient Japan who came to the fore in Japanese power politics during the Kamakura period (1185–1333). They followed a martial code known as *Bushido* — literally 'The Way of Martial Honour' — which laid primary stress on loyalty, chivalry and contempt for death. The samurai of the Kamakura period ardently espoused Zen because it helped them train themselves in their military virtues. The samurai spirit also reciprocally infiltrated Japanese Zen. Thus have arisen the so-called martial arts — kendo, aikido, karate, etc. — in which military-style training is undertaken as spiritual discipline.

58 *Bushido*: see note 57.

59 The early Buddhists trenchantly denied the reality of any *atman* (Pali, *atta*) or self (that is, any ultimate ground of being, personal or, by extension, transpersonal), and this negativistic stance was perpetuated in early Indian Mahayana – in, for instance, the Madhyamika philosophy of Nagarjuna. In later Mahayana, however, the approach to Ultimate Reality becomes more positive. Yogachara-Chittamatra philosophy, for instance, does concede that 'something' enduring and absolute is attainable through meditation practice, and this becomes more pronounced in the Tathagathagarba doctrine, which propounds the notion that each one of us is a kind of womb in which the seeds of Buddhahood are gestating. Such views influenced Chinese Zen (Ch'an), whose masters talk quite freely of a Buddha-nature and attempt, through their teaching methods, to give their students direct experience of 'it'. *'What is it?'* is a classic Zen question.

60 We have not been able to trace the author of this or the following poetic quotation.

61 Zen Master Takuan (1573–1645): an abbot of Daitoku-ji, the great temple in Kyoto, who was invited by the Shogun (Military Governor) Tokugawa Iemitsu to go to Edo, the centre of Tokugawa power, where the Tokai-ji temple was built for him. 'He was the most important Zen figure at the beginning of the Tokugawa period' (H. Dumoulin). Watts' source here was almost certainly D. T. Suzuki's *Zen Buddhism & Its Influence on Japanese Culture*, first published in 1938 by the Eastern Buddhist Society of Otani Buddhist University, Kyoto (later reissued as *Zen & Japanese Culture*). It contains chapters on Zen and

Swordsmanship, and Zen and the Samurai, in which Suzuki includes a translation of Takuan's Letter to Iemitsu's master, the swordsman Yagyu Tajima no Kami Munemori (1571–1646), on 'The Mystery of Prajñā Immovable' (Bollingen-Princeton edition, 1970; pp95–6): 'No doubt you see the sword about to strike you, but do not "stop" there...', etc.

62 Chuang-tzu (369?–286? BCE): 'the most important exponent of Taoist thought in ancient China' (Burton Watson). A native of Meng, he was for a time an official at a possibly mythical place called 'Ch'i-yüan'. According to the classic Chinese historian Ssu-ma Ch'ien, he wrote a text of 100,000 words or more 'mostly in the nature of fable.' See A. C. Graham, *Chuang-tzu: the Seven Inner Chapters & Other Writings from the Book of Chuang-tzu* (London, 1981) and the section on Chuang-tzu in Arthur Waley's *Three Ways of Thought in Ancient China* (London, 1956).

63 *Walk On!*: one of the classic Zen ripostes of the laconic Chinese Master Yun-men (Japanese, Ummon; died 949) who studied with Mu-chou (Japanese, Bokuju), a disciple of Master Huang-po (Japanese, Obaku; Master Lin-chi's teacher). When asked 'What is the Tao [Way]?', Yun-men is reputed to have replied, 'Walk On!'. This precise translation comes in Suzuki (see *Essays in Zen Buddhism* (First Series), London, 1958; p354). Christmas Humphreys took it up with relish and even used it as the title of one of his books. Yun-men's famous 'shit-stick' riposte forms Case 21 of the great collection of anecdotes of the Chinese Zen masters of the classic period called *Wu-men-kuan* (literally, 'Gateless Gate'; Japanese, *Mu-mon-kan*). 'Yun-men eschews theory and excels in originality, paradox, and trenchant repartee, in keeping with the great masters of the T'ang period' (H. Dumoulin).

64 These lines are attributed to Miyamoto Musashi (1582–1645), a great Zen swordsman and artist of the Tokugawa period, founder of the Nito-ryu school. See D. T. Suzuki, *Essays in Zen Buddhism* (Third Series, London 1953; p334).

65 Kenshin and Shingen. The source for this story must again be Suzuki's *Zen Buddhism & Its Influence on Japanese Culture* (see Bollingen-Princeton edition, 1970; pp76–77). Takeda Shingen (1521–73) and Uyesugi Kenshin (1530–78) were indeed two great generals during a period when Japan was riven by internecine strife. Both were students of Zen Buddhism.

66 We have not been able to find a source for this quotation.

67 Tsukahara Bokuden (1490–1572): according to Suzuki 'one of the greatest [Japanese] swordsmen'. Again the sources for Watts' two Bokuden anecdotes must be Suzuki's *Zen Buddhism & Its Influence on*

Japanese Culture ((Bollingen-Princeton edition, 1970; pp74–76).

68 Hinayana: the so-called 'Little Vehicle' or 'First Turning of the Wheel of the Dharma'. This represents the basic development of the Buddha's teaching following his *Parinirvana*. Traditionally, eighteen schools are said to have emerged during this phase, though actually there were more. Today only the Theravada (lit. 'Way of the Elders') survives, and does so mainly in south and south-east Asian countries, so is often known as the Southern School.

69 Mahayana: the so-called 'Great Vehicle' or 'Second Turning of the Wheel of the Dharma', This emerged in India around the turn of the Common Era and represented a whole new wave of development within Buddhism. It broadened the base, allowing greater scope for lay practice; it elevated the Buddha to a more transcendental status and at the same time spawned a vast pantheon of celestial buddhas and *bodhisattvas* whom the devotional could petition for help. It exchanged the Arhat Ideal of personal salvation for the Bodhisattva Ideal of working for the salvation of all sentient beings; it spawned new scriptures and facilitated marvellous new developments in philosophy; and it paved the way for Tantra – the incorporation into Buddhism of magico-ritual practices. It was transmitted beyond India, mainly to central, north and east Asia, and consequently is often called the Northern School. It underwent further changes in every culture in which it took root, from Siberia to Japan, and especially in China, where Zen, Alan Watts' great love, emerged.

70 Lao-tzu is in fact regarded as the reviver and reformer of Taoism; the tradition itself is said to have derived from the teachings of the mythical Yellow Emperor, Huang-ti (2698–2597 BCE).

71 Sung paintings. Watts was first deeply impressed by these paintings at the International Exhibition of Chinese Art held at Burlington House, London, under the auspices of the Royal Academy of Arts in 1935. He was given an official pass by his friend Robert Holland-Martin and returned day after day in order to 'understand and absorb the mood beneath Chinese art forms'. The memory of this exhibition was still vivid when he came to write his memoirs some thirty five years later. See 'The Genius of China. Notes on the International Exhibition of Chinese Art', London, *Buddhism in England*, Jan–Feb 1936, anthologised in *The Early Writings of Alan Watts*, ed. John Snelling, with Mark Watts, Berkeley, 1987; pp117–20. Here he writes:

> Passing out of this room to the left we come to the first gallery of the Sung dynasty. There are four galleries devoted to this dynasty, and to appreciate them properly would require several days in each. Therefore I can only mention three or four of the

astonishing collection of paintings produced by the artists of this Golden Age of Chinese culture when Zen Buddhism was at its zenith. Firstly... there is Ku An's picture of 'Bamboos and Rocks' (1130). This is so beautiful that I hesitate to say anything about it... Then there is a long scroll by Ma Fên — 'The Hundred Geese' (1387) — which is carried out in the same spirit of suggestiveness...

72 T'ien-t'ai (Japanese, Tendai) and Hua-yen (Japanese, Kegon): two Chinese transformations of Indian Buddhism. Both attempted a categorisation of the prodigious canon of Hinayana and Mahayana Buddhist teachings and texts around the centrality of one particular scripture or sutra – the T'ien-t'ai favouring the *Saddhamapundarika* or *Lotus Sutra* and the *Hua-yen* the *Avatamsaka* or *Flower Adornment Sutra*. Hua-yen propounded the interconnectedness and interpenetration of all phenomena; thus the universe in its totality is contained in even a speck of dust. This grand vision is encapsulated in the potent image of the Jewel Net of Indra, a cosmic net with a jewel at every knot, each jewel containing reflections of all other jewels as well as its own in all of them *ad infinitum*. Hua-yen was often combined with Ch'an practice, hence the old Chinese dictum, 'Hua-yen for philosophy, Ch'an for meditation'. For further reading see Francis Cook, *Hua-yen Buddhism. The Jewel Net of Indra* (University Park, Pa., 1977); and Thomas Cleary, *Entry into the Inconceivable* (Honolulu, 1983). T'ien-t'ai, on the other hand, combined philosophy with a meditation system based on the traditional Buddhist model of concentration and insight (*samatha, vipassana*); the ultimate objective here was 'to sweep away all doubts and achieve the Great Result' (i.e. the Body of the Buddha or *Sambhogakaya*). Both schools were complex and highly philosophical, and Ch'an itself was no doubt a reaction against this – a ruthless cutting away of non-essential accretions to zero in on the simple heart of the Great Matter.

73 One is bound to point out that, impressive as this is, it is all derived from secondary sources; Watts had not been to the East at this stage. He did not in fact go until 1960, but went there two or three times a year from then till 1965, leading tourist parties to Kyoto.

74 This is all very apposite to our own time. The Zen that has been transmitted to the West has been the hard-nosed Japanese Zen with its martial-feudal ambience, typified most perhaps in a rigid master-student relationship which gives the master more power than many seem able to handle. Thus there have been numerous 'crises' in Zen groups in the West. Arguably Westerners are hard-nosed enough as it is and would do better with an altogether 'softer' approach pitched at redressing the balance. Chinese Ch'an was generally softer (though by no means too soft!) and so it is a pity that we know so little of it in the West today. The reason for that is mainly political — the fall of China to the Communists. It should also be borne in mind that, at least in the early days in China, Ch'an was not for raw beginners but for seasoned practitioners, mostly monks who were up to their ears in moral precepts, philosophy, etc., and needed freeing up. The tendency for it to be practised in the West without the basis of fairly extensive previous training is probably another reason why it often tends to go awry.

75 Pali Canon: the scriptural canon of the Theravada or Southern School of Buddhism, set down in Pali, one of the ancient dead languages of India. It is also known as the *Tripitaka* on account of its trivision into three 'baskets' or compilations: 1 *Vinaya Pitaka*, containing the code of monastic discipline, 2 *Sutta Pitaka*, in which are collected the discourses of the Buddha, and 3 *Abhidhamma Pitaka*, in which are expounded philosophical systematisations of the Buddha's teachings.

76 *Karma* (Pali *kamma*): *karma* literally means volitional action. Any action that is willed will produce a fruit (*vipaka*) of similar moral complexion. Upon this is based the Buddhist theory of causation. Our present lives are thus the result of past actions. If happy, this is on account of meritorious actions; if unhappy, 'unskilful' or morally unsound actions must have been perpetrated earlier in the present or else in a previous life. Theravada Buddhist practice aims at *nirodha*: the exhaustion of personal *karma* so that no further rebirths occur.

77 Hinayana and Mahayana Buddhism: see notes 68 and 69.

78 *Tathata, Shunyata, Dharmakaya*. *Tathata* literally means 'suchness' or 'thusness' and signifies the way things really are as perceived through the enlightened eyes of buddhas. The historical Buddha is often called *Tathagata*: 'he who is thus gone'. *Tathata* is more or less cognate with *Shunyata*, literally 'Emptiness', implying that all things are empty or void of inherent existence or self-nature (*svabhava*). Or, put another way, that they do not exist independently, supported by some self-sustaining inner soul or essence, but only in dependence on other things. Both *Shunyata* and *Tathata* are in a sense Mahayana restatements of the Hinayana doctrine of *anatman* or 'not-self'. The *Dharmakaya*, on the other hand, is one of the Three Bodies of the Buddha. It is the ultimate or cosmic body, the consummation of *Shunyata*, the perfection of all buddha qualities, fully one with the eternal Dharma.

79 *Lankavatara Sutra*: an important Mahayana scripture containing expositions of the teachings of *Citta-matra* (lit. 'Mind Only'), *Alaya-vijñana* (lit. 'Store Consciousness') and *Tathagata-garbha* (Lit. 'Womb of the Buddha'). These are mainly associated with the Yogacara school of philosophy founded by the Indian sages Vasubandhu (see note 81) and Asanga (4th century CE). Yogacara is depicted by some commentators as a Buddhist equivalent of Western Idealism (Bishop Berkeley, *et al.*), though, as it was very much a meditation-based school, its philosophical ideas were not 'pure philosophy' in the Western sense but were rather linked to and conditioned by soteriological practices. Translation of the *Lankavatara Sutra* by D. T. Suzuki (London, 1932); see also Suzuki's *Studies in the Lankavatara Sutra* (London, 1930; reprint Boulder, 1981).

80 Watts is referring here to the devotional Pure Land school and its derivatives. Pure Land, another Chinese transformation of Indian Buddhism, was a Mahayana development and no doubt grew out of a call for the laity to be given a greater role in the spiritual life than was accorded them in early or Hinayana Buddhism – or indeed many of the other Mahayana schools for that matter. It is frankly devotional, or founded on faith in the intercessionary power of a benign celestial buddha or *bodhisattva*. There were in fact Indian precedents – the so-called *bhakti* cults (see note 10), which were strong in mediaeval India, for instance. In Buddhism it was linked with the notion of the Final Days of the Dharma (Japanese, *Mappo*) – that global conditions would become increasingly degenerate and inimical to practice to the point that it would eventually become impossible and the Dharma would die out, inaugurating a horrendously long dark age before the next buddha appeared. Conveniently, conditions in 6th century China, when Pure Land's star came into the ascendant, were pretty bad. The government was tyrannical, priests were degenerate, the laity were lax and general pessimism prevailed. To make things worse, in 574–8 Buddhism was actually persecuted. The Chinese cult can trace its origins back to the 3rd century, however, and among its early patriarchs may be listed T'an-luan (476–542), Tao-ch'o (562–645) and Shan-tao (613–81). T'an-luan's Five Practices include: 1 Prostrating to Amitabha and holding the wish to be reborn to his Pure Land; 2 Singing the praises of the Amitabha and reciting his name; 3 Vowing to be reborn to his Pure Land; 4 Visualising Amitabha and his Pure Land; and 5 Transferring merit to other living beings. In China, Pure Land spawned a wonderful art (e.g. at Lung-men) and many pious societies, notably the White Lotus Society which, until it was suppressed in 1322, had developed into a powerful movement dedicated to vegetarianism and good works (e.g. the construction of hostels, bath-houses, waterworks, mills, etc.). It had married clergy and allowed the participation of women in important roles. Pure Land was introduced into Japan during the Heian period (794–1184 CE), and two important cults emerged during the Kamakura period (1185–1333 CE): 1 the Jodo-shu of Honen Shonin

(1133–1212), and 2 the Jodo Shin-shu of his disciple Shinran Shonin. Honen emphasised the repetition of Amitabha's name, but Shinran went even further and declared that conditions were so hopeless that practitioners should abandon all attempts at practice and throw themselves utterly on Amitabha's mercy.

81 Nagarjuna, Ashvaghosa and Vasubandhu. **Nagarjuna**, an Indian of the 2nd century CE, was the founding genius of the Mahayana Madhyamika or 'Central Way' school of philosophy. This employed a rigorous dialectic designed not so much to deliver positive conclusions as to drive practitioners into the arms of Emptiness (*Shunyata*) by reducing all theses, both positive and negative, to absurdity. 'I do not myself have any thesis. I negate nothing,' declared Nagarjuna. **Ashvaghosa** (1st or 2nd century CE), on the other hand, is the reputed author of the *Awakening of Faith in the Mahayana*, a text in which the Tathagata-garba doctrine is expounded. This suggests that we are all 'wombs' in which the seeds of Buddhahood are gestating. Finally, **Vasubandhu** (c. 316–396? CE) and his brother Asangha (c. 310–390) were the seminal masters of the Yogacara school of philosophy, which arose possibly as a foil to the negativistic disposition of the Madhyamika. Yogacara, as its name suggests, was based on yogic practice, the devotee hoping to achieve a 'revolution at the basis' in which he would finally see that all external objects were mere projections of his own consciousness and that, as there were in fact no real objects to be grasped, there could be no grasper. With all mental agitation finally subdued, he would rest in a state of pure quiescence beyond subject-object dualism. Philosophically, Yogacara put forward the notion of 'Mind-only' (*Citta-matra*): that all things are created in and out of mind. (See also note 84.)

82 The warring opposites or dualities were a major theme in Watts' early writings. See, for example, his piece 'Man, Woman and Child', from his series *Seven Symbols of Life*, published in 1936 and anthologised in *The Early Writings of Alan Watts*, edited by John Snelling with Mark Watts, Berkeley, 1986, pp169ff.

83 *Bodhisattva*. In early Buddhism, a *bodhisattva* is a buddha in the making, so to speak. A buddha specifically is a very special person who discovers the Dharma after it has been lost during one of the long dark ages that periodically occur during the cycles of time. Siddhartha Gautama is the Buddha for our age. An *arhat*, on the other hand, is a being who opts for the personal salvation of Nirvana. In the Mahayana, however, the distinction between buddhas and *bodhisattvas* begins to blur. For a start, because of the innumerable world systems in the cosmos, there are an infinite number of buddhas in an infinity of buddha-fields and pure lands. There are also *bodhisattvas* in celestial realms. Both celestial buddhas and *bodhisattvas* can be appealed to by the pious for help. A *bodhisattva* is, moreover, not so much one who could attain Nirvana but opts to stay out for compassionate reasons; rather he has attained a higher realisation than the *arhat* who opts for Nirvana. He can in fact exist in Samsara (the cosmos of cyclic existence – see note 122) in a Nirvanic way. And anyway, as Watts points out, in the Mahayana Nirvana and Samsara are not separate.

84 *Alaya-vijñana*): more usually translated today as 'store-consciousness'. In the Yogacara/Citta-matra philosophy of Mahayana Buddhism, which maintains that all things are the product of mind (i.e. a kind of idealism), the store-consciousness theory explains how perceptions arise in the mind if they do not arise in the outside world. It postulates a kind of subconscious in which past impressions are stored as seeds which will ripen into future experience. When, through spiritual practice, all the seeds are 'exhausted', then the pulsing stream of consciousness that they engender will subside.

85 *Sukhavati-vyuha Sutra*: there are in fact two such sutras, the Larger and the Smaller. Both are of Indian origin and were subsequently translated into Chinese. It is unclear which came first, though modern Western scholarship favours the Larger.

86 See note 80.

87 See note 72.

88 Dark cycle. Actually *Kali Yuga* is a Hindu term; Buddhists more precisely think of this dark age as the 'Final Days of the Dharma' (Japanese, *Mappo*), during which, according to the devotional cults at least, things are so degenerate that one cannot hope to realise any positive results from one's own practice, hence the need for faith in the benign intercession of divine buddhas and *bodhisattvas,* and in the possibility of elevation to their pure lands. See also note 80.

89 See note 80.

90 Zen, Shingon, Tendai, Kegon, and Nichiren schools. The first four are the Japanese names of the Chinese Ch'an, Mi-tsung/Chen-yen, T'ien-t'ai and Hua-yen schools. Tendai/T'ien-t-ai and Kegon/Hua-yen are dealt with in note 72. The Ch'an or Zen school originated in China around the 6th century CE, and was an iconoclastic movement aimed at returning Buddhism to basic essentials, i.e. the Enlightenment experience itself. Ostensibly its masters eschewed scriptural study and many of the other norms of practice, seeking to give their disciples direct insight into their own true nature by often unorthodox methods. The Rinzai/Lin-chi line is traditionally reputed to have been introduced into Japan by Eisai (1141–1215) and the Soto/T'sao-tung by Dogen Zenji

(1200–1253). Japanese Zen burgeoned among the martial *samurai* during the Kamakura period. Shingon, meanwhile, is the Japanese version of the highly esoteric Tantric school or Vajrayana, called Mi-tsung or Chen-yen in China, which looked to the *Mahavairocana Sutra* as its principal text. Tantra is about transforming one's body, speech and mind into those of a fully-enlightened buddha by special yogic and magico-ritual methods. It is said by its partisans to be the fastest route to Enlightenment. The Tantric school was introduced into China during the T'ang dynasty by the Indian adept Subhakarasimha (637–735 CE). The Third Patriarch, Amoghavajra (705–774 CE) is credited with initiating three emperors. The school was carried to Japan by Kobo Daishi (774–835) and was at first very popular; especially in court circles and among the upper classes during the Heian period, when, in Suzuki's words, Japanese Buddhism was 'flooded with magic ritualism'. Finally, the originating genius of the Nichiren sect was an eponymous and controversial figure who lived in 13th century Japan. Nichiren Shonin passionately maintained that in the current dark age (*Mappo*) all practices were useless except his own, a *mantra* (verbal formula) extolling the virtues of the *Lotus Sutra*. He furthermore deemed all other schools not merely misguided but positively harmful in that they diverted practitioners from the true way that he propounded. This brought persecution upon him, but that merely galvanised his fanatical sense of mission. This school has lasted to the present and, since World War II, its various sub-sects have attracted mass followings both in Japan and in the West.

91 *Bhakti-marga*: Watts is using Hindu terminology again here. 'Bhakti-marga' means 'devotional way'. See also note 10 on *Bhakti yoga*.

92 Surely a factor that encouraged their appeal to Alan Watts!

93 *Rinzai-roku* (Chinese, *Lin-chi-lu*): the classic compilation of the sayings of Chinese Ch'an Master Lin-chi (died 867 CE), known in Japan as Rinzai. One of the two surviving schools of Zen in Japan bears his name. Rinzai Zen, unlike its more gentle Soto counterpart, is redolent with the Kamakura *samurai* spirit. It lays emphasis on intensive sitting (*zazen*) and *koan* practice. See *The Record of Rinzai*, trans I. Schloegl (London, 1975).

94 Hokoji – or Ho Koji: The Japanese name of Layman P'ang, the Chinese Zen Master who figures in Case 42 of the *Blue Cliff Record*. See note 18 and *The Recorded Sayings of Layman P'ang*, translated by Sasaki, Iriya and Fraser (New York and Tokyo, 1971).

95 George Herbert (1593–1633): English clergyman and poet. Educated at Westminster and Cambridge, he moved in court circles and took holy orders in 1630, whereafter he served as a parish priest in Wiltshire.

96 *Mu-mon-kan* (Chinese, *Wu-men-kuan*, lit 'Gateless Gate'): an anecdotal record with commentaries of the sayings and doings of some of the great Chinese Ch'an masters, with special reference to their *koans* or Dharma questions, compiled by Wu-men Hui-kai (1184–1260). See *Mumonkan*, Vol. 4 of *Zen & Zen Classics* by R. H. Blyth (Tokyo, 1966). The three individuals referred to immediately below, Joshu (Chao-chu, 778–897), Nansen (Nan-ch'üan, 748–834) and Bokuju (Mu-chou), were all Chinese Zen masters of the classic T'ang period

97 Sokei-an Sasaki (Sokei-an Shigetsu Osho, 1882–1945): pioneer teacher of Zen in the USA. Born in Japan, Sasaki was first a carver of dragons; later he was encouraged by Soyen Shaku (one of D. T. Suzuki's teachers at Engaku-ji in Kamakura) to 'carve a Buddha statue' (i.e. become enlightened himself). In 1906, he went with a group to the USA to found a Rinzai Zen monastery in California; this mission failed but Sasaki stayed on and eventually established himself in New York, where in 1931 the Buddhist Society of America was formed around him; this later become the First Zen Institute of New York, later of America. One of his chief supporters was Ruth Everett, Alan Watts' mother-in-law, whom he married in 1944. Watts studied Zen with Sokei-an for a short time.

98 This is a very important point and one frequently brought up by commentators on Pure Land teachings. If we are buddhas as we are, why then bother to do anything? Why not even live dissolute lives since we can always be saved? This could well give antinomianism its *entrée*. On the matter of spiritual effort, Suzuki also makes a relevant point in relation to Master Bankei (see note 119), who finally discovered that he always had what he had been strenuously seeking for many years (he called it 'the Unborn'), so all his years of striving had been so much waste of time. 'But without such a waste of effort could Bankei have been Bankei?' Suzuki asks; '. . . the swimming of a waterfowl looks effortless, yet would not have been possible without the accumulation of really indescribable effort . . . Without the exertion of his weight of effort, who would be able to achieve anything worthwhile?' Christian theologians have not of course been unaware of such problems. Compare, too, Watts' exact words in the last sentence here with T. S. Eliot's dictum, 'We have the experience but we missed the meaning' (*Four Quartets*, paperback edition, London, 1966; p39).

99 Huang-po (died c.850 CE). One of the great early Chinese Zen masters, he was the teacher of I Hsüan, the founder of the Lin-chi (Rinzai) line, which continues to this day. He took his name from the mountain where he lived for many years. In Japan he is known as Obaku. See *The Zen Teachings of Huang-po on the Transmission of Mind*, translated by John Blofeld (London, 1947).

100 *Pratyeka-buddha* (lit. 'Independently Enlightened One'). One who achieves Enlightenment by his own unaided efforts but does not proclaim his attainment or teach. Such are said to cherish solitude and be frugal of speech.

101 Watts describes in his memoirs how this idea was communicated to him by Eleanor Everett, a young American woman who had turned up at the Buddhist Lodge in London with her mother in July 1937. Walking home one evening from a meditation session, 'I began to discuss the method of meditation on the eternal present. Whereupon she said, "Why try to concentrate on it? What else *is* there to be aware of? Your memories are all in the present, just as much as the trees over there. Your thoughts about the future are also in the present . . . The present is just a constant flow, like the Tao." With that my whole sense of weight vanished . . .' Eleanor, the daughter of Ruth Fuller Sasaki (1883-1967), a pioneer of Zen Buddhism in the USA, became Watts's first wife.

102 Pure Land School: see note 80.

103 Actually Watts is in error to ascribe the foundation of Japanese Pure Land to Shinran. As I indicate in note 80, he founded the Jodo Shin-shu (or 'True Pure Land School'), but that was preceded by the Shin-shu ('Pure Land School') of his mentor, Honen. Pure Land was introduced to Japan during the Heian period (794-1184), when Kuya Shonin and Ryonin were active in propagating a popular form of Buddhism on the basic of the Amitabha cult.

104 D. T. Suzuki was at one stage of the opinion that the practices of Shin Buddhism might work particularly well for Westerners – better than, say, those of Zen.

105 This of course has rather grave implications ethically. If Amitabha saves everyone, why refrain from dreadful behaviour? Watts touches on this crucial point later on, but his suspicion of morality — that source of guilt, the bane and inhibitor of well-brought-up Englishmen like himself — is quite apparent throughout.

106 *Rin zai-roku*: See note 93.

107 *Satori*: an initial opening or 'enlightenment experience' requiring the maturing influence of further practice.

108 See note 97.

109 *Lankavatara Sutra*: see note 79.

110 *Mu-mon-kan*: see note 96. The particular Nansen-Joshu case mentioned here is Case 19. In R. H. Blyth's translation (details in note

96; p307), when Joshu asks, 'What is the Way?', Nansen answers, 'Your ordinary mind – that is the Way.' 'Does it go in any particular direction?' Joshu asks. 'The more you seek after it, the more it runs away,' Nansen replies. Joshu: 'Then how can I know the Way?' Nansen: 'The Way does not belong to knowing or not knowing. Knowing is illusion. Not knowing is lack of discrimination. When you get to this unperplexed Way, it is like the vastness of space, an unfathomable void – so how can it be this or that, yes or no?' – whereupon Joshu was suddenly Enlightened.

111 Notice here how Watts calls Christianity Western man's 'own religion'. This tellingly reflects how he was thinking at the time. His own freewheeling spiritual life and work, successful as they had been in their way, had nevertheless marginalised him – and hence made both earning a living and supporting a family difficult. To become a Christian and in due course a priest therefore seemed at the time a possible solution to his problems; and as he believed all religions were merely fingers pointing at the same ineffable Truths, there seemed no fundamental reason why he could not operate within the Church without any serious compromises or contortions. Later, however, he was to find out that it was not as easy as he had initially anticipated.

112 *Anatta* (Sanskrit, *anatman*): a central Buddhist doctrine, one of the so-called Three Signs of All Existence. Basically this asserts that the things of the world are not self-causing and sustaining, do not spring from some kind of innate essence or soul hermetically insulated from the rest of creation. Instead they are causally produced and sustained in dependence on other conditions. In Mahayana Buddhism the concept is developed into that of Emptiness (Sanskrit, *Shunyata*): lack of inherent existence, or self-nature (*svabhava*). In the magnificent Chinese Hua-yen philosophy, meanwhile, it is asserted that anything that exists in the universe is caused and sustained by everything else and is in turn their cause and sustainer.

113 We have not been able to identify the origin of either this or the following verse.

114 By the time that he wrote this item, Alan Watts had dropped his unhappy masquerade as 'paradox priest' in the Episcopalian Church and was back as a freewheeling man of the Way on the West Coast of the USA, back with Zen, Taoism and the other Oriental traditions that he loved – and their hour was about to come, too . . .

115 See note 112.

116 During his Christian phase, Watts had published a translation of Dionysius: *Theologia Mystica: being the treatise of Saint Dionysius the Pseudo Areopagite on Mystical Theology, together with the first and fifth*

Epistles, translated from the Greek with an Introduction by Alan W. Watts (New York, 1944).

117 Ananda Coomaraswamy (1877–1947): influential Sinhalese art historian and religious thinker. Born in Sri Lanka of Anglo-Indian extraction, he was educated in England and graduated from London University. Returning to Sri Lanka, then Ceylon, to practise geology, he was soon captivated by the indigenous traditions of art and also began to call for political and cultural independence, though he kept up a home in England where he spent periodic sojourns. Early influences included William Morris and, after he moved to India where he developed his true vocation as an art historian, Rabindranath Tagore. Between 1917 and 1931 he was curator of Indian and Muslim art at the Museum of Fine Art in Boston, Massachusetts, during which period he produced more important works of art history. Gradually his field of interest widened to include religion, philosophy, aesthetics, symbology, mythology and the traditional culture of India and mediaeval Europe. Then, after a transformation in 1932, he became more of a religious and philosophical thinker, urging modern man to seek again the roots of the spiritual and cultural traditions which he has abandoned with such catastrophic consequences. His books include *Mediaeval Sinhalese Art* (1908), *Indian Drawings* (1910), *Rajput Painting* (1916), *Myths of the Hindus & Buddhists* (with Sister Nivedita; 1913), *Buddha & the Gospel of Buddhism* (a book that was a crucial influence on Watts' mentor, Christmas Humphreys) (1916), *The Dance of Shiva* (1918), *The Transformation of Nature in Art* (1934), *Elements of Buddhist Iconography* (1935), *Christian & Oriental Philosophy of Art* (1943), *Am I My Brother's Keeper?* (1947).

118 Rinzai (Lin-chi): see note 93.

119 Bankei Yotaku (1622–93): a Japanese iconoclast who challenged orthodox Zen teaching. Having spent many years strenuously pursuing Enlightenment, he at last had the powerful insight that he already possessed the very thing he was seeking — which he called the 'Unborn' — and that all the years of struggle had been so much waste of time. Accordingly, as an alternative to the rigours of formal Zen training he advocated discovery of the Unborn amid the flux of ordinary, everyday life. This naturally did not please the Zen establishment, but Bankei was charismatic and attracted a large following, notably among the laity. His teaching was very much dependent on his own personality, and his 'school' did not survive long after his death. See *Bankei Zen*, translations from the Record of Bankei by Peter Haskel (New York, 1984).

120 Kichibei: 'A wealthy farmer of Idzumo province' who, when his religious consciousness was awakened, sold up and became a wandering student of Shin Buddhism. At the age of 70 he was earning a scant living selling fish. Thus it was said that 'Kichibei goes around in sandals made of gold', i.e. all his worldly wealth had gone into his spiritual quest. For more information, see D. T. Suzuki, *Essays in Zen Buddhism* (Second Series), London, 1950; pp275–6.

121 *Koan* (Chinese, *kung-an*): in Zen Buddhism, particularly the Rinzai school, a cryptic 'problem' to which the practitioner applies him or herself assiduously both during and outside formal *zazen* practice. It focuses concentration in a very active way on the key issue: *Who or what am I?* Yet the only acceptable 'answer' will be an existential, never a conceptual or verbal, one.

122 The Buddhist Wheel of Becoming – usually now called The Wheel of Life (Sanskrit, *Bhava-chakra*): a great wheel or mirror clamped in the jaws and talons of Yama, the grisly Lord of Death. In it are vividly depicted the five or six 'destinations' – the realms of the cosmos in which it is possible for beings to be born, i.e. the hells, the heavens, the world of humans, of animals, of hungry ghosts (*preta*) and of titans (*asura*). Within this there is another ring depicting humans ascending into pleasant destinations and descending into unpleasant ones. On the periphery, meanwhile, there is a circle of twelve panels symbolising the twelve phases of the *Pratitya Samutpada* (the Buddhist doctrine of Dependent Origination, or creation by causes): a blind man, potter, monkey, three men in a boat, house, etc. Finally in the centre a rooster, a pig and a snake chase each other, symbolising the doctrine of the Three Fires or Poisons (i.e. greed, hatred and delusion). Altogether, the Wheel of Life symbolises the Buddhist notion of *Samsara* – of endless rebirth in a range of situations, most of them unpleasant and some dreadful. The Buddha, however, is depicted off the Wheel and points to an Escape Route. Thus the traditional goal of Buddhism was escape from cyclic existence. See *The Buddhist Handbook*, by John Snelling (London, Century Hutchinson, 1986; pp75ff).

123 Ishvara: a Hindu name meaning 'Lord'; also 'a title given to Shiva' (J. Dowson).

124 'Secret Doctrine' – the use of these words suggests the writer was a Theosophist, for Madame H. P. Blavatsky, the founder of the movement, gave one of her great works precisely that title.

125 Hoxton. An underprivileged area in the (at one time) bleak East End of London, just north of the City.

126 Toc H: a society, originally of ex-service personnel, for fellowship and social service. The name is derived from Talbot House, a soldiers' club started on the Front during World War I by Rev. P. Clayton in memory of one Gilbert Talbot.

127 See note 31.

128 Religion. The usual derivation given is the *re-ligere* one, meaning to 'bind back' (to the basic Ground of Being, etc.); but I have also heard it asserted that the *ligion* component has affinities with the *glect* of *neglect* etc., so in this sense 'religion' is to 're-glect' as opposed to 'ne-glect' – i.e. to pay attention, or be aware. This would of course fit in nicely with Buddhist and allied meditation practices, to all of which awareness is central.

129 See note 32.

Select Bibliography

•

Alan Watts Autobiography/Biography

In My Own Way. An Autobiography. Alan Watts. New York, 1972
Alan Watts. David Stuart. Radnor, Penn., 1976
Genuine Fake. A Biography of Alan Watts. Monica Furlong. London, 1986

Books by Alan Watts

The Spirit of Zen. London, 1936
The Legacy of Asia & Western Man. London, 1938
The Meaning of Happiness. New York, 1940
The Early Writings of Alan Watts. Edited by John Snelling, with Mark Watts. Berkeley and London, 1987

Dimitrije Mitrinović & the New Britain Movement

Certainly Future. Selected Writings by Dimitrije Mitrinović. Edited with introduction by Harry C. Rutherford. Boulder, 1987.
Initiation & Initiative. An Exploration of the Life & Ideas of Dimitrije Mitrinović. Andrew Rigby. Boulder, 1984
The Religion of Logos & Sophia from the Writings of Dimitrije Mitrinović. Harry C. Rutherford. Sausalito, 1973
World Affairs. M. M. Cosmoi. Reprinted from *New Britain*, May/July 1933, for the New Europe Group for private circulation. Undated.
World Senate. Unite in Heroic Love! Testament to the Kingly of Spirit. Frederik van Eeden. London, undated.

INDEX

•

Judaism 256
ju-jutsu 177–8, 209
Jung, Dr. C. G. 5, 13, 16, 21, 29,
72–77, 135, 151, 281n, 286n

Kandinsky, Wassily 13, 290n
karma (kamma) 209, 218
karuna, see compassion
kendo 177–8, 194, 209, 292n
Kenshin 197–8, 293n
Kerouac, Jack 33
Kegon school, see Hua-yen
Kichibei 263, 302–3n
King's School, Canterbury 3–6, 11,
29, 287n
Kipling, Rudyard 45, 131
Koestler, Arthur 14
Krishna 49–53, 111, 279
Krishnamurti, J. 5, 7, 8, 13, 67–71,
281n

Lankavatara Sutra 214, 217, 221, 222,
248, 296–7
Lao-tzu 49, 58–62, 127, 128, 155, 202,
254, 294n
Lawrence, D.H. 166
letting go 108, 144–5, 250, 251–2
Lewis, Wyndham 149, 286n
Lin-chi-lu, see *Rinzai-roku*
Lindworsky, J. 73, 282n
Lotus Sutra, The 295n, 300n
Lucretius 86, 284n

Madhyamika ('Central Way')
philosophy 298n
Mahayana Buddhism 28, 201ff, 211ff,
244, 256, 282n, 294n, 295n, 296n,
303n
Mahaparinibbana Sutta 211
Mansfield, Katherine 166
Manu, Laws of 48, 63, 152–3, 279
March, A. C. 7
Marxism 156, 157–8 (see also
Communism)
materialism 98, 101, 189 (see also
science)
Maugham, Somerset 3
McElwain, Bishop 30
meditation 202, 210, 295n, 306n
Merry, Eleanor C. 11, 116ff, 271–8,
285n
metaphysic 255
Middle Way, The 54, 72, 111, 229
Middle Way, The 30
Watts's contributions to 255–266

militarism (see war)
Mitrinović, Dimitrije 5, 7, 13ff, 15,
279n, 287–8n, 288–91ns
his influence 149–186
Modern Mystic, The 11–13, 271ff
Watts's contributions to 41–145
Moeran, Edward 185, 288n
money 17–18, 160
Moral Rearmament 13, 283n
morality 112, 119, 122, 227–9, 248–9,
258, 302n
Mu-mon-kan 213, 248, 293n, 300–1n,
302–3n
Murry, John Middleton 266–7

Nagarjuna 298n
Nansen 248, 302–3n
Nazism 33, 171–80 (see also Fascism)
New Age, The 17
Nembutsu 220
New Albion 152–3
New Atlantis Foundation 22, 24,
187–8n
New Britain Movement 14, 21–3,
185–6, 287–91ns
New Britain Quarterly 13, 21, 22, 290n
New Order, The 22, 153, 171, 181–4
Nichiren school 218, 299–300n
Nichiren Daishonin 299–300n
Nietzsche, F. 154
non-attachment (see also letting
go) 204
non-duality 126, 224, 226, 229
Northwestern University 32
Nukariya Kaiten 229n

occultism 12, 119, 136ff, 140, 271ff
opposites 55–56, 111, 118, 120, 122,
127, 131–2, 143, 173, 234ff, 276,
298n
Orage, A.C. 17
'Oxford Groups' 13, 65–72, 267–8,
283n

pacifism 10, 176
P'ang, Layman (Hokoji) 283n, 300n
Pavlov, I.P. 73, 281n
Plato 159
Plotinus 91
politics 17ff, 103, 104, 149–86
primitive religion 45, 75–6
Psychoanalysis 135ff, 189 (see also
Freud, Sigmund)
psychology 5, 16, 26, 72-77, 135–40,